CHE GUEVARA AND THE
LATIN AMERICAN
REVOLUTIONARY MOVEMENTS

CHE GUEVARA AND THE LATIN AMERICAN REVOLUTIONARY MOVEMENTS

Manuel Piñeiro
("Red Beard")

Selected and edited by Luis Suárez Salazar

Translated by Mary Todd

OCEAN PRESS
Melbourne • New York

in association with Ediciones Tricontinental

ISBN 1-876175-32-X

First printed 2001

Printed in Australia

Published by Ocean Press
GPO Box 3279, Melbourne, Victoria 3001, Australia
• Fax: (61-3) 9329 5040 • E-mail: info@oceanbooks.com.au

Library of Congress Catalog Card No: 00-112187

OCEAN PRESS DISTRIBUTORS
United States & Canada: LPC/InBook,
    1436 West Randolph St, Chicago, IL 60607, USA
Britain and Europe: Global Book Marketing,
    38 King Street, London, WC2E 8JT, UK
Australia and New Zealand: Astam Books,
    57-61 John Street, Leichhardt, NSW 2040, Australia
Cuba and Latin America: Ocean Press,
    Calle 21 #406, Vedado, Havana, Cuba
Southern Africa: Phambili Agencies,
    PO Box 28680, Kensington 2101, Johannesburg, South Africa

www.oceanbooks.com.au

Table of Contents

Epilogue

Manuel Piñeiro Losada

MANUEL PIÑEIRO LOSADA was born in Matanzas, Cuba, on March 14, 1933. In September 1953, after participating in student protests against the military coup of Fulgencio Batista on March 10, 1952, his family sent him to study in the United States in order to isolate him from the Cuban political situation. He continued his studies at Columbia University in New York.

According to his own accounts, while studying and working in New York he reaffirmed his political beliefs, in particular his rejection of the social inequalities and racial, national and cultural discrimination typical of U.S. society.

After returning to Cuba in 1955 he participated in the founding of the July 26 Movement in Matanzas, where he was subsequently detained by Batista's repressive forces.

He continued with underground activities in Havana until he joined the rebel fighters in the Sierra Maestra as a combatant in the column led by Fidel Castro.

Recognizing his strengths, Piñeiro was chosen to join the group led by Commander Raúl Castro, who in March 1958 formed the Frank País Second Front in Oriente province.

He participated in various actions and later had the task of supervising both Cuba's Intelligence Services and the Rebel Police.

Following his role in the battle to take Santiago de Cuba, Piñeiro was named as a Commander of the Rebel Army.

After the triumph of the Cuban Revolution, the military plaza in Santiago was named after him. It was there that photographers fought for the first time to capture his image: a face dominated by a ginger, bushy beard that since his days in the Sierra Maestra had earned him his legendary nickname: Red Beard.

Later he moved to Havana, where he worked at establishing Cuba's organs of State Security. On June 6, 1961 he was named Vice-Minister of the Ministry of the Interior and head of the 'Specialist' Vice-Ministry: a body responsible for developing intelligence strategies and implementing Cuba's international policies and solidarity with the Cuban Revolution.

An elected member of the Central Committee of the Communist Party of Cuba in 1965, he remained so until 1997. In 1970 Piñeiro became the First Vice-Minister of the Ministry of the Interior and head of the then nascent General National Liberation Department (DGLN) of the Ministry of the Interior (MININT). He directed numerous Cuban solidarity activities with popular and revolutionary movements in many diverse countries, especially those in Latin America and the Caribbean.

Early in 1975 he was appointed to the position he held for over 17 years: head of the Americas Department of the Central Committee of the Cuban Communist Party.

Manuel Piñeiro Losada died in a car accident on the night of March 11, 1998, only hours after receiving an award at an activity marking the 40th anniversary of the Rebel Army's Frank País Second Front.

Acknowledgments

To those at the Organization in Solidarity with the Peoples of Asia, Africa and Latin America (OSPAAL) and at the magazine *Tricontinental*, who all welcomed enthusiastically the idea of preparing this book and who transformed all related tasks into a priority of the organization. In particular, to Ramón Pez Ferro, Ana María Pellón, Lourdes Cervantes, Mayra Oramas, Gladys Acosta, Mario González, Nectalí Corso, Sigrid Wilson, Ibolya Virág, Arleen Rodríguez and Teresa Valdés.

To Marta Harnecker, Manuel Piñeiro Burdsall (Manolito), Lorna Burdsall, José Arbesu Fraga, Zenaida Llerena, Juana Morera (Jenny), Luis Hernández Ojeda, Jorge Ferrera, Sergio Cervantes and Francisco Delgado (Panchito), for their never-ending help in locating a large part of the materials that make up this book.

To Hilda Betancourt, who transcribed many of the interviews and public appearances made by the author of this book, Manuel Piñeiro.

To Carlos Oliva and Jorge Bousoño from the Association for the Unification of Our America (AUNA) for their contribution in scanning the speeches that appear in this book, given by the author between 1972 and 1990.

To the journalists Claudia Furiati, Lucía Newman, Faride Zeran, Ana María Lobouno and Francisco Loquercio, each of whom have generously given their permission to publish interviews undertaken individually with Manuel Piñeiro Losada.

To Tahamí Suárez, Yaser Barroso and the other members of the group *Che Vive* at the University of Havana, for their initiative and dedication in the organization of an activity that became a homage from a new generation of students to the author of this book.

To Dr. Andrea Salvagno, for the wonderful decision to press play on her tape recorder in the precise moment Commander Manuel Piñeiro Losada spoke publicly for the last time about Che in Bolivia – words that have since passed into history. Without her immediate choice to bring forward this tape, it would not have been possible to recover the fragments of the exchange that appear in the form of an epilogue in this book.

To Ramiro Abreu, Armando Campos, Omar Córdova, Néstor León Sobral, Leonel Urbino, Jorge Luis Joa, Carlos Antelo, Fernando Ravelo, Santiago Salas Ochoa, Patricio Etchagaray, Claudia Korol and Iván Vázquez, who helped me in any number of ways, and, perhaps without realizing it, gave shape to the original text and notes that appear in this book.

To Martica, Vivian, Beatriz and Lorena, all linked with the group, Popular Latin American Memory (MEPLA), who diligently gave me all the help they could give in the compilation and preparation of this volume.

To my wife and colleague Tania García Lorenzo and to my children Ernesto Javier and Haydeé Tamara, who, united by the memory of the author of this book, made it possible for me to have the time, space and silence necessary for the reading, selection and preparation of the text, prologue and notes that are included in this book.

Luis Suárez Salazar

Introduction

This book, like many others, has a sad history. Like other social scientists and countless Cuban and foreign journalists, I spent more than a decade asking Commander Manuel Piñeiro Losada to give me an interview on the many activities that the Cuban Revolution carried out in solidarity with the peoples' revolutionary movements in various parts of the world, especially Latin America and the Caribbean.

In order to continue advancing in my unfinished research on the strategy and different stages of Cuban relations with the rest of Latin America and the Caribbean,[1] I had to have access to the information, opinions and testimony that Piñeiro and many of his comrades in the Technical Deputy Ministry, General Intelligence Department and General National Liberation Department of the Ministry of the Interior and in the Americas Department of the Central Committee of the Communist Party of Cuba (PCC) could provide.

In my humble opinion, all of us who are linked in one way or another to that work should pass on to the new generations — especially those in Cuba — our experiences and what we have learned about the basic theory and practice to which hundreds of Cuban and other comrades from other parts of Latin America, the Caribbean and the rest of the world have — often anonymously — devoted their lives.

By doing so, we would add to our peoples' collective recollections of history the selflessness, spirit of solidarity and internationalism that have accompanied and continue to accompany the main protagonists in

---

[1] See Luis Suárez Salazar, "La política de la revolución cubana hacia América Latina y el Caribe: notas para una periodización" (The Cuban Revolution's Policy on Latin America and the Caribbean: Notes for an Update), in *Cuadernos de Nuestra América* (Havana: July-December 1986), Vol. III, No. 6, 137-80; "Las relaciones de Cuba con América Latina y el Caribe: posibilidades y retos" (Cuba's Relations with the Rest of Latin America and the Caribbean: Possibilities and Challenges), in *Cuadernos de Nuestra América* (Havana: July-December 1990), Vol. VII, No. 15, 144-69; *Cuba: ¿aislamiento o reinserción en un mundo cambiado?* (Cuba: Isolation or Reinsertion in a Changed World?) (Havana: Editorial de Ciencias Sociales, 1997); and "Las relaciones interestatales de Cuba: desde la Helms-Burton hasta la visita de Juan Pablo II" (Cuba's Intergovernmental Relations: From the Helms-Burton Law to the Visit of John Paul II), in *Enfoque* (Havana: IPS, July 1998).

the revolutionary events in Cuba and the rest of Latin America in their unfinished striving to reach the goal that José Martí set us a century ago: that of bringing about the real, definitive independence of Our America.

This is especially important because, in spite of everything that has been written about the Cuban Revolution in the past 40 years, and in spite of the countless documents, essays and articles that have been published about its foreign policy, there isn't any text that analyzes or places in context the details and alternatives of the policy of the first socialist government in the western hemisphere toward the rest of Latin America and the Caribbean.

Moreover, since both humans and nature abhor a vacuum, it was only to be expected (as, in fact, has happened) that certain texts (some of them by "renowned authors") would be published about the motivations of the Cuban revolutionary leadership — especially those of Fidel Castro — in drawing up and implementing that important facet of our country's foreign policy. These texts are frequently filled with distortions, simplifications, ruses and vulgarizations.

In addition, as time went by without any clarification of the details and decisions regarding those events, the inexorable laws of life and death meant that a risk was being run that memories would fail or that the comrades who had had the privilege of playing a part in those important events and decisions — which have unquestionably had a lasting influence on the recent history of the Latin American and Caribbean peoples' anti-imperialist struggles — would die.

In spite of his stated agreement with these arguments and our long and close personal and work relations, Piñeiro kept turning down my reiterated requests for an interview, saying, "That isn't declassified yet"; "Another comrade should tell you that part"; "That should be told by a representative of the Latin American peoples' revolutionary movement"; "I had nothing to do with that"; "The time isn't ripe for talking about that yet"; "Give me an outline of your research and your main questions"; "I can't talk about that until Fidel does"; or "My current responsibilities don't allow me to talk about those things."

He repeated some of those arguments when he handed over the reins of the Americas Department of the International Relations Department of the Central Committee of the Communist Party of Cuba in March 1992 and entered what someone has described as his "industrious retirement" — his final years.

Even so, a few weeks after that decision, during one of our frequent meetings in his house or in the offices of the Center for the Study of the Americas (CEA), I asked him again. Together with my friend Fernando Ravelo, former Cuban Ambassador to Colombia and Nicaragua, I even made an outline of the questions I would like to ask.

But, once again, nothing happened — until one day (I can't

remember exactly which day it was) I asked Piñeiro yet again and he said, "I'm putting my papers in order, beginning with all the ones linked to Che. After I've finished, I'll give you your interview." Even with that promise, I was pessimistic, thinking that it was just another pretext for indefinitely putting off the interview. The passing years seemed to confirm that premonition.

But, in early 1997, when the 30th anniversary of the Heroic Guerrilla's[2] death was approaching, I returned to the attack. This time, I did so not only on my own behalf but also implementing a resolution of the Advisory Council of *Tricontinental* magazine, together with Ana María Pellón (its editor in chief) and Ivette Zuazo (editor), solemnly promising that all of our questions would be related to Che's internationalist missions in the Congo and Bolivia and to Piñeiro's views on the timeliness of Che's actions.

Since he who perseveres is nearly always rewarded, after several changes in the time and place of the interview (which sometimes made us think that, in the end, he wouldn't grant it), we finally managed to meet with Manuel Piñeiro Losada on a rainy afternoon in June 1997 and set down for posterity his authoritative, vivid testimony about Che's feats and his own participation in them.

After that meeting, we drew up the first rough draft of the interview. This was followed by many intensive work sessions in which, either on his own or after consultation with other comrades, he asked us to expand or amend (even at the page-proof stage!) some of the answers he had originally given us, playing down his own importance and, as always, being meticulously correct in presenting events exactly as they had happened.

Finally, the "exclusive" that he described as "My modest tribute to Che"[3] was published in issue 137 of *Tricontinental*. Its presentation in the Cuba Pavilion on July 31, 1997, as part of the 14th World Festival of Youth and Students was like a call to arms. More than a dozen alternative media papers reproduced it in whole or in part, in various languages. Some editors asked us to extend its contents with a view to larger editorial efforts. With greater or lesser credits for its authors and for the magazine, some major media mentioned the interview, sometimes incorporating other texts, questions and answers. Several foreign journalists posted in Havana and elsewhere took the opportunity to obtain and publish interviews that, on other occasions, he had refused to grant. We learned from various means that they had sent him new lists of questions.

For my part, recognizing the difficulties of holding another formal

---

[2] Che Guevara is commonly referred to as the Heroic Guerrilla.

[3] See Luis Suárez Salazar, Ivette Zuazo and Ana María Pellón, "Mi modesto homenaje al Che" (My Modest Tribute to Che), included in this book.

interview in such a short time, I began asking him to allow me to attend his meetings with select audiences interested in learning firsthand of the experiences and views of someone who had legitimately become a part of the legend of the Cuban and Latin American revolutions.

Sometimes — as during an international conference on Che Guevara held September 25-27, 1997, by the Organization of Solidarity with the Peoples of Africa, Asia and Latin America (OSPAAAL) — I managed to tape his address and the question-and-answer period following it; edited it; got him to check it by supplying him with plenty of bitter coffee and cigars, which he always needed while working; and guaranteed its subsequent publication.[4]

At other times (as in his address to the participants in the National University Seminar on Che and the Challenges of the Third Millennium, that was held at the University of Havana in late February 1998), I took notes of what he said, with a view to finding an opportunity for checking and/or enlarging on his new revelations and assessments. I even gave him 17 new questions, which he agreed to answer as soon as he found the time to study them and document his replies.

During the February 1998 Book Fair of Havana, with his consent, the *Tricontinental* team and I promised to prepare all of that material and get one of our publishers — which included Ocean Press of Australia — to print it in the form of a book. We wanted the volume to come out (at least in Spanish and English) in honor of the 40th anniversary of the triumph of the Cuban Revolution.

Aware of that commitment, he reiterated to us by phone on the afternoon of Saturday, March 7, 1998, that we could begin to work on that text as soon as he got back from the ceremony held on the 40th anniversary of the founding of the Frank País Second Eastern Front.

At close to midnight on March 11, just a few days before our next meeting, news reached us that Manuel Piñeiro Losada — "the fearsome Red Beard," as Nobel Prize laureate Gabriel García Márquez and his wife, Mercedes, affectionately called him — had died an hour earlier in an automobile accident.

The harsh impact of that news and the grief it caused stayed with me after his burial and led me to keep going over his appearances and interviews (both with me and with others), which events had turned into messages from the grave. As I wrote:

> Reading them over, listening once more to his distinctive voice, his sometimes hesitating words, his witty remarks, his irony and the strong flow of his arguments; looking over everything that remained

---

[4] See "Inmortalidad del Che" (Che's Immortality), *Tricontinental* (Havana: 1998), Year 31, No. 138.

unpublished and the notes of everything that we still had to do; and trying to make out his nearly illegible writing, I was convinced yet again — a conviction I share with many — that Piñeiro was an irreplaceable link in history, in our histories.

Without his competent information and assessments; without his stupendous memory; and without his ability to call other anonymous, known or little-known participants together, it would be very difficult to reconstruct the full story of the last four decades of Cuban, African and Latin American internationalism and the very diverse links between his beloved island and the rest of Latin America and the Caribbean.

In his enriching relationships with Fidel, Che and other outstanding leaders of our homeland, the Americas and other parts of the world, Piñeiro was a pioneer and builder. In his absence and that of other more or less outstanding protagonists, it would also be very hard to reproduce the full chronicles of the revolutionary movement of the peoples of our region and, perhaps, of another part of the world.[5]

Starting with these painful thoughts, many other comrades and I began to think about how we could preserve the legacy of Manuel Piñeiro Losada. It seemed to me that it would be impossible to write a biography — at least, in a short period of time. Unfortunately, the details of his life were and remain shrouded — even from his comrades — in the discretion that always accompanied him in his tremendous revolutionary political work.

However, it seemed relatively easy to gather together and publish in a single volume all of his addresses and the interviews which, just before and after July 31, 1997, he had granted to distinguished journalists from different parts of the world.

Thus, in his absence, but trying to continue as he would have wished, we would keep the pledge to the publishers. Moreover, we were sure that, by so doing, we would express his gratitude to all of the men and women of the press (with whom Piñeiro had excellent relations), who, for decades, complying with the best ethics of their profession, had respected his silence — and especially to those who, when he decided to break that silence, had neither twisted his words nor engaged in speculation with his revelations.

With the immeasurable help of Marta Harnecker, his comrade for life and in the struggle, and with that of Hilda Betancourt, we began to list, locate, transcribe and digitize everything that had been published and —

---

[5] See Luis Suárez Salazar, "Un hombre que derrotó a la mediocridad" (A Man who Defeated Mediocrity), *Tricontinental* special supplement (Havana: 1998), Year 32, No. 139, 6-8.

in close contact with their respective authors — everything that was still awaiting publication. In the course of that search, we found two essays on the situation of Latin America and the Caribbean that Piñeiro had published in the 1980s. We also found some of his addresses that had been reproduced in full during those years.

Basing ourselves on those findings, we began to toy with the idea of finding and publishing all of the addresses he had given at different times and places. The problem lay in how and where to find them.

But chance came to our aid. Acting on something that his son, Manolito, had told us, Marta Harnecker came across a folder on a shelf in their house that contained copies of the addresses that Piñeiro was assumed to have given between 1972 and 1990. Vidalina Valledor, the head of his office for nearly three decades and one of the people closest to Red Beard, had patiently and meticulously put them in order.

Even though we knew from our own experience that most of the writings and addresses we had found were the fruit of his characteristic methods of collective work, we also knew that he never signed or expressed verbal support for anything with which he didn't fully agree. The file even contained suggestions for talks that he had rejected and texts with handwritten notes in which he changed the proposals that had been made by some of his subordinates. Therefore, it was possible to discern which of all the manuscripts we had found were (and which weren't) in accord with the view of reality that Piñeiro had at the specific historical moment in which each of those texts had been written.

The book that we now present to our readers is the result of a critical review and painstaking editing of all that material. Its second section contains a chronological selection of the addresses that Manuel Piñeiro Losada made between 1972 and 1990 and the two essays he published in the 1980s — one of them together with his close friend and comrade. Commander Jesús Montané Oropesa.[6] The first section contains nearly all of the interviews and talks that Piñeiro gave in the period just before and after the 30th anniversary of Che's death,[7] including excerpts from

---

[6] Jesús Montané Oropesa was one of the young people who attacked the Moncada Garrison in July 1953 and founded the July 26 Movement. After the triumph of the revolution, he held various important political and governmental posts, including that of minister of communications and alternate member of the Political Bureau of the Central Committee of the Communist Party of Cuba. From 1965 until his death in 1999, he was a member of the Central Committee of the Communist Party of Cuba. He was also a deputy to the National Assembly of People's Power and an assistant to Fidel Castro.

[7] Because of problems encountered in the taping, we decided to exclude the round-table discussion that the Fernando Ortiz House of Advanced Studies of the University of Havana sponsored on Che's struggle in Africa. Papito Serguera and Léster Rodríguez (a revolutionary combatant who has since died) took part in the round-table discussion along with Piñeiro. For reasons beyond our control, the biographical

his February 28, 1998, speech at the National University Seminar on Che and the Challenges of the Third Millennium and on Che's struggle in Bolivia — Piñeiro's last such intervention.

All of these speeches and interviews provide an assessment of some of the events linked to the internationalist trajectory of the Heroic Guerrilla as well as the documented, authoritative criticism that Piñeiro made of some of the twisted versions and lies that are being spread in the latest biographies of Ernesto Che Guevara.

In most cases, the interviews are published just as they appeared in the various newspapers in several countries throughout the world. In others, what appears in the book corresponds to the transcript and editing I did — with authorization by their authors — of important unpublished parts of the interviews that Piñeiro had given which had been left out for reasons of space.

My purpose when it came to editing these last was to try to reduce, as much as possible, the repetition of some questions and answers, but, in order to preserve the coherence of those texts, it wasn't always possible to do so.

From the foregoing, you can see that this volume is not a compilation of the complete works of Manuel Piñeiro Losada. The addresses he gave between 1959 and 1972 (and especially between 1961 and 1970, when he headed the Technical Deputy Ministry of the Ministry of the Interior of the Republic of Cuba) are missing, as are some of the talks on the situation of Latin America and the Caribbean which he gave to carefully selected audiences during the more than 15 years (1975-92) when he headed the Americas Department or Americas Area of the International Relations Department of the Central Committee of the Communist Party of Cuba.

For editorial reasons, this selection also leaves out some of the addresses that Piñeiro gave between 1972 and 1990. Only those that are linked to important Cuban and Latin American events or which bring out an important facet of the history of the Cuban Revolution's solidarity with the rest of Latin America and the Caribbean are included.

In spite of these gaps, we are confident that readers of this book will find many pages of interest for reconstructing the bases of the Cuban Revolution's internationalist and Latin Americanist policies and, perhaps for the first time, for drawing closer to the world view that characterized the selfless, brilliant revolutionary activities of Commander Manuel Piñeiro Losada.

This is especially true of his constant identification with the thinking

---

interview which the outstanding Cuban social scientist Fernando Martínez Heredia made of Manuel Piñeiro and the as yet unpublished interview that Mexican journalist Mario Menéndez made of him concerning aspects related to the 1960s are not included.

and actions of Fidel Castro; his permanent praise for the life, work and example of Che; his anti-imperialism; his internationalism; his Latin Americanism; his work to unite the peoples; his constant warnings — even at times of victory — not to underestimate the many forms that actions by counterrevolutionaries in the United States and the ruling classes might take; and his unlimited confidence — even at times of the worst defeats — that the causes of the peoples of the world would emerge triumphant.

Finally, we invite readers to view this book as a tribute by OSPAAAL and *Tricontinental* magazine to Commander Manuel Piñeiro Losada — and, through him, to all of the comrades who anonymously accompanied him in the internationalist tasks to which he devoted his long and fruitful life as a revolutionary: especially to all of the comrades in the Technical Deputy Ministry and General National Liberation Department of the Ministry of the Interior and of the Americas Department of the Central Committee of the Communist Party of Cuba who dedicate their lives to struggling, as Fidel Castro said in *History Will Absolve Me*, to make Cuba a bulwark of freedom rather than a shameful link of despotism in the Americas.

Luis Suárez Salazar

Interviews
on Che Guevara

My Modest Homage to Che

Interview with Commander Manuel Piñeiro Losada by Luis Suárez, Ivette Zuazo and Ana María Pellón [1]

A heavy thundershower lets loose just as we turn on the tape recorder, as though the heavens are trying to drown us out. But we are undaunted. The world has waited too long for this interview. The subject of our interview grumbles in mock protest: "You folks are putting an end to my virginity." We acknowledge the deed. Although Manuel Piñeiro has occasionally spoken with reporters, this is the first time in 30 years he has agreed to be interviewed about Che Guevara.

The requests have been abundant, from Cuban as well as foreign journalists and writers. The reason is simple: Manuel Piñeiro, whose friends and enemies all referred to him as "Barba Roja" (Red Beard) in the turbulent 1960s, was an active witness to Che's international actions from 1959 up until his assassination in Bolivia in 1967.

Throughout those years, Piñeiro headed the Intelligence Department of Cuba's Interior Ministry. Among other things, he was responsible for maintaining ties with Third World revolutionary movements. The liberation insurgency was then at its height. Among Che's many tasks within the leadership of the Cuban Revolution were the promotion of anti-imperialist solidarity and the preparations to extend the struggle to other lands. In this, Piñeiro was very closely associated with Che.

Manuel Piñeiro earned his position primarily during the anti-Batista guerrilla struggle led by the July 26 Movement in the Sierra Maestra mountains, having arrived there from Havana in May 1957. Piñeiro started out as one of the local leaders of the movement in his native province of Matanzas, but was forced to relocate to Havana when his propaganda and sabotage actions began to draw too much heat. In

---

[1] This interview was first published in *Tricontinental*, Number 137, 1997.

Havana, he sent arms shipments to the Sierra, then asked to be allowed to join the guerrillas in the mountains.

Once there, he joined up with guerrilla Column One, led by Fidel. In March 1958 he transferred to Raúl Castro's column, which opened up the "Frank País Second Eastern Front," named after the underground leader assassinated by Batista's forces in Santiago the year before. While in the Second Front, Piñeiro was Chief of Staff and headed the unit that maintained contact with the various July 26 Movement guerrilla groups spread out through the mountains. He also ran the movement's intelligence services and the Rebel Police.

By the end of the war, he wore the insignia of commander [then the highest rank in the Rebel Army]. In 1961, Manuel Piñeiro helped establish the Ministry of the Interior, where he was to remain until 1975. For nearly a decade of that time he headed the Technical Vice-Ministry, and later served in the General Headquarters of National Liberation.

For the next 15 years, he was in charge of the Americas Department of the Cuban Communist Party's Central Committee. Piñeiro has been a member of the Central Committee since its founding on October 3, 1965 — the day that Fidel made public Che's farewell letter.

Today, at 64 years of age, with his beard and hair turned gray, Piñeiro still works until all hours of the night, whether in the Central Committee offices where he goes each afternoon or in the simple terrace of his home, where we are now meeting. His work habitat is revealing of the man: tables covered with documents and publications about Latin America; a red pole lamp standing guard over a white, oval-shaped work table; a long hammock swinging against the backdrop of the profuse greenery of his back yard. But it must be said that amidst all this intense focus on his revolutionary life, his family occupies a special place: his *compañera*, Marxist Chilean writer Marta Harnecker; their daughter Camila, and his son by his first marriage, Manuel, who is a lawyer.

We've been talking with him for almost four hours and Piñeiro is as fresh as he was at the beginning. He hasn't been able to keep the promise he made to himself at the beginning — to be brief — but he makes up for this with a sharp memory for details.

After so many years of silence, Manuel Piñeiro says that granting this interview is his way of paying tribute: "my humble homage to Che Guevara."

* * * * * * *

How and when did you meet Che?

Piñeiro: The first time I saw him was in passing, when our columns passed by each other after the battle of Pino del Agua (September 10,

1957). I had already heard from other combatants, who spoke of him with great love and respect, that he was a brave, audacious Argentine blessed with a great intellect and solid political ideas.

Later, I encountered him again in El Hombrito, another site in the Sierra Maestra where his command post was located. This included an armory, a bakery and a post for medical and dental services — of which he was the dentist, with a pair of pliers as his only instrument. Coincidentally, the day I went there I had a tremendous toothache, but when I went looking for Che I heard a man screaming and moaning, and I saw him holding a peasant farmer by the head and, pliers in hand, extracting a molar. I said to myself right then and there: I will never fall into the hands of that man. I don't think I'll ever forget that image.

Beyond that first shock, what kind of impression did he make on you?

Piñeiro: That of a serene man, very self-confident, a man who inspired respect. In the beginning he would seem serious or introverted, but once you got to know him personally he was very communicative, with a sharp sense of humor, sometimes touched with irony.

I think that some *compañeros* didn't understand his jokes because his psychology and idiosyncrasies were different from ours; he had a different cultural upbringing. Some thought his jokes were very acid, very "Argentine." It's true his jokes sometimes had a biting edge, but they were always affectionate and educational; they were never meant to offend anyone, but rather to appeal to one's personal sense of dignity.

When was the first time you ran into him after the triumph of the revolution?

Piñeiro: On May 1, 1959 — International Workers' Day — he attended the parade in Santiago de Cuba, which was the capital of what was then Oriente Province. I was the military chief of Oriente Province at that time, so I welcomed him and we met in my office at the Moncada Barracks. But my close relationship with Che began in the second half of 1959.

Is that when you began to work together on activities linked to solidarity with revolutionary struggles in the Third World?

Piñeiro: Yes. That year I moved from Oriente to Havana to help set up the intelligence and security structures that preceded the creation of the Ministry of the Interior on June 6, 1961. The ministry was then headed by Comrade Ramiro Valdés. These incipient structures, and later the Technical Vice-Ministry of MININT [Ministry of the Interior], which I was appointed to head up, were also responsible for dealing with revolutionary and political leaders of other Third World countries who came to learn from the experience of the Cuban Revolution. Of course, they wanted to talk with its principal leaders, first of all, with Fidel and

Che. Che gave them what little free time he had, especially at night, just as he did for any *campesino* [peasant farmer] or rebel combatant he had known in the Sierra who asked to speak with him.

The meetings with these leaders — most of them from the Caribbean or Latin America — lasted until well into the early hours, and sometimes until the first rays of the sun. They were carried out in safe houses, in Che's successive offices in the National Institute of Agrarian Reform [INRA], the National Bank, and the Ministry of Industry and occasionally in his home.

Did you take part in all of them?

Piñeiro: Almost always. If not, there would be some other *compañero* who was responsible for taking care of that visitor.

What do you most remember of those meetings?

Piñeiro: I remember the ever-present thermos of hot water, the *maté* [a strong, Argentine tea] with its wooden gourd and straw, the cigar in Che's mouth...

I was struck by Che's eternal capacity for listening, his respect for the opinions of the speaker, even when that person's ideas didn't coincide with his own. But that didn't mean he failed to present his own viewpoints, and very convincingly. And even if he didn't know the visitor, he was able to create a relaxed atmosphere, a sense of trust and fraternity, which enabled them to speak freely with each other.

Although he was usually on top of the political situation and the actions of the revolutionary movements in the Third World, especially in Latin America, Che always read as much material as we had about the economic, social and political situation of the country in question before each meeting. It was inconceivable to him not to have a map of that country on top of the table because, as someone very concerned with detail, he liked to analyze the geography, the topography of the territory, the characteristics of the rural population, the forms of land ownership, the social struggles and their antecedents, the peasant, worker and student movements, the political organizations, the intellectual world... He was extremely meticulous in seeking data and details on all those topics.

In a pedagogical fashion, without any dogma or rigidity, he would explain the Cuban revolutionary experience — not just his own, but that of other leaders like Fidel and Raúl Castro, Juan Almeida, Camilo Cienfuegos. He never failed to point out to the visitor that whenever there was the minutest chance for engaging in legal activities, they should take advantage of that — but without any illusions. They should also always be aware, he told them, how indispensable it was to strengthen their forces as much as possible and prepare militarily for the repression of the popular and revolutionary movement that would occur as soon as these became a serious threat to the ruling system. He would warn them of the probable aggressive reaction of the imperialists when confronted with the advances of the revolutionary struggles. Sometimes he would get into philosophical or cultural discussions.

Could you mention some of the Latin American leaders who came to make contact with him?

Piñeiro: It would be impossible to mention all of them, but among the many I recall were the Nicaraguans Carlos Fonseca, Tomás Borge, Rodolfo Romero and the former officer in Somoza's army, Somarriba, who led an attempt at armed struggle in Nicaragua — which failed in the end, and in which two Cuban *compañeros*, Onelio Hernández and Marcelo Fernández, died.

I also remember the Guatemalans Turcios Lima, John Sosa, Rolando Ramírez, Pablo Monzanto, Julio Cáceres (Patojo) — an intimate and much-loved friend of Che; the Peruvians Luis de la Puente Uceda, Héctor Béjar and Javier Heraud; the Peronists William Cooke and Alicia Eguren; the Colombians Fabio Vázquez (who became the leader of the National Liberation Army); the Liberal Party guerrilla leader Ricardo Franco, the La Rota brothers (who founded the Colombian Worker-Student Movement) and the secretary general of the Communist Party of that country, Gilberto Vieira.

There was also the Uruguayan Communist Party secretary, Rodney Arismendi; the principle leaders of the Chilean Socialist and Communist parties, especially Salvador Allende, who was then a senator, and Jaime Barrios; Venezuelans Eduardo and Gustavo Machado, and Gallegos Manceda of the Venezuelan CP, and the congressman from that country, Fabricio Ojeda; various Paraguayan, Haitian and Dominican leaders; Brazilian *campesino* leader Juliao and Brazilian Communist Party Secretary General Carlos Prestes…

In general, all the leaders of the left and of the communist parties of the region who passed through Havana met with him. Remember, Che participated in the Conference of Latin American Communist Parties that was held in Cuba in 1964.

Can we say that from the very beginning of the revolution there was a convergence of the Cuban practice of political solidarity toward other countries of the region, with Che's idea of eventually joining the battle for liberation in other Latin American countries?

Piñeiro: You shouldn't forget two things: Ever since he wrote "History Will Absolve Me" in 1953, Fidel has made clear that this revolution was seeking the liberation and integration of Latin America. He himself had participated in the "Bogotazo" [a popular uprising in Bogotá, Colombia],

and in actions on behalf of Puerto Rican independence, for the
sovereignty of the Malvinas, for the recovery of the Panama Canal; he
had also taken part in the Confite Key expedition, which was an
unsuccessful attempt to overthrow the Dominican dictator Leonidas
Trujillo. In Che, Fidel found someone who shared this same
determination and who came here already marked by his experience
during the CIA's overthrow of Guatemalan President Jacobo Arbenz in
Guatemala in 1954. Che had met many Latin American revolutionaries
in Guatemala, and that strengthened his anti-imperialist and Latin
Americanist convictions.

The other thing is that before setting out for Cuba in the *Granma*, Che
told Fidel that as soon as he had fulfilled his responsibilities to the
Cuban Revolution, when the right moment came, he wanted to be free
to join the revolutionary struggle in another Latin American country,
preferably Argentina. He was always interested in any plan that showed
some possibility for the development of revolutionary armed struggle —
whether in Nicaragua, Venezuela, Colombia — and in the possibility of
being accepted as a participant in the struggles of other countries.

For example, as early as 1959, Che sent a note with a Cuban emissary
to the anti-Somoza leader Somarriba, in which he expressed his
willingness to join that struggle as soon as the guerrilla column could
create the necessary conditions in that country. To Che's sadness, that
early attempt failed.

*How did Che see the development and dissemination of the revolutionary
struggle in Latin America?*

Piñeiro: His concept, rooted in the Cuban liberation war, consisted in
founding a "mother column" made up of revolutionaries from various
Latin American countries. Once they had overcome the initial period of
basic survival and had combat and leadership training, they would enter
the next stage of growth and development, during which they would
create the conditions for initiating other columns. Thus they would
spread the battle to other countries throughout Latin America, especially
those whose governments had united with U.S. imperialism against the
cause of the people.

As the Cuban experience demonstrated, the original guerrilla
nucleus, if well-directed, could be the small motor whose political and
military actions could set in motion the big motor of the masses of
people. Che's anti-imperialist, continental concept of armed
revolutionary struggle was based on this. It is essentially a political and
military concept based on the masses, which contradicts that narrow
interpretation of the "guerrilla foco" that has been falsely attributed to
Che. He always spoke of an insurrectionary guerrilla foco linked to the
people, not of a small group of armed men who acted divorced from the

popular movement and from the people in general.

He also said that a guerrilla struggle couldn't be carried out in countries where the governments were the result of some form of popular choice, and where all possible forms of civic struggle had not been exhausted.

There's one basic idea of Che's that should be emphasized: it is not necessary to wait for *all* the proper conditions to exist before starting the revolutionary struggle; the struggle itself will create the conditions as it goes along.

Che, therefore, is not responsible for the oversimplification of the Cuban experience and the misinterpretation of his ideas expressed by some Latin American revolutionaries, albeit with the best of intentions.

Was Che's preference for Argentina the origin of the guerrilla force led by his compatriot Jorge Ricardo Masetti in 1963? What was Che's role in that?

Piñeiro: Che met Masetti when he came to the Sierra Maestra as a journalist. After January 1959, Masetti returned to Cuba; he carried out some missions in support of the Algerian Revolution with the National Liberation Front (FLN) there, so he had acquired some combat experience. He received some military training in our country and then Che gave him the task of organizing a guerrilla column whose main mission was to install itself in Argentine territory near the border of Bolivia, in a place called Salta, with the idea that when the minimum conditions had been achieved, he would join them, to initiate armed struggle in Argentina. Che dedicated a lot of time to preparing that detachment, called the Guerrilla Army of the Poor. Masetti was accompanied (among others) by two Cubans: Hermes Pena (who died in battle) and Alberto Castellanos, who was captured and spent four years in Argentine jails without his captors being able to identify his real nationality.

When Masetti left for Salta he was called "Segundo" (Second); was this because he was only going to head the group for a short while?

Piñeiro: Yes, because the "First" was Che — that was the meaning of Masetti's pseudonym. Che wanted to be the one to initiate it, but Fidel persuaded him that he should only return to Argentina after an advance group laid the groundwork. That is, he shouldn't be there during the riskiest and most difficult stage faced by any guerrilla movement, that of survival, when the guerrillas are basically left to their own devices.

That criterion has its antecedents in the cadre policy Fidel developed in the Sierra Maestra. He always tried to preserve the best of the intermediate-level column leaders for later actions. This policy was shown to be correct during our war. Fidel didn't want to risk losing someone with the experience and continental stature of Che in the first stage of the guerrilla struggle.

Nevertheless, that effort had Cuba's solidarity?

Piñeiro: Yes — at all stages. First, it was necessary to establish a logistical support base from the Bolivian side, and there were Cubans assigned to do that: Abelardo Colomé Ibarra (Fury), who is now General of the Army Corps [and Minister of the Interior], and José María Martínez Tamayo (Papi), who died a few years later in the Bolivian guerrilla struggle. They went to Bolivia to receive Masetti and his group, with the aid of the Peredo brothers and Rodolfo Saldaña (members of the Bolivian CP), in coordination with a group of *compañeros* we sent to La Paz. At the same time, at Che's request, the Argentine couple William Cooke and Alicia Eguren was asked to serve as backup in Argentina, although they weren't fully aware of all the plans, or about Che's eventual participation in the guerrilla movement.

We also should acknowledge here the cooperation provided at all times by the leadership of the Algerian FLN.

Eventually Masetti's insurgency was discovered and almost all its members were killed or disappeared. What affect did this have on Che?

Piñeiro: It had a profoundly emotional and human effect: it meant the deaths of *compañeros* he had worked with through many years of struggle. He said more than once that what most upset him was the idea that while this was happening, he was here in an office. When we lost contact with Masetti in April 1964, Che made every effort possible to find out what happened, to learn if there were any survivors and, if so, to reorganize them. William and Alicia were involved in this attempt. Later on, other Argentine friends kept looking for the remains of Masetti and his *compañeros*, trying to reconstruct the events, but up to now nothing has been found to indicate how that guerrilla effort ended or about Masetti's death.

During that same period Che was very interested in the progress of the Peruvian insurgency. Is it true that Peru was another of the alternatives considered before he selected Bolivia?

Piñeiro: Argentina, Peru, Bolivia... they were all part of his strategy to spread the revolution to the rest of Latin America.

Parallel to the Salta Operation, a group of Peruvian combatants led by Alain Elías, which included Javier Heraud and Abraham Lamas, tried to initiate armed struggle in January 1963, entering Peru through the Puerto Maldonado area bordering Bolivia. Heraud, a young Peruvian poet, died there, along with other *compañeros*.

They had the support of various Bolivian communists, especially the Peredo brothers, who gave them logistical support and served as guides for the column to infiltrate Peru from Bolivia. Years later the ELN reinitiated the struggle under the leadership of Héctor Béjar. The guerrilla movements of Luis de la Puente Uceda and Guillermo Lobatón, leaders of the Revolutionary Left Movement (MIR), emerged then, too. Che met with all of these Peruvian leaders at one time or another.

That is, there was a certain amount of organization and popular movement in Peru, social struggles, such as the land takeovers led by Hugo Blanco. Peru also held an attraction for Che because it was closer to Argentina. Besides, there was a democratic government in Bolivia at that time, which had arisen out of the 1952 revolution and lasted until 1964. But both the guerrilla movements of the MIR and the ELN were wiped out. Luis de la Puente Uceda died in November 1965 and Lobatón in January 1966. Héctor Béjar had already been captured in 1965 and the guerrilla column he led had been beaten...

How did Che react to all these setbacks, which obviously interrupted his plans for the continent?

Piñeiro: You could see he was very impatient. He never stopped exploring the possibilities of joining the armed struggle in other countries, such as Venezuela and Colombia. But none of them achieved the favorable conditions needed to incorporate a revolutionary of his political and military stature into their movement, with all that that implied.

When did he start to think of Bolivia as a possible scene of struggle, and not just as a support zone? Why did he decide on that country?

Piñeiro: In 1964 General Barrientos staged a coup d'état. That initiated a period of intense repression in Bolivia, but at the same time, of resistance by the popular movement, particularly the miners and students. From then on, Che began closely observing the unfolding of events. Two years later, while he was in Tanzania, Che decided to send Papi to Bolivia to evaluate the situation. He confirmed that Bolivia was the only option, in the sense that the minimum political conditions existed, and there were Bolivian cadre with experience, who had helped Masetti and the Peruvian guerrillas. That is, they were people who had been trained in combat and who had a political-ideological commitment to solidarity with any revolutionary movement that should appear in the area.

How did Che's plans for Bolivia fit into his continental strategy?

Piñeiro: From his viewpoint, this guerrilla struggle should be a training school for Latin American cadre, above all those from the Southern Cone — among them, Argentines — which would help to extend the armed struggle to bordering countries. At the same time, it gave him the chance to gather political and military forces and to wait for a more opportune occasion to move on to his native country.

This would depend on the growth and development of the "mother column" based in Bolivia. Without that, it would be impossible to continue toward Argentina, where there was also a vicious military dictatorship installed by the United States and repudiated by the most militant sectors of the Argentine people.

Che analyzed realistically what would happen if other guerrilla columns, made up of combatants from various countries of the Southern Cone, were to develop and emerge from the Bolivian experience. The reaction to this would be an alliance among the governments and armies of the bordering countries, supported by U.S. imperialism. That, in turn, would contribute to the spread of revolutionary armed struggle in the region, which would produce a scenario of long, bloody and difficult battles that sooner or later would lead to Yankee intervention. That would constitute, therefore, another of the "Vietnams" he called for in his historic "Message to the Peoples of the World" disseminated by *Tricontinental*.

Was the original idea and plan for Bolivia entirely Che's?

Piñeiro: Yes, the selection of the place, the combatants, the design and preparation of that plan were all conceived by Che. Of course, Fidel offered all the support and cooperation possible. He again urged that Che not be among the first group, but to join in when they were installed and had created the minimal conditions: logistics, armaments, urban support networks and the incorporation of some Latin American cadre, especially the Bolivians. The idea was also to wait until they had sufficient information and had adapted to the terrain; in short, to wait until the guerrilla movement had passed the initial survival stage. But Che was already eager to begin the struggle, especially in a country neighboring the one where he most desired to carry the revolutionary battle: Argentina.

Furthermore, from the psychological viewpoint he felt very pressured by the passing of the years. He knew more than anyone that you need certain basic physical conditions to engage in guerrilla warfare, and that it wouldn't be an easy task to carry out that struggle at this particular conjuncture in Latin America. Remember, this was when the United States had just initiated the destabilizing "Alliance for Progress," and at the same time was carrying out a counterinsurgency campaign to aid the regimes in the area, supplying them with weapons, money and training for their armies. The United States wanted at all costs to halt the spread of the example of the Cuban Revolution.

Some people say that after his farewell letter was published, Che felt that he had a moral commitment to never return to Cuba or, if he did so, to not hold any visible leadership position...

Piñeiro: In my opinion, with or without a farewell letter, Che's plans were unalterable. He was determined to fulfill what he had set out as his historic and strategic objective: to wage an anti-imperialist struggle throughout the Americas.

Not counting Ciro Bustos,[2] there was only one other Argentine, Tania, in the Bolivian guerrilla movement. Why do you think there were so few Argentines involved?

Piñeiro: Bustos operated as the liaison for a whole series of interrelated networks provided by Che to contact Argentines from various organizations and take them to the area where Che was operating in Bolivia. When Bustos was captured and turned traitor — offering data, maps and drawings identifying Che and the guerrillas and showing where they were — that "froze" Argentina. Remember, too, that when the Bolivian Army discovered the guerrilla base, the whole plan unraveled precipitously. The guerrillas had to be constantly on the move, and in this stage it was very difficult to maintain contacts with the urban base and with those abroad.

I think that if this hadn't happened, once Che's presence in Bolivia was known, cadre and combatants from various revolutionary forces in Latin America would have sought some way to link up with them and to participate. Che's call had great influence on many revolutionaries inside and outside of Latin America.

What do you think of the story spread around the world that Cuba's political leaders abandoned Che in Bolivia and didn't give him the support necessary for the success of his operation?

Piñeiro: From the very beginning of the Cuban Revolution — and long before, from the time of our wars of independence — the strategy of the U.S. empire has been to attempt to divide the revolutionary forces. First, they initiated a campaign saying that the disappearance of Commander Camilo Cienfuegos, whose plane was lost at sea in 1959, was the intentional result of contradictions within the revolutionary leadership. Later they spoke of supposed differences between Fidel and Raúl; and later, between Fidel and Che. They mounted a disinformation campaign that still persists today, trying to create confusion not just in Cuba, but also in the Latin American and worldwide revolutionary movements, and international public opinion in general. One of the centerpieces of these slander campaigns is the alleged "abandoning" of Che's guerrilla

---

[2] Bustos, an Argentine artist, and French writer Régis Debray had gone to the guerrilla camp in Bolivia in March 1967 at Guevara's invitation to discuss international support work for the guerrilla movement. The two were trapped in the zone of operations after the onset of combat, and were arrested in April.

movement, questioning why Cuba didn't send in military reinforcements to aid him and to break the Bolivian encirclement.

Anyone who knows the laws of guerrilla warfare knows that, in the initial and most difficult phase, the column has to be constantly on the move to prevent ambush by the enemy army, especially if it is outnumbered. During this phase, the guerrillas must depend on their own strength, plus the backing they can get from the urban networks — which at that time had been beaten. So the idea that we could have just sent in military reinforcements is absurd; it was logistically impossible — that's pure fantasy.

And is it also fantasy to compare the alleged lack of support for Che with the successful Cuban efforts to rescue the officers who were trapped in Venezuela under similar circumstances?

Piñeiro: I can assure you, based on my own knowledge and responsibility, that the two situations were completely different. Although the militants [who were backing up the guerrillas] from the Venezuelan Communist Party, the MIR and other revolutionary forces had suffered some defeats, they maintained enough clandestine structures and operational resources to facilitate the patient and thorough operation of extracting these *compañeros*. Those circumstances were not duplicated in Bolivia.

Going back to 1965: you were heavily involved in the preparations for the Cuban internationalist mission in the Congo that Che led that year. In your opinion, what did that stage mean for him in relation to long-term strategy?

Piñeiro: At that time, there were certainly signs of revolutionary movement throughout the world, impelled by the heroic example of the Vietnamese, and the heady success of the Cuban Revolution. But the minimal conditions still didn't exist for Che to be able to carry out his plans in Latin America. Given that, and the request for help that the Congo Supreme Revolutionary Council had transmitted to Cuba via Che, Fidel suggested to Che that the best thing he could do was to lead a group of Cuban military advisers who were heading for that African country. That would give him time to acquire more experience, again prepare himself militarily, and at the same time train some Cuban cadre and combatants who later would accompany him to Bolivia.

For Che the Congo phase was like a rung in a ladder, an intermediary phase to prepare himself for the final goal, waiting for events in Latin America to evolve enough to create favorable conditions for carrying out his long-term plans. So much so that, at his departure from the Congo, Che asked Harry Villegas, Carlos Coello and José María Martínez Tamayo, if they were willing to continue fighting alongside him in another country, where the struggle would be long, complex and difficult. Those *compañeros* later on formed a part of the Bolivian guerrilla movement using the noms de guerre Pombo, Tuma and Ricardo.

What was the role of the vice-ministry you headed in the delicate operations of getting Che and his compañeros *to Africa, bringing them back to Cuba and later getting them into Bolivia?*

Piñeiro: Our department was in charge of all the technical and operational preparations for the Congo mission: getting them their documents, preparing their travel itineraries, their cover stories. We formed a support group based in our Tanzanian embassy, which was responsible for information gathering and help in moving logistical support from there to Che's base in the Congo. They were also in charge of training the radio operators and for other forms of communication and contact with Che.

Following Fidel's instructions, MININT's Technical Vice-Ministry provided backing for Che in everything he asked for in relation to his future mission in Bolivia. We worked in securing documents, falsifying passports, got him the information he asked for about specific situations in Bolivia, provided training in various specialties such as communications and security.

All the technical details were worked out by our officers, but each and every one was analyzed and approved by Che: the routes chosen, and who would go on them; how to go through airports unnoticed, descriptions of the airports and the border posts, reports on how strict the immigration controls were, what were the days and times when the authorities were less vigilant. To do this we carried out a prior study of the operational situation, the borders, immigration control, and methods applied by the counterintelligence agencies of the countries Che and the other combatants would pass through.

Some day, when the moment is ripe, we should tell this story in greater detail, to give recognition to the *compañeros* who worked on those operations, which all went according to plan. We sent 140 Cubans into Africa, and more than 20 into Bolivia, without any of them being spotted by Yankee espionage agencies or by the security apparatus of the countries they were going through. These *compañeros* worked very meticulously, with a great deal of professionalism, compartmentalization, and, above all, with tremendous motivation because it involved Che and those who accompanied him.

We were living under a great deal of tension at that time; I'm speaking for the entire team that was entrusted with these tasks. We knew that any kind of error could cost the life of some member of the mission. It was a time of permanent vigilance and anxiety until we received confirmation of the arrival of Che and the rest of his group at their destination. I'll never forget those moments, or any of the *compañeros* who anonymously carried out that difficult internationalist task.

What was Che's mood in the months between his return from the Congo and his departure for Bolivia? He was coming from a defeat in Africa...

Piñeiro: Well, it was a defeat whose causes he explained, with ample self-criticism, as was typical of his personality, his ethics. But we have to remember that he was there to pass on his experience and to advise, not to lead that war of national liberation. In the Congo he confronted the problems of religious and cultural traditions, contradictions among the Congolese leaders, the lack of combat experience. It was a very difficult situation for our combatants — especially psychologically — who were tried and tested men, who had experience in battle and who wanted to not only advise but also participate in direct combat against the enemy. Obviously, it wasn't easy.

That's why Che became directly involved in the fighting, and he was willing to go all the way. But the decisions made by the Congolese leadership and African governments created a situation in which there was no alternative but to organize his departure from the Congo, along with many other *compañeros*.

What was Che's frame of mind prior to leaving for Bolivia? He was like a kid with a new toy. He was euphoric, happy because he was with the group he had chosen and trained. He treated the *compañeros* like brothers, although he was also very disciplined and demanding. They carried out a rigorous program of physical, military and psychological training; studied documents about the country; learned Quechua; had classes in mathematics. Che was very concerned about improving the educational level of those combatants who fought under him.

In April 1967, while Che was in Bolivia, our magazine [Tricontinental] published as a supplement his "Message to the Peoples of the World." Some say this document wasn't written in Bolivia, but in Cuba. What can you tell us about this?

Piñeiro: I think that's right; he wrote it while he was in the training camp in Pinar del Río, before his departure for Bolivia in November 1966.

There was a lot of comment about the fact that Che, who was so well known for his internationalist thoughts and actions, hadn't attended the historic African, Asian and Latin American Peoples' Solidarity Conference in January 1966. Can you tell us why not?

Piñeiro: He couldn't attend because he was in Tanzania when the Tricontinental Conference was held. But he received all the materials and evaluation of that meeting.

What impact did Che's farewell message have on you?

Piñeiro: I knew about it before Fidel read it to the first Central Committee of the Communist Party in October 1965. Nevertheless, every time I hear it I tremble as it brings back many memories, both of Che and his *compañeros*, since I knew all of them and had close personal ties and working relations with some of them.

When was the last time you saw Che? Did you think it would be last time?

Piñeiro: I saw him after midnight on the day he left for the airport to join the guerrilla struggle in Bolivia. It was in a safe house where he had what I think was his last talk with Fidel. Raúl Castro and Vilma Espín were there, too. Fidel and Che were sitting on a sofa in the living room, speaking alone, in soft voices, for a very long time.

I didn't think it would be the last time I would see him, although those of us who commit ourselves to this kind of struggle know that we will either win or die. We were very optimistic and had lots of confidence in the determination, will and capacity of Che and the Cubans who accompanied him, and of the Bolivians who had been tested in other tasks. We believed they would be able to achieve their objective, overcoming whatever obstacles or dangers they encountered. Actually, the Bolivian guerrilla struggle succeeded in carrying out a number of successful military actions, inflicting casualties to the Bolivian army and capturing some of their soldiers.

It's not true that Che felt "a certain mysticism about death," as some writers have claimed. Even if he had been the last one left, or if he was left with just one combatant at his side, he would have tried to reorganize the guerrilla movement and continue fighting. He wasn't a man who would easily let his enemies take his life, nor did he have a martyr complex. Proof of that is that when he was wounded and his gun useless, he tried to escape the encirclement to regroup with his men. He never felt defeated or demoralized; he defended his ideas with his body, not caring that he might lose his life in the effort.

Did Che say goodbye to you? What was his farewell like?

Piñeiro: He said goodbye at the safe house I mentioned. He was happy, smiling, because he was about to set out toward his long-awaited final goal.

It was a simple farewell, he was not an effusive person. He carried his feelings inside, you had to know how to read him. But as always, the expression on his face conveyed great strength and conviction.

How did you hear the news of his death?

Piñeiro: By a wire photo that I received on October 10 [1967], in which Che's body appears on the table in the hospital washroom in Vallegrande. I called Fidel and he came to my house. I remember Fidel's face, dubious. Although the photo looked something like Che, he wasn't convinced. He went back home and was there with *compañera* Celia Sánchez when I took him a second wire photo I had received, which left no doubt that it was Che. That moment is engraved in my mind like an unforgettable image. There was a profound silence in the room. Fidel sent Celia to locate Che's wife, Aleida, who was doing historical research in the Escambray mountains. Celia sent a plane to bring Aleida to Havana, and picked her up at the airport. From there, she took Aleida to a house where Fidel was waiting to break the news to her in person. Meanwhile, Fidel called other party leaders and began to give instructions about how to transmit the information and prepare our people for this harsh news.

It was a tremendous blow. But on these revolutionary missions, we say, "you leave your life under the pillow."

When did you learn there had been survivors?

Piñeiro: A short time later, when Pombo, Urbano and Benigno (who has since turned traitor) were able to break out from the encirclement. More specifically, it was when Inti Peredo was able to make contact with some members of the Bolivian Communist Party and the ELN, who subsequently took him to the Chilean border. I always recall with great warmth the role of Salvador Allende, then-president of the Chilean Senate, who despite criticisms from the right wing, offered the three survivors all his support and protection. Allende contacted our ambassador in France, Baudilio Castellanos, who had the three survivors relocated to Tahiti. Our ambassador went there to pick them up, took them back to France, and from there to Cuba.

We should also note the collaboration offered by the Chilean Communist and Socialist parties, by Beatriz Allende and — among many other *compañeros* — that of the journalist Elmo Catalán, who later died in battle along with Inti Peredo, trying to reinitiate the armed struggle in Bolivia.

You read the recently published testimonial of Chilean Manuel Cabieses, in the magazine Liberación *about how Che's [Bolivian] diary was taken to Cuba. What can you say about that?*

Piñeiro: It's very objective. Cabieses is a serious journalist who is rigorous in his articles and analyses, in addition to being a consistent revolutionary who demonstrates fraternity and solidarity toward Cuba and the Latin American revolutionary movements.

That question reminds me of the participation of many *compañeros* in the publication of the diary in various languages: the Italian Feltrineli, a friend of the Cuban Revolution and admirer of Che; the Frenchman Francois Maspero; Arnaldo Orfila of Siglo XXI in Mexico, Bob Scheer and the staff of *Ramparts* magazine and Bantam Books in the United States. Along with editors and publishers in other countries, in coordination with Rolando Rodríquez, then-president of the Cuban Book Institute, they made an extraordinary effort to distribute Che's diary in Cuba and throughout the world, before the U.S. intelligence agencies could publish a false and apocryphal version of their own. Because of them, we won that battle.

What is your opinion of the various biographies of Che that have appeared recently?

Piñeiro: Well, I haven't read them all. I've seen some commentaries published in Latin American newspapers in which one of them in particular tries to present Che as just a cultural symbol — above all, among the young; it tries to obliterate his political-ideological message and his example. Not all the biographies are bad, of course. But some of them claim that all of Che's economic, political and military theses have failed, are out of date, and that the course of the Cuban Revolution has abandoned his ideals. In my opinion, if the Cuban Revolution had abandoned Che's ideals, it would not be the bastion it is for the popular anti-imperialist, anti-capitalist, pro-socialist struggles that are still being carried out in the world. Even under the harsh circumstances of economic, political and ideological aggression by imperialism, the Cuban people today exhibit the heroism that Che called for, and that Fidel — whom Che referred to as his "teacher and guide" — still calls for every day.

The proof that Che's ideals, thought, action and example have not failed and that they are spreading — now and into the future — is that every day there is growing interest and awareness in Cuba and the world by people who want to study and interpret his writings, recover the essence of his ideas, taking into account the historical differences between the times he lived in and those of today.

In many countries, consumer societies have tried to turn him into merchandise, but the paradigmatic force of Che rises above these attempts, much to the chagrin of the triumphalist neoliberals and the powerful of this world.

To try to reduce him to a mere cultural symbol is a vulgar over-simplification. Che's attraction to young people all over the world, within the revolutionary movements and the progressive and democratic sectors of the earth — and the solidarity inspired by his character — does not correspond to that narrow perception of his legacy. Rather, they see Che as a person of tremendous moral strength, very honest, sensitive, humane, capable of putting his convictions to the test through his actions; as a symbol of internationalism, anti-imperialism, of solidarity, of genuine socialism. Finally, Che is an example for present and future generations, who see him as a standard of revolutionary intransigence, ethical values and social justice.

I think that Che's ideas and example will survive while there are oppressed and oppressors, social injustice and imperialist domination — as long as there is also hope for a more just world, with fraternity and solidarity among men and women, people and countries.

That's why I agree with what Fidel stated on October 12, 1987, during the commemoration of the 20th anniversary of the death in combat of Che and his *compañeros*: "Now more than ever, Che is alive; he is with us; and he is a more powerful adversary of imperialism than ever before."

Red Beard, Che's Partner

By Claudia Furiati [1]

A master of the unforthcoming reply, with a somewhat dry smile, he never let anybody interview him, and to think that he would agree to such a thing would be a mistake. I am referring to the engineer of Che Guevara's guerrilla operations, both in Bolivia and in the Congo; to the man who coordinated the training of the armed-struggle groups in Latin America; to the man who built the relations between the Cuban Revolution and the leftists in the Americas; to the trainer of Cuban spies; and to the man with strategic information about — and for — Che Guevara and Fidel Castro.

I am referring to Commander Manuel Piñeiro Losada, known by both friends and enemies alike as Red Beard. In the language of his environment, everything related to him has to be secret and on a need-to-know basis, except for what follows: his previously unpublished revelations about the links between the Cuban Revolution and Brazilian leaders and organizations — both those for and those against armed struggle — and a reply to the accusation that he participated in the kidnapping of Brazilian industrialist Abilio Diniz.

Even though he is 64 and his hair and beard are beginning to turn gray, a reddish tone still predominates. The nickname Red Beard comes, first of all, from his red hair, though it would be just as suggestive an expression — and just as apt for the spiritual guide of a transgressing sect or for an eminence of the secret apparatus — if he weren't who he is. Commander Piñeiro is an incorrigible night owl; he thinks and is creative in the early morning hours and has, for decades, been used to long night sessions and also to dozing for 15 minutes at a time, his hand over his eyes so as not to bother others, to recharge his batteries.

He speaks English very well and was looking for a good detective movie to watch while resting in a hammock on the terrace of his pleasant, unostentatious home. Camila, his daughter, says he *always* finds out who the murderer is halfway through the movie. With Marta

---

[1] Excerpts from the interview appeared in the daily *O Globo* of Brazil on October 8, 1997.

Harnecker, the Chilean writer whom he married some years ago, he shares, among other things, a bottomless and constant interest in political theory. Like his partner, Che, Red Beard — this figure who looks you in the face and whose glance can cut off discussion — often uses a tough demeanor to hide his tenderness.

A few days ago, when the mortal remains of Che Guevara arrived in Cuba for burial, Piñeiro decided to pay tribute to his dead friend. In addition, as a result of the recent increase in biographies and essays about Che, 30 years after his murder in Bolivia, Piñeiro began to consider the possibility of speaking out to counter what he considers historical inaccuracies and to express his disagreement with certain points of view. So, we decided to begin there.

"One of the biographers tried to present Che as nothing but the embodiment of a cultural product. It is a base simplification to reduce his legacy to that. I think that young people — who didn't experience that era — see in him what we call real socialism and the moral force of a sensitive person who coupled words with deeds... Another biographer claimed that his economic, political and military theses failed and that, immediately after the triumph of the Cuban Revolution, he abandoned his ideals. In fact, his ideals and actions live on today in the enormous interest in Cuba that exists throughout the world and in the parallel desire to be familiar with Che's work," he said.

When I asked if the two authors to whom he referred were Jorge Castañeda and John Lee Anderson, he opted for an ethical silence.

The guerrilla Piñeiro, who hadn't yet grown his red beard, first met Che Guevara, after an ambush that Fidel had laid in the foothills of the Sierra Maestra mountains. Che was known as the "daring Argentine." The second time they met was the following year, 1958, when Piñeiro, with the rank of commander, headed the Intelligence Service and the Rebel Police in the Second Front.[2] That day, Piñeiro had a terrible toothache and had to go to Che's camp, where he had set up a tent as a dental clinic. When he got close, he heard excruciating screams and saw Che holding a farmer firmly by the head with one hand and brandishing some pliers — the only instrument the clinic had — in the other. "Right there, I said I'd never fall into that man's hands," he recalled — and, in fact, he never did.

His ties with Che were strengthened in mid-1959, after the triumph of the revolution. At that time, Commander Piñeiro was a member of the

---

[2] We have respected the text of the interview as prepared by its author. However, as can be seen in the interview which *Tricontinental* magazine published under the title "My Modest Tribute to Che" and which is included in this book, the anecdote told here took place before Piñeiro was in the Frank País Second Eastern Front. It really occurred in the Sierra Maestra before Piñeiro was promoted to the rank of commander in the Rebel Army.

Special Operations Department (DOE), an intelligence structure the preceded the founding of the Ministry of the Interior (MININT), whose function was to serve leaders and other VIPs from the Third World and, in general, all Latin Americans who came to Cuba. Che Guevara spent hours talking with them after his normal work day, the talks sometimes lasting till dawn. Nearly always, Piñeiro accompanied him. The talks took place in "safe houses," Che's office at the National Institute of the Agrarian Reform (INRA) or at the National Bank or in Che's home.

"Wherever the meetings took place, he always had a thermos near him, some hot water, a gourd cup, some *maté* and some good cigars," he recalled. "While sipping *maté* and exhaling smoke, he impressed me with his ability to listen and respect the other man's opinions, even when they were very different from his own. He created a climate of calm and camaraderie that facilitated direct dialogue..." The leaders he met during those early years included the Nicaraguans Tomás Borge and Somarriba, a former officer in the dictator Somoza's army; the Peruvian leaders Héctor Béjar and Javier Heraud; the Peronists William Cooke and Alicia Eguren; Salvador Allende, who was a Senator of the Republic in Chile at the time; the Venezuelan leader Fabricio Ojeda; the Guatemalan Julio Cáceres ("The Kid"), who became a close friend of Che's when the latter was in Guatemala in 1954; and the Brazilians Luis Carlos Prestes, general secretary of the Brazilian Communist Party (PCB), and Francisco Juliano, leader of the Farmers' Leagues (LC).

****

What did Prestes come to Cuba to do?[3]

Piñeiro: His interest was political: to get to know the Cuban process at close hand and establish contacts with Che and other leaders. He talked a lot about the Brazilian situation, defending the principle of an alliance with sectors of the nationalist bourgeoisie and expressing optimism about the conditions for the development of socialism in Brazil. He came back after the 1964 coup and stayed here for a while.

What about Francisco Juliano?

Piñeiro: Juliano was very interested in the plans for developing rural guerrillas and talked about that with Che Guevara, who told him about the experiences of the Cuban revolutionary war, based on our specific

---

[3] Luis Carlos Prestes (1898-1990), an outstanding figure in the Latin American communist movement, was general secretary of the Brazilian Communist Party until 1983. The 1964 military coup made him go underground again. He spoke out against armed struggle, the trend that was headed by the communist Carlos Marighella at that time. Prestes lived in the Soviet Union from 1971 to 1979, then returned to Brazil when the amnesty was declared. [Footnote by Claudia Furiati]

conditions.

Did Che do any studying in preparation for those meetings?

Piñeiro: He always went through all the available information on the situation in the country or countries involved. What was unpardonable was if there was no map he could lay out on the table — he liked to make comments based on some knowledge of social and economic geography, the urban movements and aspects regarding the farmers and land ownership...

Was that when he gave his opinion about the forms of struggle or combat?

Piñeiro: He said that every existing possibility for action through institutional channels should be used, but without any illusions. In addition, it was absolutely necessary to gather together as many forces as possible and for them to be given military training so they could confront the repression to which the people's movement would be subjected as soon as it began to challenge the system.

In short, what was Che's plan for expanding the revolution?

Piñeiro: Based on his experience in the war in Cuba, he planned to found a mother column that would be composed of revolutionaries from various Latin American countries. As soon as it had gone through its survival stage — that is, when the combatants were trained and had adapted to the territory and the leadership cadres had been formed — and was in the second stage, that of development, other columns would break off from the mother column and expand through other parts of Latin America, especially in those regions where the people's cause was being crushed.

Would that be within the principle that is known as "guerrilla focism," centered on an armed nucleus toward which the movement converged or from which it spread?

Piñeiro: No. His concept was political, military and of the masses, contradicting the interpretation of the "guerrilla foco" that is attributed to him. He said that the mother column was a small motor that, when it functioned well, would start up the larger motor of the masses. What he proposed was not a small group of armed men acting in any way divorced from the people's movement but rather an insurgent focal point linked to the masses.

Did he consider the existence of some kind of people's movement to be a prerequisite for armed struggle?

Piñeiro: This appears in a dialectical form in his thinking. He didn't think it was necessary for all of the initial conditions for the struggle to be present. He thought that, in the course of its development, the struggle could create those conditions. However, he also said that guerrilla warfare couldn't be carried out in countries whose governments were the fruit of some kind of popular consultation or where there were still possibilities for civilian struggle. Therefore, he isn't responsible for the simplifications that were made of the Cuban experience and of his own concepts, even though those simplifications may have been made in good faith.

****

Che Guevara explained the general outlines of his plan to Fidel Castro months before the [1956] expedition on board the *Granma* — the cabin cruiser that brought the original guerrilla nucleus to the Cuban coast — set out from Mexico. He told him that, as soon as he could be freed of his responsibilities in Cuba and the conditions were ripe, he wanted to go to another Latin American country — preferably Argentina, where he had been born — to assist in the making of a revolution there. According to Red Beard, Che began to take preparatory steps for the project immediately after the rebel victory in Cuba.

Masetti, the Argentine journalist[4] who had met Che in the Sierra Maestra mountains, returned to Cuba at that time to receive military training and then carry out a mission in support of the National Liberation Front (FLN), which was directing the struggle for Algeria's emancipation. Fidel managed to persuade Che to stay in Cuba and delay his departure for Argentina until the conditions had been created, because he didn't want such a valuable cadre to be exposed to the risks during the first stage, that of survival. They convinced him, but he remained restless, wanting to take command of everything right from the start.

When Masetti returned from Algeria, Che called him "Second Commander" and gave him the task of organizing a guerrilla column on Argentina's border with Bolivia. A group of Cubans, who also received assistance from the Algerian National Liberation Front, left for there. Some time later, in April 1964, when contact with Masetti was lost, Che felt trapped in an office and did everything possible to clear up what was happening. Nothing was ever known for sure, but Masetti was probably killed between April 15 and April 25, 1964.

At the same time, ever since 1959, Che Guevara had been alert to other possibilities — Nicaragua, Venezuela, Peru and Colombia — for participating as a simple combatant. In 1959, he sent a message to the

---

[4] Masetti went to live in Cuba after the revolution and founded the Prensa Latina news agency.

Nicaraguan leader Somarriba, a former officer of the dictator Somoza's army, placing himself at his disposal for joining his guerrilla group. The message was given to Somarriba in Honduras, where a group of Cubans went to give him their support. That effort quickly failed, however.

As for Peru, it was felt that the sociopolitical effervescence there was propitious to the conditions for an armed movement. Paralleling the operation in Argentina, a group of Peruvians headed by Alain Elías[5] entered Argentine territory from Bolivia in January 1963 to direct the guerrillas. Che Guevara had held meetings with all the Peruvian leaders of the National Liberation Army (ELN) and of the Movement of the Revolutionary Left (MIR) who continued the armed struggle, supported by the Bolivian Communist Party. The Peredo brothers played an especially important role. But those attempts also failed.

Thus, Che Guevara became more and more impatient as the days went by, while, in his opinion, Bolivia was being reaffirmed as a center where the mother column could be developed, according to his plan. Motivated by that idea and observing how matters developed, in 1964 Che learned about the coup in Bolivia that had installed a repressive regime. In early 1965, the possibility of joining the struggle in the Congo arose, and he decided to do so immediately.

His mission was handled by the Intelligence Department [which Piñeiro headed], with the technical and operational aspects — documentation, travel itineraries, field information, etc. — prepared with the help of the Cuban Embassy in Tanzania.[6] For Fidel, the option of Che's going to the Congo as a military adviser also provided a way of controlling him until the minimal political conditions existed in Bolivia.

Nearly two years later, after the Congolese conflict, when Che was in Tanzania, he decided to send Papi (José María Martínez Tamayo) to evaluate the situation. He immediately confirmed that Bolivia was the only option, because it had the following conditions: a logistic support structure and the contacts and guide provided by the communist cadres

---

[5] Alain Elías was one of the founders of the National Liberation Army (Ejército de Liberación Nacional, ELN) of Peru. Together with the poet Javier Heraud, he was killed in combat in the Puerto Maldonado area of Peru on May 15, 1963, having entered that country from Bolivia. The founders of the Movement of the Revolutionary Left (MIR) of Peru included Luis de la Puente Uceda, who was killed in combat in 1965.

[6] As on earlier occasions, we have respected the text of the interview, but, in the interests of historical accuracy, it should be stated that the Technical Deputy Ministry, which Commander Manuel Piñeiro headed at the time, was in charge of only a part of the operation in the Congo. Other entities of the Cuban Revolutionary Armed Forces (FAR) also played an important part in the selection of the combatants and in the preparation and shipment of the weapons that the Cuban combatants used. Those interested in going more fully into this subject should consult William Gálvez's *Che in Africa* (Melbourne: Ocean Press, 1999).

who had already supported Masetti and the Peruvians.

****

So Bolivia was the option?

Piñeiro: Yes, depending on its development. First of all, it should be a school for training Latin American cadres — especially those from the Southern Cone, including the Argentines — that would facilitate extending the armed struggle to the bordering countries. According to Che's analysis, if other guerrilla columns could be created from the one in Bolivia, that would cause a chain reaction of governments and armies of countries supported by the United States, which would help to spread the revolutionary struggle in the region. It would immediately become the scene of long and hard battles that, sooner or later, would lead to U.S. intervention, creating another Vietnam, in the spirit of his "Message to the Peoples of the World" in *Tricontinental.*

What did Fidel Castro think of this?

Piñeiro: He offered all the cooperation he could and reiterated that Che shouldn't go at the beginning but should wait until the column had logistics and arms, had adapted to the terrain, had urban support networks and when some Latin American cadres had joined. In line with Fidel's orientation, our agency gave Che support in everything he asked for. Our officers drew up all the technical details, but Che analyzed and approved each step, from the training in the various specialties — communications and conspiratorial methods — to the falsification of passports and the selection of how to get there and who would go by each route. Therefore, we made a prior study of the operational, border and migratory situation and of the methods applied by the counterintelligence agencies of the countries through which Che and the other combatants would have to go.

Bolivia failed, too.

Piñeiro: When the Argentine Ciro Bustos was captured and became an informer, giving details about Che and the guerrilla group, Argentina was "frozen." Later, the Bolivian Army found the guerrilla base and everything happened very quickly: the guerrillas had to keep moving all the time, which made it very difficult for them to keep in contact with the urban base and abroad.

Some people have accused Fidel of having abandoned Che to his fate.

Piñeiro: That stemmed from their interpretation of the farewell letter that Che left. But, with or without any letter, Che's decision had been irrevocable for a long time. The claim that Che's guerrilla group was deserted was also based on the fact that we didn't send him military reinforcements to help him break through the Bolivian Army's encirclement: the guerrillas were at a disadvantage, forced to keep moving all the time to avoid ambushes, and were utterly dependent on their own forces and on the support that the urban networks, which had already been hard hit, could give them. Critics say it would have been easy for us to send him military reinforcements, but that wasn't so. Those claims are nothing but fantasy.

Let's go back to the Brazilians. It is known that when Carlos Marighella[7] decided to found the National Liberating Alliance (ALN) guerrilla organization he came to Cuba. How and when was that?

Piñeiro: Marighella came to Havana in January 1966 to attend the Tricontinental Conference. He had some meetings with Fidel Castro and other Cuban leaders and impressed all of them that he was a resolute revolutionary.

In your opinion, did Marighella want to establish a clear distinction between his point of view and the Guevarists' theses?

Piñeiro: Well, as already explained, Che Guevara concentrated on rural guerrillas as a revolutionary lever. Marighella's theses referred to urban guerrillas as a form of struggle and also as a means of confronting the regime of political-military repression, which is normally described as terrorism. You also have to remember that the two never met, because, when Marighella was in Cuba, Che was in Tanzania, after the war in the Congo. However, we know that in the months prior to his death Marighella had also drawn up a plan for organizing rural guerrillas.

Other members of Marighella's ALN sought exile in Cuba after the kidnapping of U.S. Ambassador Charles Elbrick in 1969 — which, it is said, was a combined action by the ALN, the October 8 Revolutionary Movement (MR-8)[8] and the Revolutionary People's Vanguard (VPR)…

Piñeiro: Among the members of the ALN, José Dirceu, who is now president of the Workers' Party (PT), was in Cuba as a political exile, along with Glauber Rocha,[9] whom I remember with affection.

---

[7] Carlos Marighella (1911-69), led the Brazilian Communist Party to break with Luis Carlos Prestes, in particular, by adopting the line of armed struggle against the military regime in Brazil. In 1968 and 1969, he organized several guerrilla actions in Brazilia territory. Members of the security bodies shot him down in a São Paulo street in November 1969. [Footnote by Claudia Furiati]

[8] Carlos Marighella founded the ALN after attending the Conference of Solidarity with the Peoples of Africa, Asia and Latin America, which was held in Havana in 1967. The October 8 Revolutionary Movement was founded by Carlos Lamoner, a former captain in the Brazilian Army.

[9] Glauber Rocha, a Brazilian movie director. Some of his films (such as *Dios y el Diablo*

Carlos Lamarca[10] was also in Cuba.

Piñeiro: He was trained here in 1970 and 1971; then he went back to Brazil to carry out his plans. I remember Lamarca as a patriot determined to fight against the military dictatorship. He constantly reiterated his confidence in the nationalist sectors of the Brazilian Armed Forces.

Did you learn at any time before it was proved that Corporal Anselmo, who was supposedly an ally of Lamarca, was a CIA agent?

Piñeiro: We heard it a little before, when many Brazilian leaders accused him of having infiltrated their ranks, but there wasn't any proof.

It is said that Fidel Castro financed the first revolt that was attempted against the military — the one that the Caparaó guerrillas, headed by Leonel Brizola,[11] carried out in 1966...

Piñeiro: That's an interesting question. I can confirm that we always got along well with Brizola as a Brazilian leader, but an ethical question is involved here: Leonel Brizola is alive and active and can tell you about it if he wants to, better than I. As for me, I would like to take this opportunity to acknowledge the attitude of solidarity with Cuba, Fidel and other democratic Brazilian leaders that he always maintained.

Do you confirm that the VPR and MR-8 also had relations with Cuba?

Piñeiro: We had relations with those and other organizations in that stage, but we weren't involved in the kidnappings they carried out. We always respected the decisions that the various organizations made in their battle against the military dictatorship, because they were mature enough to assume their own responsibilities and decide where they were going.

Did those going to Korea for training come through here and get Cuban

---

en la Tierra del Sol [God and the Devil in the Land of the Sun]), are considered classics in the history of Latin American and world cinematography. His profound critical view of Brazil's socioeconomic reality led him to undertake clear political commitments to the Brazilian people's struggles for a better life and especially against the military dictatorships that vented their cruelty on that country between 1964 and 1983.

[10] Carlos Lamarca was a candidate officer in the Military Academy of Agulhas Negras and a Second Lieutenant in the UN intervention troops in the Suez Canal Zone in 1962. In December 1964, when he was an army captain, he rebelled against the regime. At Christmas 1968 he sought exile in Rome and then traveled to Cuba. He was killed in an ambush in Baia on September 17, 1971. [Footnote by Claudia Furiati]

[11] Leonel Brizola was a founder of the Democratic Workers' Party (PDT) of Brazil and is still a leader of it. Historically, he has maintained a position of solidarity with the Cuban Revolution. He has also held important positions in the Socialist International.

passports?

Piñeiro: Yes, that's so; that was part of the agreement between the Brazilian groups and the Korean party.

Commander Piñeiro, according to commentaries that have reached me, your name appears in two indictments related to the kidnapping of Brazilian industrialist Abilio Diniz in 1989, as one of those who planned the action. At the time, Brazilian justice considered the kidnapping to be a nonpolitical crime, so those who were convicted didn't have the right to extradition. Do you have anything to say about this?

Piñeiro: First of all, it should be publicly stated in which indictment, in which declaration or in which document my name appears, and how. Cuba had nothing at all to do with the kidnapping of that Brazilian citizen. Second, it doesn't surprise me that Cuba should be linked, yet again, to that kind of action; it is just one more example of the CIA's policy of accusing Cuba of being a center for planning and carrying out such actions. You should ask the CIA about that kidnapping and so many others, the assassination attempts against political leaders that it has planned and carried out throughout Latin and Central America by means of the manuals it has drawn up and sent to other security bodies.

In spite of the CIA's recent "declassification" of materials on assassination attempts against Fidel, that policy stopped being anything new a long time ago.[12]

---

[12] Abilio Diniz was kidnapped on December 11, 1989, just before the second round of presidential elections in which Fernando Collor de Mello emerged the victor. Nine of the 10 participants in the kidnapping who were sentenced to between 26 and 28 years in prison were foreigners: five Chileans, two Canadians — Christine Lamont and David Spencer — and two Argentines. The Chileans are in the Carandiru Prison, while, under an agreement between Argentina and Brazil, the Argentine brothers were transferred to prisons in their own country. The case of the two Canadians has hurt the diplomatic relations between Brazil and Canada, because the Brazilian Government doesn't plan to transfer them, in spite of strong pressure by the Canadian Government and Canadian public opinion.

In May 1996, it was announced that four people had been sentenced in Nicaragua for having blown up an arms depot — which contained documents on kidnappings that had taken place throughout Latin America, including that of Abilio Diniz — three years before.

In December 1996, the Movement of the Revolutionary Left (MIR) guerrilla organization in Chile announced that its political leadership, together with the People's Liberation Forces (FPL) of El Salvador, had decided to carry out the operation and that this had hurt the presidential hopes of Luiz Ignacio "Lula" da Silva, in Brazil. The Chilean MIR had connections in Nicaragua, and the FPL was one of the armed branches of the Farabundo Martí National Liberation Front of El Salvador — which, the kidnappers stated, was to receive the money obtained in the negotiations for freeing the industrialist. [Footnote by Claudia Furiati]

CNN Interview

Interview with Lucia Newman, CNN's Correspondent in Cuba [1]

C ommander, before beginning to speak about Che, I'd like to ask you, is it true that you studied at Columbia University in New York?

Piñeiro: Yes, I was also a waiter in New York. I was a master of ceremonies and did some bilingual comedy numbers in a hole-in-the-wall theater — we would call it a dive in Cuba. That was after I began my studies; I made contact with revolutionaries from other countries, and it occurred to some of my comrades (almost as a joke) to propose me as general secretary (or president) of the foreigners who were studying at that university. When my family found out about all that, they thought I was on the wrong path and should be brought back to Cuba in order to save me... First they sent me out of Cuba to New York to save me, and then they had to bring me back to save me yet again...

What was harder for you: being a waiter or being a guerrilla?

Piñeiro: Being a waiter was hard. I'll never forget the trays I had to carry in that restaurant — or the customers' bad manners... I spent hours and hours carrying trays and dishes. It was a tough experience... a real struggle.

How, in your view, did Fidel and Che differ?

Piñeiro: Rather than differ, they always complemented each other. At the beginning of the revolution, Fidel had the strategic task of uniting all the revolutionary forces and of educating our people about the revolution and its measures, of helping them to understand through his educational speeches and his very direct communication with the

[1] A shorter version of this interview was used in a CNN report on the 30th anniversary of Che's murder. So as not to repeat things contained in the other interviews that appear in this book, and with the author's consent, we have selected those questions and answers in which the dialogue took new turns.

people. At that time, he didn't have enough time to systematize and elaborate on our experiences theoretically. Meanwhile, because of his talent for theoretical work, his skills and his capacity for reading, Che spent more time conceptualizing the strategy and tactics that had led our movement — the July 26 Movement — to victory.

Che heard the speeches, ideas and talks that Fidel had with the people; understood the measures that the revolution took; and systematized them from the theoretical point of view. The books Che wrote in the first few years after the triumph of the revolution — books such as *Guerrilla Warfare: A Method*; *Strategy and Tactics of the Latin American Revolution* and *Socialism and Man in Cuba* — were the product of that effort.

Speaking of the new man, Che was very critical of the former Soviet Union and the system he saw there. He saw that the model new man that he wanted for Cuba wasn't really being created there. Do you think that the present leaders of the Communist Party of Cuba should have paid more attention to Che back then?

Piñeiro: First of all, you should keep in mind that Che, we and the rest of the progressive world owe a lot to the Soviet Union. The Soviet Union had made a revolution and wrought a thorough change to meet the people's needs, to guarantee health and free education, to develop an advanced industry and to guarantee strategic nuclear parity with the United States; it had also sent the first man into space. In short, it had achieved social and technological advances that attracted interest and admiration for a nation that, after the October Revolution, had leaped straight from feudalism into space.

At the same time, in his meetings with the Soviet leaders and in his tours of various socialist countries, Che began to see the subjective problems that existed, the need for moral motivation to get people to work not only as a right but also as a social duty to benefit others and, thus, to slough off their selfishness and individualism and feel love and solidarity toward others and all humankind — to have an internationalist conscience.

Che began to see that this hadn't come about as he had imagined it would, and he began to express criticisms — constructive ones, which he didn't voice behind people's backs but rather stated in his meetings with the Soviet leaders and with the leaders of other socialist countries in the framework of the exchanges that we had with them. Che had formed those opinions on the basis of our experience and on the basis of our contacts with Soviet society.

At the time of the Sino-Soviet conflict, some people began to use the constructive criticism that Che had made to the Soviets (criticism which wasn't made public during the first few years) in order to speculate —

by means of propaganda, the press and some publications aimed at revolutionaries — saying that Che was leaning toward the positions of the Communist Party of the People's Republic of China at the time and that, therefore, he caused (as some historians claim) adverse reactions by the Soviets.

This led to the intrigue that was manipulated by the mass media in the West to the effect that Che had decided to leave our country because of his criticism of Soviet foreign policy and of socialist construction in the Soviet Union...

But if the Sino-Soviet conflict was not the basis for Che's departure for Africa, what was?

Piñeiro: Che's departure for the Congo in 1965 was the result of the tour he had made of several African countries and the meetings he had held with the leaders of the national liberation movements in those places. On that occasion, Che reached the conclusion that the Congo was the best place in Africa for initiating revolutionary armed struggle.

The recently triumphant Algerian Revolution and its president, Ben Bella, were willing to give that effort their political support. Several other progressive governments in Africa also pledged to help the Congolese people's struggle against the dictatorship that was headed at that time by Kasavubu, Tshombe and Mobuto. They all remembered the murder of Patrice Lumumba — a people's leader who was popular throughout the world — and the fact that his supporters had taken up arms and revolted. That struggle also had the support of the progressive movement and of many African and European governments.

Because of those factors and the requests that several leaders of the African liberation movements (including those of the Congo) made for Cuban military advice and logistic support, Che saw that that was the best place for continuing the anti-imperialist struggle in Africa, and the leaders of the Cuban Revolution decided to give the Congolese combatants support and advice. You should remember that Che didn't go to the Congo as just one more fighter or as a leader of the Congolese combatants; rather, he went as the chief of a group of Cuban military advisers to help them, to convey technical experience to them and to train them in the use of the most complex weapons. All the problems that we already know about came later.

At that time, Latin America didn't have the political conditions required for Che to implement his historic decision, which he had said to Fidel in Mexico — that as soon as the Cuban Revolution had triumphed, he would continue the revolutionary struggle in another Latin American country (especially in the Southern Cone and preferably Argentina). Fidel persuaded him that the mission in the Congo would allow him to gain time, get in shape, train cadres, etc. while the political possibilities of beginning the struggle in a Latin American country ripened.

Let's go back to the Soviet Union. In view of Che's opinions concerning the deficiencies of the Soviet system, weren't there any differences among the top leaders of the revolution — between Che and yourself, for example?

Piñeiro: No. I think that Fidel and the other Cuban leaders understood Che's point of view. But, of course, understanding it is one thing and it is another to take political steps that might be interpreted as an act of intervention in the internal affairs of a friendly country — a strategic ally that maintained an attitude of close solidarity with us; that was providing us, at no cost, with the weapons with which to defend the revolution; and that was carrying out a program of cooperation to promote our country's economic development while we were subjected to a blockade, left without oil and isolated from all of the other Latin American governments (except for that of Mexico, which always maintained diplomatic relations with Cuba) because of the decision that the OAS made under pressure from the United States.

Within that framework, you must see that, for ethical reasons and out of respect for the Soviet Union, though we could make some critical observations, we couldn't go beyond presenting them to the Soviet leadership frankly and directly, leaving it to make the final decisions.

But the things that Che had said — I think his exact words were that the European socialist system was bound to be a dead-end street...

Piñeiro: What you're quoting is a press version... What Che really said was that the methods that were being applied in the construction of socialism in the Soviet Union and some measures of a capitalist nature that were being applied were going to produce a situation in which it would be necessary to back up a bit...

At that time, did the rest of you share that view?

Piñeiro: Well, we had close relations, exchanges, scholarship students, students of economics, technical missions and an embassy. We knew that a great discussion was going on there about the concept of the transition from capitalism to socialism, about the role of moral and material incentives, about the role of the market and planning, etc. That discussion was reproduced in the other socialist countries... But what I want to convey is that some people incorrectly confused those criteria, the constructive criticism that Che made to the European socialist countries, with a political and ideological position connected with that of the People's Republic of China at that time in its confrontation with the Soviet leaders.

Then, when Che left for the Congo with the Cuban military advisers, there was a vacuum. For some months, the people in general didn't know where Che was, and the international mass media came up with the story that the Soviets had pressured us, and that opportunistically, in a dehumanized way, without any ethics or principles, we had sold Che like merchandise and had thrown him out of our country so that he wouldn't upset our relations with the Soviet Union. I remember that some other newspaper articles said that during an argument that Fidel and Che had in an office, Fidel had pulled out a pistol and killed him and that we had buried him secretly. That's how one of the most incredible tall tales of all time was created.

Speaking of that, there's a lot of speculation that the Cuban Revolution betrayed Che in Bolivia — more specifically, that Fidel Castro betrayed him, took away his support and didn't give him the logistic support he needed. You're familiar with these accusations. Was there any such betrayal, or not?

Piñeiro: That's a very popular theme right now, among both historians and journalists. The Cuban position is clear, and Fidel has stated it many times...

When Fidel and Che met in Mexico, after several hours of exchanging views and after Fidel had explained the plans for freeing Cuba, Che said he wanted to join the *Granma* expedition, but he also told Fidel that, if the revolution triumphed, he wanted to be freed of all governmental, political and military commitments so he could carry out his mission of fighting for the liberation of other peoples in Latin America, especially Argentina...

You have to remember that, before coming to Cuba, Che had been in Guatemala at the time of Castillo Armas's invasion. There, he became very politically aware and suffered when he saw that the people were not organized to fight against the U.S. intervention. In Guatemala, he met many Central American, Peruvian and other Latin American exiles, and many of them came to Cuba after the triumph of the revolution, both to learn about the revolution's achievements and to ask for solidarity and help with their revolutionary plans in their own countries.

Thus, as I have said in other interviews, Che had already committed himself personally and directly — as far back as March 1959 — to a group of Nicaraguans led by Somarriba, a former officer in Somoza's army, who went into Nicaraguan territory from Honduras to begin the guerrilla struggle against Somoza.

Che had been restless ever since March 1959; the revolution had triumphed, and he was taking part in the revolutionary construction of our country, but he wanted to keep on struggling for the liberation of other Latin American countries. He tried — but failed — to realize that goal in 1964 by working on the preparations for a guerrilla column that would operate in Argentina under Jorge Ricardo Masetti and which Che planned to join later on. That's why he called Masetti the Second

Commander. When there's a second, it's because there's a first, and that first commander was Che.

The failure at Salta was a harsh blow. He always said — he told me this himself — that he felt terrible because comrades with whom he had very close ties had died while carrying out a revolutionary mission, which he should have led. Yet he was sitting in an office, not knowing what had happened to them. He worried for months, trying to think of a way to help any survivors. Many efforts were made to try to reconstruct what had happened; it traumatized him and wounded him deeply.

Since the conditions for initiating guerrilla struggle didn't exist at that time in the Latin American countries in the Southern Cone, he decided to go to the Congo. When that effort failed (because of the contradictions within the Congolese leadership and the resolutions that the OAU adopted), Che went to Tanzania. He spent two or three months there analyzing the experience in the Congo, which, as always when Che made an analysis — and especially the analysis of an activity in which he had participated — was very self-critical.

While in Tanzania, he became eager to find a way of going to Latin America to continue the revolutionary struggle, but Fidel convinced him that the conditions had to be created and that he should wait until at least the minimal conditions existed for carrying out his mission, doing what he wanted and advancing his ideals. Fidel convinced him that he should return to Cuba, to be trained and to choose the men who would go with him on that revolutionary undertaking. At the same time, the conditions would be prepared for providing him with logistic support and for receiving him and the other comrades in Bolivia.

Che realized that it was necessary to come back to Cuba; choose the Cuban and Bolivian combatants who would go with him; get more training; prepare himself physically; and teach the comrades about the economic, political and social features of the country, which included learning about the different ethnic groups, the language — Quechua — the geography, and the customs, habits and traditions of the farmers and Indians in that rural area.

Why Bolivia?

Piñeiro: I'll tell you… Apart from the political situation caused by General René Barrientos's coup, the students and miners began to participate in movements of protest and resistance, using some forms of violence. An interesting political situation was created. In addition, some of the cadres of the Bolivian Communist Party, with the authorization of their leadership, had cooperated with the Peruvian revolutionaries in their plans for initiating guerrilla struggle in their country. They had also provided logistical support for Comrade Masetti's attempt to organize a guerrilla movement in Salta, Argentina, from Bolivian territory. Those cadres were politically reliable. They were trained and were eager to do something in solidarity with Cuba. There was that advantage.

That group of comrades — headed by the Peredo brothers, Inti and Coco — bought the Ñacahuazú Farm; they obtained weapons that were modern for that period, logistical support, medicine, munitions and uniforms and took it all to Ñacahuazú. Thus, they had the logistical support not only for guaranteeing the reception and transfer of the men but also for equipping them and placing them on a combat footing.

And it was the Cuban Revolution that provided that logistical support?

Piñeiro: Of course. It was obtained with our cooperation. They didn't have the economic resources for doing that. All they had were the contacts. Naturally, the Cuban Revolution gave them all the resources they needed when they began to work with Che. As I have said on other occasions, Fidel told Che that we were willing to give him all the help and cooperation we could.

That's why, whenever anybody says that Cuba didn't do everything possible to rescue Che in view of the difficult situation he was in and that we abandoned and betrayed him, I say that, first of all, you have to consider the difficulties involved in sending a group of men, providing them with documentation, preparing them to cross several borders and equipping them with the logistical support and weapons they needed to go into the area where Che was. From the operational point of view, it would have taken months.

Anybody who knows what a guerrilla movement is and how the enemy army acts knows that, when there is a guerrilla area, the first thing the army does is set up a strategic encirclement — hold all the points of entry, roads and transportation and control the movement of the farmers — to deprive the guerrilla movement of a possible base of support.

The only other thing the Cuban Government could have done would have been to declare war on the Bolivian Government and land an airborne division in the area — a scandalous thing that would have provided a marvelous pretext for holding an OAS meeting and for the United States to join in the defense of the Bolivian Government against an attack by the Cuban socialist revolution with "the support of international communism." Anything else that's said is nothing but hogwash.

But did Che ask for help?

Piñeiro: No. That's another thing that people ask: whether Che had an escape plan, an emergency plan, or not. First of all, any revolutionary with strong convictions, who is determined to fight for their ideals, knows that an undertaking of this kind is no picnic; it's not a matter of fun and games. You go into the struggle with arms in hand, determined to win or to die in the attempt. Therefore, with the experience he had and with his Latin American stature, Che knew better than anyone else that there are no escape or rescue plans in a guerrilla struggle.

Anybody who is familiar with the laws of the guerrilla movement knows that, in the first phase, the guerrillas must rely on their own resources. That is the survival phase; the phase of exploration; of getting to know the terrain; of toughening the combatants; of seeing if they are psychologically, politically and morally ready. They are days of hunger, of difficulties, of lack of food, when diseases appear... It is a phase of self-cleansing, and only the staunchest, the most convinced and the most determined remain. Che was in that survival phase.

As I've already said, Fidel didn't want Che to be in at the beginning of the guerrilla struggle in Bolivia; he wanted him to wait, for an advance group to go and for Che to go later, when the guerrilla column had been somewhat consolidated in the terrain and the cadres had been toughened — beginning with the Bolivian cadres, who, in the end, would take over the leadership of the guerrilla struggle in their country. The combatants from other countries in the area who were trained in Bolivia would, with their respective leaders, join the struggles in their own countries later on. The Argentines would go to Argentina with Che; the Brazilians, with their own leaders, would go to Brazil. That was the strategic concept of the development of the guerrilla movement at the continental level, based on applying the Cuban experience.

In our experience, the first thing we formed was what we called the mother column, which Fidel headed. All of the other cadres (Raúl, Camilo, Che, Almeida, etc.) went out to head other columns later on, implementing the same concept and knowledge of how to move, how to test cadres, which cadres should be protected and not exposed to battle, how to treat the farmers, how to do political work, what kind of educational work to do and how to provide medical attention... In short, they had a concept because they had already done their apprenticeship... That's how the columns headed by Che and Camilo that advanced through Cuba were formed, though each leader had his own personal characteristics...

So Fidel Castro advised Che Guevara not to go to Bolivia?

Piñeiro: No. What he advised Che to do was wait until the first advance group had arrived and had created the necessary conditions before entering Bolivian territory.

The Cuban advance group, or the Bolivian one?

Piñeiro: The Cuban-Bolivian advance group.

Many people say that it was a group of military adventurers, a project that wasn't linked to the masses, one that had no political links. They forget that Mario Monje, the general secretary of the Bolivian Communist Party, had pledged to support the initial plan headed by Che. Monje didn't keep those pledges, and that held back the revolutionary movement that Che headed, depriving it of political support right from the beginning. It also caused difficulties with the urban networks, which were hard hit. Some members of the Bolivian Communist Party wanted to join the guerrilla movement, but Monje placed obstacles in their way. For example, when Che left Cuba, there was a group of around 15 or 20 Bolivians here who had completed their training, but Monje didn't give them the facilities for joining the guerrillas.

All of those factors, plus the early discovery of the camp (which wasn't an area of military operations but was rather a rearguard area for logistics, for storing medicine and for messengers to go to), created very difficult conditions and changed all of Che's plans. He hadn't planned to begin operations immediately.

Sometimes it's forgotten that, during the few months Che was there, he inflicted more than 50 losses on the Bolivian Army and captured over 200 weapons. That created serious concern in the Bolivian Army and its U.S. advisers, because symptoms of demoralization were noted in the Bolivian military high command — which is why the first Rangers were sent to Bolivia.

How was the mission in Bolivia planned? How were the cadres who took part in that mission selected?

Piñeiro: Che chose Bolivia, drew up the plan, designed it, chose what kind of logistics he needed and selected the Cuban combatants. Some people don't understand this; they say: so didn't Fidel participate at all? Naturally, Fidel talked with and had fraternal discussions with Che, but Fidel knew that Che had military experience (gained not only in Cuba but also in the Congo) and that, therefore, he was capable of making the best decisions.

This doesn't mean that, when they saw each other at the farm where Che and the other comrades whom he had selected were training, they didn't toss ideas back and forth. That was only natural between two men who had a very fraternal relationship, and Che (like Raúl and all the other leaders) always expressed his point of view...

Moreover, fortunately, Che had great respect and admiration for Fidel; he always considered him a man of exceptional qualities who nearly always convinced us that his view was correct... This explains how this tiny country [Cuba] has managed to hold out against all kinds of acts of aggression for over 37 years. This is why Fidel is now a world figure who is respected even by his adversaries, a man who says what he thinks, accepts all risks and is ready to die in the defense of his principles — the principles of the revolution — without making concessions.

Did you contribute to that mission?

Piñeiro: I was responsible for sending comrades there to make an analysis of the situation: border controls, the counterintelligence apparatus, airports, the security bodies, etc.; their mentality, their doctrine, their strengths and their weaknesses — in short, in professional terms, I was responsible for studying the operational situation. That study led me to believe that the Bolivian Army was weak from the viewpoint of its combat preparation and weaponry. It wasn't an army that had been trained in the counterinsurgency techniques in which, after its defeat in Vietnam, the United States trained other Latin American armies.

My next question is obvious: If the Bolivian Army was so weak, why did Che fail?

Piñeiro: In addition to the factors I've already mentioned, I think that one of the negative factors was the division of the guerrilla column. When Che and Vilo Acuña's group separated, they planned to rejoin each other 15 days later. That didn't happen, and Che spent six months moving around, trying to find him in an unfavorable area; he wore out his group there, and there were losses that drained the fighting ability of the guerrilla column.

Now, I'm sure that, if Che had managed to break through the encirclement at Quebrada del Yuro — even if it had been with only two or three men — he would have reorganized the guerrilla movement. While retaining his critical capacity and recognizing his weak points at any given moment, Che was also a very confident person; he had a lot of confidence in himself, in his convictions, in his decisions.

Then all of you thought that Che's operation was going to be successful?

Piñeiro: I'll tell you: when I went to that house where he was with Fidel, Raúl and Vilma to bid him farewell, Fidel and Che talked together in low voices for a long time. When Che was about to go to the airport, I said a few words to him — he wasn't very effusive; he had other ways of expressing his affection and feelings for his comrades. I thought the chances of his getting through the initial stage of the guerrilla struggle were very good because of his ability, his experience, his determination, the mystique that he generated around the men who went with him and his happiness (he was happy; he was like a child with a new toy). He had a capacity to create a sense of solidarity and fraternity among the combatants. He'd learned that from Fidel. Fidel was like that, and he taught us all to be that way.

Why do you think the impression was created in some circles at that time that Cuba betrayed Che?

Piñeiro: That distortion was an effort to try to present Che as being opposed to Fidel, to make people think that Fidel betrayed Che because of political and ideological differences and because the Soviet Union was pressuring him to get rid of Che, who was an obstacle hindering the relations between the two countries and parties. That distorted view was promoted in the press, in documentaries, in the biographies that have been written about Che (there are around 29 of them, if I'm not mistaken) and in several movies, both full-length features and shorts that have marked the 30th anniversary of Che's death and the discovery of his remains.

Let's go back to Cuba now. What was Che's role in the executions that were carried out immediately after the triumph of the Cuban Revolution?

Piñeiro: Che was eminently ethical and humane. He was very demanding with the lawyers and prosecutors who were applying revolutionary justice against the most notorious police officers and criminals who had been responsible for torturing and murdering combatants and women and for doing other things that were even worse than the things I saw described in documents about Hitler's Germany.

All of us know that he demanded to be shown files with data, witnesses and verifications and that the death penalty wasn't applied unless he was fully convinced of the prisoner's guilt. Moreover, revolutionary justice wasn't applied to many in La Cabaña. That was another distortion that was made in a deliberate attempt to present Che as heartless, violent, lacking in human sensitivity and love for his fellow beings, an ogre capable of assassinating people with little or no justification. It's just one more distortion spread by those who have tried to present Che as a violent, narcissistic, authoritarian militarist.

In your opinion, what was Che Guevara's greatest contribution to the Cuban Revolution?

Piñeiro: I think of the contribution he made to the theory of the construction of socialism in the conditions of an underdeveloped, Third World country 90 miles from our main historical enemy. Che also contributed to the political economy of socialism. As a minister, he helped to consolidate all of the country's industries, applying his concepts on planning, incentives and the role of the individual in the construction of socialism. He couldn't finish his theoretical work, but he left us his example, which was and is of fundamental importance. He practiced what he preached, and this inspired a lot of respect and admiration in all of us who worked with him.

Che also had the virtue of inspiring organization and cohesion. He practiced conscious austerity. He made those who worked with him and the other Ministry of Industry workers aware of their social duty; stimulated their spirit of solidarity; informed them about the international situation; awakened their internationalist conscience regarding other, more backward peoples that had greater difficulties; and opposed all acts of injustice, no matter where they took place in the world.

This shows you his universal outlook, which was based on love for and solidarity with his fellow human beings. It was expressed in his decisions to go and fight in the Congo and Bolivia.

Thirty years have passed, and Che's image has become one of the most commercialized, "in" things now. What do you think about this?

Piñeiro: I ask myself: Are those millions of people moved only by the attractive, photogenic aspect of Che? Are they simply going to concerts given by famous singers? What is the real motivation of the thousands of young people who attend the cultural activities that are held in memory of Che?

I think that, apart from the fact that those cultural activities do generate mass interest, there is a feeling of respect and admiration for someone who left behind his family, his powerful position and the affection that this people and the revolutionaries and other progressives in this and other parts of the world felt for him... There is respect and admiration for someone who risked their life in the defense of the freedom of other peoples. There is respect for his intellectual contribution, for his conduct as a revolutionary and as a champion of the most legitimate causes in the world.

For example, take the 70,000 Chileans who went to the stadium where [Cuban singer] Silvio Rodríguez and other Latin American singers performed recently. Were they motivated only by Silvio's music, or did they also go as a means of expressing their solidarity with Che?

This is why I think that the efforts of those who have distorted Che's image — trying to reduce him to a cultural icon, in order to strip him of his ideological, political, humanistic message of solidarity — have boomeranged. All of that consumerism using Che's image, that massive consumerism of objects and posters, has had the opposite effect to what they intended. Those who wanted to manipulate Che as an object of consumption must have realized by now that Che has broken through that image, those limits, and that he is just as alive as ever, just as influential as ever, and has become a powerful enemy of imperialism.

With ever increasing frequency, you see young university students and members of the people's movements who don't belong to any party with pictures of Che. He is a real symbol in his example and his thinking. His ideas are still studied. And, even though this is a different era — and, therefore, his ideas must be viewed dialectically and applied according to the specific situation in each country — in essence, it contains lasting general principles for the struggle for human liberation, for improving human beings, for struggling for justice and for doing away with social inequalities.

That message has had repercussions in religious sectors in the United States — not just in the solidarity that they are giving Cuba but also in the example they see in Che, in his moral and ethical values, in his love for his fellow human being and in his struggle against individual selfishness. This is why I consider Che to be more than the cultural symbol that those who want to divest him of his revolutionary essence seek to portray him as...

Not long ago, I saw a copy of *Newsweek* with a very attractive cover that said "Che Lives," but when I read the article I realized that its main purpose was to present Che as a brave, selfless romantic without any ideological-political message. They didn't present Che as he was: a social fighter ready to risk his life for the liberation of other peoples. Instead, they emphasized the secondary aspects, the frills — not his political and ideological message, his thinking.

Commander, what would Che have thought of the Cuban Revolution now?

Piñeiro: I think that, if Che had stayed in Cuba, he would have been of extraordinary help right now, because of his authority — created by means of his example and his links with the people: his very simple, frank, direct, self-critical, close links with the masses. He would have been of tremendous help to Fidel and the other leaders of the revolution, because of his intelligence, his practical experience, his knowledge gained while serving as a minister and while taking part in drawing up the revolution's strategy and in defense of the revolution. If Che were here now, he would be helping to make the people more politically aware and mobilizing them — especially the younger generations, who didn't experience the heroic stage in which it was our fortune to live — for another kind of heroism: the heroism required in daily life.

But do you think he would have agreed with the path taken by the revolution he helped to build?

Piñeiro: You don't have to view Che schematically, by means of dogma. Independently of his ideals and of his readiness to risk his life anywhere in the world, Che was a realist.

In this changed situation in the balance of power at the world level — with the collapse of the Soviet Union, the destruction of the other socialist countries, the universal trend toward U.S. hegemony and the strategy of "neoliberal globalization" — in this objective situation, in which our small and underdeveloped country 90 miles from the United States must confront difficult conditions, Che would have been enough of a realist to see that, while upholding our principles and not making concessions, we have had to develop our creativity and imagination, seeking solutions that strengthen rather than weaken us and that, rather than making us give in to capitalism, help us to advance toward socialism.

Legendary Cuban Guerrilla Speaks

Interview by Chilean journalist Faride Zeran [1]

He fought in the Sierra Maestra mountains alongside Fidel Castro and Ernesto "Che" Guevara, whom he met in the midst of the struggle and whom he feared when, nursing a toothache in the guerrilla camp, he heard the yells of a farmer on whom Che was working as dentist, armed only with a pair of pliers. Therefore, though he knew that Che was a courageous, daring man with a high cultural level and solid political ideas, his first thought was that he would never let himself fall into his hands — never imagining that, 10 years later, he would be seeing him off on each of his journeys, including the one from which he didn't return.

Manuel Piñeiro, 64, the husband of Chilean intellectual Marta Harnecker and the father of Camila, is a key figure not only in Che's internationalist activities until his murder in Bolivia but also in the development of all the revolutionary movements in the Third World in the 1960s and 1970s, especially in Latin America. This is why he appears in the views of Che presented in the writings of Mexican intellectual Jorge Castañeda and in the statements of Régis Debray, who he referred to disparagingly as a protector of "deserters."

A former Deputy Minister of the Interior of Cuba who headed the Americas Department of the Central Committee of the Communist Party of Cuba for 15 years, the legendary "Red Beard" took his time replying to a questionnaire sent by fax three weeks earlier, perhaps because he had only recently begun to break his silence — in July, in an interview given to *Tricontinental* magazine, of Cuba; a few weeks ago, with CNN's representative in Havana; and now, with *La Epoca*. It is the testimony of a witness for the prosecution in the history of the Latin American left in the latter half of this century.

****

---

[1] *La Epoca*, Santiago de Chile, October 26, 1997.

You broke your long silence with a published interview called "My Modest Tribute to Che." Why? What aspects did you want to bring out?

Piñeiro: As part of the 30th anniversary of the deaths in combat of Che and his comrades, I felt I should make a modest contribution to clearing up the circumstances surrounding the Heroic Guerrilla's internationalist feats. Like other comrades, I considered it necessary to leave the younger generations some testimony and assessments of the present meaning of Che's thinking and revolutionary actions of solidarity.

How do you feel about Che's final return to Cuba? What do you think about this historic coincidence: that, on the 30th anniversary of his death, when his myth is stronger than ever before, his body has been found?

Piñeiro: Independently of the coincidence that Che's remains and those of his comrades have been located close to the anniversary of their murder — which was ordered by the CIA and carried out by the Bolivian military high command, headed by General Barrientos — I feel that his strength and example are an incentive for continuing our struggle today. As Comrade Fidel said, the return of Che and his combatants gives us and our people strength to continue our 100-year-long anti-imperialist struggle to defend our homeland; to work for social justice and the construction of a better society; and to guarantee the preservation of the social and political achievements of socialism, which is being built in our country.

What recollections do you have about the man who made you forget your toothache when you saw him doubling as a dentist in the Sierra Maestra mountains?

Piñeiro: I could go on forever, recalling anecdotes about Che's life, work and example. Right now, I think it is important to place emphasis on his ethics, his values, his internationalism, his anti-imperialism, his Latin Americanism, his revolutionary humanism and his conviction that the cause to which he gave his life would emerge victorious in the end. Even in the worst conditions, Che always placed his trust in humankind, confident that people would be able to keep improving themselves until they became new human beings; confident that they could create a better, fairer world of solidarity without any selfishness or alienation. Those were Che's highest hopes.

Why do you oppose writer Castañeda's view of Che as a "cultural symbol"?

Piñeiro: To reduce Che to a "cultural symbol" is a gross simplification. Che's political legacy and example can be seen clearly in the many acts of tribute to Che and of solidarity with Cuba that were held in many parts of the world — in Latin America, the Caribbean and Africa. What can that so-called political writer say about the more than 70,000 people in Chile who, while remembering Che, expressed their repudiation of Pinochet, their admiration for Fidel and President Allende and their solidarity with Cuba? Was that a mere cultural manifestation, or was it an unequivocal political message: that, as long as there is injustice, social inequality, impunity, corruption, politicking, demagogy, hunger and poverty in the world, Che's political legacy and example will live on in the awareness, admiration and respect given them by worthy, honest men and women in this world?

Speaking of biographies, in his book, Castañeda included several statements about the abandonment of Che by Cuba and Fidel. One of them is the testimony of Gustavo Villoldo, the main CIA agent in Bolivia, who said that Fidel "was afraid of creating anything else that might also be identified by our groups. So, that kept him from taking the initiative to help Che — not because there had been a schism or any split or problems between Havana and Che. No, the system simply failed them, and, when the system failed, they didn't know what to do. In such cases, either you're very aggressive or you do nothing at all. And he opted to do nothing..." What do you think of these words?

Piñeiro: I think that that so-called, libelous thesis is a bunch of political and intellectual crap. He tries too hard to make his point. It is in line with the permanent goal of imperialism and its allies to confuse, disinform and raise doubts, sweeping under the rug the impressive relations of loyalty and respect that always existed between Che and Fidel, which were confirmed in Che's farewell letter when he said, in closing, "If I should die in combat, it will be for Fidel and the Cuban people, who are now my people."

Anything else that is said is simply a matter of intrigue — an attempt to divide and create confusion among Cuban revolutionaries, to raise doubts about our policy of solidarity, to isolate us from international solidarity and to present Fidel and the other historical leaders of the revolution as traitors to Che and his internationalist mission to Bolivia. But they haven't achieved their goal. Their efforts have boomeranged. Nobody believes that lie.

Concerning this topic — Fidel's supposed abandonment of Che — both Castañeda and other biographers of Che also present the thesis that the Soviet Union was pressuring Cuba not to get involved with revolutionary focal points in Latin America. Was that so?

Piñeiro: The enemies of the Cuban Revolution have used the development of this so-called theory more than once in an attempt to show that our internationalist policy wasn't independent. I don't know of any official document or statement by the Soviet Government or Communist Party that made their assistance to Cuba conditional on our abandoning our solidarity with the oppressed and exploited peoples of the so-called Third World.

This doesn't mean that we may not have had different approaches toward various international or Latin American problems, but we always upheld positions of mutual respect, without any impositions. Our party's, government's and people's sovereign right to develop our line of solidarity with the revolutionary struggles of the Latin American and other peoples was always clearly respected. Anyone who is familiar with the history, thinking and actions of Fidel and other historical leaders of the revolution should know that they have never accepted pressures that threatened our revolutionary principles. The facts bear this out.

Now, the Soviet Union no longer exists, and the revolutionary thesis of creating one, two, three Vietnams isn't in vogue. What comments would you make on the Soviet Union and on the whirlpool of a time that called for revolutionary change?

Piñeiro: We are living in a unipolar world presided over by U.S. hegemony. In this era, the circumstances are different, and the slogans and tactics that Che taught us should be adapted to fit the new situation. However, this doesn't exclude the need to keep struggling to bring about revolutionary transformations; the frustrations and partial defeats of the people's revolutionary movement shouldn't make us lose hope. As stated in the Second Declaration of Havana, we revolutionaries have the duty to promote revolution, and this duty is much more pressing in this globalized world in which, every day, capitalism demonstrates its inability to solve the terrible problems that weigh on humankind.

Exploitation, poverty, racial, economic, social, ethnic, religious and sexual discrimination and homeless children are a part of daily life. The only way to try to change this situation is to keep on fighting against imperialism. There's no one formula or dogma. The social and political movements, their leaders and the revolutionary organizations should decide how to develop this struggle, depending on their specific circumstances, but we won't be able to change anything if we don't demonstrate our will and determination to change the present status quo.

The tactics of struggle may change, being adapted to accord with the present moment and era, but what should never change for a revolutionary is one's determination to keep on struggling to seize political power.

In this context, how can the revolutionary ideas of Cuba — a country that is being subjected to terrorist attacks that threaten tourism, one of its most important sources of hard currency — survive?

Piñeiro: We are surviving because of our people's strong unity and political awareness under the leadership of Commander in Chief Fidel; because the majority of the Cuban people know that only socialism can guarantee our homeland's independence, social advances and the construction of a democratic order in which our men, women and young people are protagonists in the work of the revolution; and, because our people are armed, they and our revolutionary army are ready to fight to defeat any aggressor that may try to seize our homeland.

Every day, Fidel and Che's examples are multiplied in our people's daily heroism. If this weren't so, it wouldn't be possible to defeat the imperialist aggression; the blockade; and the plans of subversion drawn up by the counterrevolutionary sectors that act with impunity in and from the United States.

Most recently, the world could see the Cuban people's fervor, unity and revolutionary firmness in the Fifth Congress [of the Cuban Communist Party] — in which everyone participated, giving opinions, criticism and suggestions concerning its documents — in the mass meeting in which the people paid solemn tribute to the memory of Che and his comrades who were killed in combat; and in the last election of delegates to the municipal assemblies of People's Power, in which more than 97 percent of our citizens voted, once more ratifying that the majority of our people support the political system built by the revolution.

In the interview you gave in Cuba, you said that Che spoke of an insurrectional focal point linked to the masses, "not of a small group of armed men acting in any way divorced from the people's movement." How much voluntarism and divorce from the masses was there in the Latin American revolutionary movements that have led you to make this statement 30 years later?

Piñeiro: Such a statement is never out of place. History shows that without the unity of the revolutionaries, without the people's support and without the timely use of weapons it is not only very difficult but also impossible to bring about the revolutionary transformations that make it possible to achieve a fairer society, one of solidarity and without exploitation or discrimination. It's not up to me to make a critical analysis of the political-military experiences in Latin America; I have the greatest respect for the men and women who, using various forms of struggle, have given their lives for their revolutionary ideals.

You know about myths. In fact, your mystique and your legendary red beard make you one of the key figures in the Latin American revolutionary utopia of the last few decades. What was lacking for that utopia to be made a reality?

Piñeiro: I think that, even though they acted with the best intentions, the revolutionaries didn't always bring about unity — the people and weapons, together creatively — without schemata and dogmas. But that doesn't mean that a liberating utopia hasn't been achieved in various parts of the world.

In spite of all their difficulties and problems, the Cuban people are standing firm against all acts of U.S. aggression and are continuing to build their socialist society. Didn't a revolution triumph on the tiny island of Grenada, which was destroyed only through the massive intervention of U.S. imperialism? Didn't the Sandinista Revolution put an end to one of the bloodiest dictatorships in Latin America? Wasn't the Farabundo Martí National Liberation Front of El Salvador on the point of winning, in spite of massive U.S. military assistance to the genocidal and counterinsurgent "democracies" installed in that country? Didn't the people of Guatemala throw out the heirs of the regime that the United Fruit Company and the CIA installed in 1954?

And what about the defeat of apartheid in South Africa and the defeat of Portuguese colonialism in Angola, Mozambique and Guinea? And the liberation of Namibia and Zimbabwe, and the end of Mobutu's dictatorship in what is now the Republic of the Congo? Have you forgotten about the victory of the Vietnamese and Lao peoples over the brutal U.S. aggression? And what about the Chinese people's achievements under the banners of socialism?

All these things demonstrate the failure of those who go around proclaiming "the end of history" and "the end of the utopias." The fact is, there is no law of history, no universal law, which says that failures and defeats won't be succeeded by future victories. As always, they will depend on the peoples' and revolutionary leaders' intelligence and willingness to fight. Sooner or later, they will find the paths that will make our dreams a reality. I have confidence in the dialectics of history.

What about the wave of neoliberalism that is sweeping Latin America?

Piñeiro: It is the best proof of capitalism's inability to solve the terrible economic, social, political and moral problems that affect most of the peoples of the world. More than 1.5 billion human beings live in conditions of critical and chronic poverty. The basic human rights of close to 260 million people in Latin America and the Caribbean are not respected. The wealth of Latin America is being privatized and denationalized. Discrimination continues against women, indigenous populations, young people and homeless children... Nature, the air and the water are being increasingly eroded and contaminated... The underdeveloped countries are being exploited more and more. The foreign debt and unequal terms of trade are increasing. Our very future is mortgaged.

What alternatives do we have? Can we stand by with folded arms in the face of this reality? Should we accept the neoliberal thesis that the "free market democracies" can solve all these problems? In my opinion, the only alternative is to keep on struggling as best we can in the specific circumstances in each of the countries in the region. As Che said, you don't have to wait for all the conditions to be ripe or to be created spontaneously... The struggle itself will speed the creation of alternatives to the various kinds of current neoliberal capitalism.

In an interview given in Paris a year ago, Régis Debray stated, "Havana needs a Parisian devil to explain the desertion by Benigno and other revolutionaries; I was the first to be surprised by that." This was in response to the accusation that Che's daughter Aleida made, saying that he had betrayed her father. Would you like to comment on this?

Piñeiro: It doesn't deserve any comment; Aleidita has already answered it. Moreover, I find the testimony of a man who has changed his political convictions more than once hardly credible. When there are deserters, there's no need to look for a "devil." They sell their own souls and drag their protectors into hell. That's all.

What about critical thought, which used to be very important to Latin American leftists but is now lacking?

Piñeiro: I don't agree with your supposition. After the initial confusion created by the collapse of the false European socialists, a rebirth of critical thought and practice is beginning. There is still much to be done, but nothing indicates that that critical practice and thought have disappeared.

I feel optimistic about the positive signs that are expressed in growing protests; strikes; demonstrations; struggles for land and home ownership; participation in democracy and human rights; and the struggles against discrimination of all kinds that are developing in different parts of the world. They show that the daily struggles against capitalism, neoliberalism and imperialism are providing and will continue to provide a reorientation of critical practice and thought of many true leaders and representatives of the left... This process is virtually inevitable. Sooner or later, the sharp contradictions of capitalism will generate new ideas, new practices and new solutions for the terrible problems in today's world.

Posters in Latin America proclaim, "Che lives." How? Where? Why?

Piñeiro: Che lives wherever there is a wrong to right and wherever there is a man or woman willing to dedicate his or her energy, efforts, intelligence and even life to the immense task of building a more worthy, humane, better society and a world of solidarity...

Che and Bolivia

Interview by Italian journalists Ana María Lobouno and Francesco Loquercio [1]

W ould you tell us something about the contacts Che had with the European revolutionary movement and how important he considered the help it could give the Third World?

Piñeiro: I would say that Che's tour of several African countries, which lasted several months, and his contacts with various leaders of the national liberation movements of that continent led him to think that Africa — with all its poverty, colonial exploitation and especially the struggle that was waged in the Congo after Patrice Lumumba's assassination — had the conditions for extending the revolutionary struggle. Lumumba's murder had a powerful political impact throughout the world, especially in Africa.

In view of that reality, Che saw that there were possibilities for developing the national liberation struggle in the Congo with the support of world public opinion and some African governments — especially the Algerian Revolution, which had just emerged victorious; the Government of Mali; Nyerere's administration in Tanzania; Nkrumah's in Ghana; and Sékou Touré's in Guinea. All of them had made the political decision to help the Lumumba forces keep fighting against the dictatorship of Moisés Tshombe and Mobutu. And, if they managed to survive the first stages, to call for European and Latin American international brigades.

That is, Che's theoretical plan included the incorporation of not only African and Algerian combatants but also European and Latin American revolutionary combatants, depending on how the struggle in the Congo developed. As you can see, it was a continental, tricontinental, Third

---

[1] When these journalists of the Il'Papiro publishing house in Italy learned of Commander Manuel Piñeiro's death, they sent this unpublished interview to *Tricontinental* magazine. What appears here is an edited version made by the compiler of this volume, with their authorization.

World strategic idea based on his deeply rooted internationalist and anti-imperialist concepts. Therefore, I would say that Che's strategic idea included the possibility of the presence of European revolutionaries in the national and social liberation struggles in the Third World, either as combatants or in providing logistic support. I think that was one of the ideas he had about the contribution that Régis Debray could make.

When — more or less in what period — did Che meet Debray?

Piñeiro: Che met Debray through a book that Papito Serguera, Cuba's Ambassador to Algeria at the time, sent us. Debray had just published *The Long March of Castroism in Latin America* and was working on a text that would later be called *Revolution in the Revolution?* At that time, he was studying and analyzing various Latin American political topics. I think that was how Debray first became known in Cuba — as a courteous, sensitive student of Latin American problems who upheld positions favorable to the Cuban Revolution. So Che first met Debray through his book and then met him in person in Bolivia.

At that time, did Debray represent any European organization or party?

Piñeiro: No, he was an intellectual and a student of Latin American topics, but he never spoke on behalf of any French or other European political force.

What was Debray's task in Bolivia?

Piñeiro: It was to meet with Che, interview him, spend some time with the comrades and then go out with a plan for publicizing and obtaining European solidarity for the revolutionary struggle in Bolivia and in other South American countries. That was the main idea and the one that most suited to his personal characteristics. Debray wasn't in very good physical condition, nor could he withstand the demands of being a guerrilla — especially in the initial stage, which is always the most complex one.

A short while ago, a dispute arose between Debray and Che's daughter Aleida about whether or not Debray was responsible for the discovery of Che's camp. Was he responsible for that, or not?

Piñeiro: I view Debray on two historical planes: the Debray of those years, who was a solid radical in solidarity with the anti-imperialist struggles and eager to contribute to the discussion of theory in the Latin American left, and the later Debray, whose political and ideological positions have been critical of the Cuban Revolution. That is, I see two Debrays: the early one and what he is now.

Was the early Debray in any way responsible for the discovery of Che's camp?

Piñeiro: You have to consider that in terms of what really happened. When Debray was captured (I think it was in April 1967), three Bolivian combatants had already deserted and given information to the army and to the Bolivian intelligence services. Therefore, Che's camp had already been detected. After his capture, members of the Bolivian intelligence services tortured Debray, along with the Argentine Ciro Roberto Bustos. The latter, who is a painter, made drawings of the guerrillas he had met, including Che. So, what Debray did was confirm that Che was in Bolivia.

Personally, I don't think he should have done that. It isn't the way a revolutionary should behave when captured by the repressive forces. I think he should never have confirmed Che's presence, much less spoken about the Latin American strategy that was behind the beginning of the guerrilla struggle in Bolivia. In any case, some aspects of the interrogations to which Debray was subjected prior to his trial have still to be investigated.

To be fair, it must be said that in his trial Debray defended his revolutionary positions, especially in response to the challenging questions that one of the lawyers asked him. The press commented on that. This is why I insist that there are two Debrays: the one of the revolutionary stage and the Debray who came out of jail and, with the passing of the years, has adopted a critical political-ideological attitude, describing Fidel and the Cuban revolutionary process as authoritarian and repressive and denying that there are democratic freedoms in Cuba. In my opinion, this "second Debray" has descended to a low-level argument which, in essence, places him on the side of the counterrevolution, very closely linked to the deserter and traitor Benigno and to a group of French intellectuals who have an extremely critical position regarding the Cuban Revolution.

How do you explain the betrayal by Benigno?

Piñeiro: Benigno is very backward, both culturally and politically. He has behavioral and psychological problems. He is a very complicated man, and some intellectuals — especially French ones — noted the weak points in his personality and fed his ego, his personal vanity, leading him to think that the positions, tasks and posts he had in Cuba weren't high enough, in view of the fact that he had taken part in the guerrilla struggle at Che's side. They fed his belief that the revolution hadn't been generous to him and hadn't accorded him the importance he thought he deserved.

As a result, he entered into a process of political and ideological decay and wound up becoming a tool of some of those French intellectuals and of others who wanted to slander the history of the revolution and of Cuban internationalism. This is the reason for his statements about the criteria and comments he claims he heard Che make (either to himself or to other comrades close to him) about disagreements within the leadership of the Cuban Revolution and especially with regard to the supposed contradiction between Fidel and Raúl on the one hand and Che on the other concerning the Sino-Soviet conflict.

Later, the same thing happened to Benigno as happens to all traitors: they stop thinking and acting on their own and become mouthpieces of the interests that pay them and tell them what to say. This was expressed in the book Benigno published recently, which is filled with distortions about the relations Che had with the other leaders of the Cuban Revolution. But no obstacles were placed in the way of Benigno's leaving Cuba. He asked to go to France to write and launch his book, and he had no difficulties.

After his departure, he asked that his wife and children join him, and no obstacles were raised to that. Of course, nobody imagined that he would end up betraying the revolution, and it's lamentable that it happened, because Benigno had been a good combatant. He was a man of rural origins who became the worst thing a human being can be — a traitor to his homeland; to his comrades; and to Che, who did so much to help him to improve himself and become a better person.

Benigno was in Bolivia some months ago. There, he lent himself to all kinds of manipulations. Following that, he even had the effrontery to appear on French television together with Félix Rodríguez, a CIA agent of Cuban origin who was linked to Che's murder. And he publicly joined that individual for the alleged purpose of learning what Che's last words had been. Thus, Benigno once more demonstrated his lack of ethics and of political and human sensitivity.

The 1960s was a period of revolutionary effervescence in Latin America, but also of counterinsurgency by imperialism. Do you think that Guevara's strategy of extending the revolution throughout Latin America would have met with enough supporters and forces to ensure that project a certain future?

Piñeiro: Che always thought that his project of extending the anti-imperialist struggle throughout Latin America would come up against great difficulties — especially stubborn political and military opposition by imperialism and its allies. This would be particularly so in Bolivia, because it has borders with many other Latin American nations which, at that time, had military dictatorships and very despotic governments that were sure to side with the United States for the purpose of wiping out the revolutionary movement.

However, I am absolutely sure that if Che had managed to get through the most difficult stage — that of the guerrilla group's survival — that movement would have attracted many Latin American combatants. Some of the members of the revolutionary organizations in Argentina and Brazil were already holding meetings, analyzing and discussing how best to participate and support the guerrillas in Bolivia. Several of them even went to La Paz, but they couldn't reach Che because the guerrilla base had already been detected. It wasn't easy to get there at any time, but especially then, because the Bolivian Army immediately isolated the area, setting up control posts to prevent access to it; the army controlled the roads, transportation, etc.

What support did Cuba give to that project of Che's? Did the leaders of the Cuban Revolution share his ideas?

Piñeiro: Obviously. Just think of the close relations that always existed between Fidel and Che and the loyalty and appreciation that Che expressed for Fidel as the leader of the Cuban Revolution. Because of Che's international experience, we had great confidence that his concept of struggle would be applied successfully. However, our own experience had made us aware of the great difficulties involved in the first stage of a guerrilla struggle. That was why Fidel always insisted that Che not go at the beginning. But Che wanted to begin the revolutionary armed struggle in the Southern Cone himself — especially because the failure of Jorge Ricardo Masetti's guerrillas in Salta, Argentina, affected him emotionally and psychologically. Che wanted to begin it himself, to be there right from the start.

Does anyone know what happened to Masetti?

Piñeiro: It's still an enigma. It was around April 20, 1964, when we stopped receiving reports about where he was and didn't know if he was alive or dead. Masetti was a cadre with very good qualities as a political and military chief. He knew that he had the great responsibility of becoming familiar with the area; scouting; toughening the combatants; and creating, under his command, the conditions that would allow Che to join the guerrilla struggle. Unfortunately, they were infiltrated and hit hard right from the start. It seems that Masetti's health problems, especially with his back, contributed to the failure of that attempt. It is said that he had several falls, which caused him great pain and kept the group from moving as quickly as necessary.

Was his body ever found?

Piñeiro: No, never. There are several versions of what happened: one is that he was wounded and that, because of his poor physical situation — the sharp pain he had in his back — he couldn't walk as quickly as necessary. After the comrades in the vanguard fell into an ambush, they fell back, and more comrades were wounded. In that situation, Masetti would have sent men out to make contact and seek support. One combatant stayed with him, and both of them disappeared. That's the most credible version. In any case, several Argentine comrades and friends have been trying for many years to obtain information about what really happened and to confirm one of the several versions. As I told you, so far, nobody knows what really happened.

In other interviews, you spoke of Che's idea that it wasn't necessary for all of the conditions to exist to begin the revolutionary struggle in a given country. Was that the case in Bolivia?

Piñeiro: In Bolivia, all of the minimum objective and subjective conditions existed for beginning guerrilla armed struggle. The military coup led by General René Barrientos had led the people — mainly headed by students and miners — to resist. In addition, there were the relations and agreements with Mario Monje, general secretary of the Bolivian Communist Party, and with other leaders of the forces of the Bolivian left. That is, there were political channels for providing political and logistic support and for sending in combatants who wanted to join the guerrilla struggle. Many grassroots cadres of the communist youth and other organizations and many miners wanted to join the guerrilla movement headed by Che.

Monje had pledged to support Che?

Piñeiro: Yes. As general secretary of the Bolivian Communist Party, he had promised to give Che his full support, provide him with every logistic facility and help members of the communist youth and of the party itself to join him, but he didn't keep his word.

Other leaders of the party were very willing to support Che, whether or not they agreed with the strategy and tactics he had drawn up for the struggle. The fact that uprisings and insurrection by the masses, supported by a sector of the army, were deeply rooted in the political culture of the Bolivian revolutionaries was a factor in their disagreement. Their concept of struggle was very similar to that of urban insurrection. Unlike Che, they lacked experience in waging a rural guerrilla struggle.

Is it true that there were contradictions between Monje and Che and that that was why Monje didn't keep his word?

Piñeiro: That is stated in Che's *Diary*. It contains the analysis he made of his December 31, 1966, meeting with Monje. Apparently, Monje went there with a decision that he knew Che wouldn't accept. Hidebound by established procedures as general secretary of the Bolivian Communist Party, he wasn't aware of the continental dimensions of Che's plan. He didn't know (or didn't want to know) that Che would be in Bolivia only until the Bolivian combatants had been forged in the struggle and had gained enough experience to enable them to take over the leadership of the guerrilla movement in their country. Che's idea, as I've said in other interviews, was to go on — along with some other cadres — toward his final goal: Argentina.

Why do people speak of betrayal by Monje rather than betrayal by the Bolivian Communist Party?

Piñeiro: Because it isn't fair to involve the other leadership cadres and all the members of that party. We know that some of them didn't agree with Monje's position. Moreover, Monje made almost all of the decisions related to support for the guerrilla struggle. As we were told later on, he never consulted with the other leaders of the Bolivian Communist Party. To doubt those statements and debate how true they are would lead us into the realm of speculation, and I don't like to speculate.

What we know officially is that the general secretary of the Bolivian Communist Party didn't tell the other leaders of the party what pledges he had made to the leaders of the Cuban Revolution. Monje (apparently behind the backs of the other leaders of the Bolivian Communist Party) even received military training in Cuba, along with a group of Bolivian scholarship students — for whom he later created serious obstacles that kept them from joining the guerrilla struggle.

What, in your opinion, were the factors that made the Bolivian guerrillas fail?

Piñeiro: First of all, the fact that Monje didn't do what he had promised the leaders of the Cuban Revolution.

Second, the guerrilla base was detected prematurely. Ñacahuazú wasn't the area of operations. In Che's plans, it was only a rearguard area for training combatants and storing logistic supplies. Other areas, such as Alto Beni and El Chapare, which had better conditions for the operations of a guerrilla detachment, were being studied. They had a greater population density and a longer tradition of social struggle, and members of various organizations of the Bolivian left lived there. Che had received information about those areas before leaving for Bolivia.

The third factor was the division of the column. Che left Comrade Vilo Acuña (Joaquín) in command of a small group of comrades, who were sick or whose fighting spirit was at a low ebb, and took another group of combatants elsewhere to allow Debray and Bustos to get out and go to the city. Che and Joaquín were to have joined forces again in 15 days but didn't do so for around six months, which meant that Che spent all that time moving around in an inhospitable area, trying to find Joaquín's group in order to unite the column. That went against Che's strategic plans.

Most of the military operations that Che carried out were successful, however. This was so because of his long experience as a guerrilla, because of the training the Cuban combatants had received and because of the actions of the Bolivian combatants who were beginning to emerge as good guerrilla cadres. The brothers Coco and Inti Peredo were among them...

Would another form of military leadership have enabled them to escape, regroup and save Che's life? Could Che and the other combatants have found a way out and saved themselves?

Piñeiro: After what happened, the question should be: Was it necessary for Che to remain on the front line, with the sick comrades, to allow the others to take up positions and regroup? The correct thing in terms of the tactics for waging a battle, according to theory — what the manuals say — was that Che had to be in a position that would guarantee him at least a minimum of safety (to the extent that any position is safe in a guerrilla battle) for directing the battle and, in the end (or at the right moment), falling back to save his life and the lives of the other combatants.

But Che had a great sense of personal ethics and surely thought that, as the leader, he should set an example and personally contain the attack of a unit of the Bolivian Army so that the other comrades (including those who were sick) could fall back. Che's response in running the greatest risks and, as leader, always setting an example, was logical in view of his personality. He did that more than once in the guerrilla struggle in Cuba. That's why Fidel has always said that Che's Achilles' heel was his courage.

Now, some people try to psychoanalyze that characteristic of Che's, saying that he sought death as a means of "running away" from the conflictive situations that surrounded him. That has no relation to reality. Che defended his life right up to the end and did everything he could to keep the enemy from capturing or killing him easily. This is shown by the fact that, when he was shot in the leg and his rifle jammed, he and a Bolivian comrade tried to break out of the encirclement and go back to the place where his comrades were to regroup. But, obviously, the military situation was already very difficult; Quebrada del Yuro had become a deathtrap...

While those military operations were being carried out, did Che remain in contact with the leaders of the Cuban Revolution? When was that contact lost?

Piñeiro: Contact between Cuba and Che began immediately and lasted until the camp was seized and the radio was put out of commission; after that, he couldn't receive our messages. The group included comrades who had been trained in how to work the radio and, when conditions permitted, establish two-way communication. However, you have to keep in mind how far apart Bolivia and Cuba are and understand what a guerrilla unit is like in the initial stage. You have to carry everything, and everything apart from food and ammunition becomes an impediment.

In that first stage, contact between Cuba and Che wasn't of decisive importance. This was so, first of all, because Che didn't have an escape plan. He knew that, in that kind of revolutionary struggle, you either win or die. So, in practice, the radio didn't play an important role — especially because, with the presence of the U.S. advisers, if any security measures were skipped, the use of the radio to send messages could enable the enemy to pinpoint the movements of the guerrilla column. Those movements depended on Che's leadership and on his evaluation of the adverse circumstances that had arisen.

I know that some biographers have placed a lot of emphasis on communications. They link it very subtly to the "theory" that our country either abandoned Che or didn't provide him with even the minimum means needed for the success of his endeavor. For the same purpose, they have placed great emphasis on the urban network and on the question of why Comrade Renán Montero, known as Iván, returned to Cuba. (He came back because he had to renew his undercover documents.) In the meantime, events didn't develop as planned. Che's plans were changed, as were his calculations concerning how many months it would take to become familiar with the terrain and receive logistic support, medicine and more Bolivian combatants.

Moreover, after the camp was discovered, sending Iván back to Bolivia wouldn't have solved anything. First, because the guerrillas were moving in a large territory, and, second, because the members of the urban underground — who belonged to the communist youth organization and the Bolivian Communist Party — were psychologically reeling from the identification and capture of some of their members. They were stunned by that situation. In addition, it wasn't easy — even for them — to penetrate the area of operations to get a feel for what was going on, learn of the army's movements and hear what the farmers and traders were saying. It would have been much more difficult for a foreigner to try to enter an area that was completely controlled and was a military zone.

Even so, those situations have been combined and used as a basis for the "theory" that Cuba didn't send the reinforcements that had been planned, both because of the impact that the Sino-Soviet conflict had had on the Cuban leadership and because of the pressure that the Soviets had supposedly brought to bear on Fidel and the revolution... All of those speculations and inventions were aimed at sowing the idea that Che was a hindrance to Cuba and that Comrade Fidel had therefore abandoned him to his fate.

As you can see, that line of thought also sought to smear Fidel, presenting him as an insensitive person totally lacking in loyalty and with no revolutionary principles — as someone who was so heartless and insensitive that he was capable of abandoning a comrade such as Che and the other Cuban comrades. That is the main thesis of the books by Ricardo Rojo, of Argentina, and Daniel James, of the United States, which present that "theory." The only thing that some of the other biographers have done is include arguments of various kinds and, working from those basic premises, repeat the same lies they've been telling for the last 30 years.

Some people think that the urban network fell apart because its members wanted to join the guerrillas. Is there any truth in that?

Piñeiro: You have to separate the problems of the urban network from the specific situation of Tania. The urban network was hurt by its inexperience in underground work, and Tania remained with the guerrillas for totally unforeseen reasons. It is true that she had an inner contradiction. She had more of a vocation for being a combatant than for doing underground work in the city, but she was working well, sending us the information gained in her underground work. She knew how important it was, but she had already given indications that she wanted to do something more active. For her, that meant joining the guerrilla column as a combatant.

She didn't go to Ñacahuazú with the idea of staying, however; she went to take Debray and Bustos in, because, at that time, there was no one else in the urban network who could do it. In view of that specific situation, she volunteered and took them to where Che was.

Some people say that Tania left all the documents in the jeep on purpose. The only documents she left there were related to her cover story, to the personality she had assumed in Bolivia. Those documents fell into the hands of the enemy by chance. Tania was a very responsible, disciplined woman who came from a communist, internationalist family that was in solidarity with Third World peoples' struggles. She wanted to contribute to the revolutionary struggle, and she threw herself body and soul into preparing to carry out her revolutionary task.

What do you think of the hypothesis that Tania was an intelligence agent of the German Democratic Republic?

Piñeiro: I've heard those lies. I believe that, moved by her revolutionary ideas and sense of duty, Tania cooperated — as is perfectly logical and understandable — with the security bodies of her country: the German Democratic Republic, which, at that time, was being harassed by imperialism and has since disappeared.

Since she spoke Spanish perfectly; was a German; came from a communist family; and had many ties with various people, including

VIPs, in Latin America, I don't doubt that she helped the political or security bodies of the GDR. But cooperating with them doesn't mean that she was an agent or official of the Ministry of Security of the GDR. Even if that dubious hypothesis had been true at any time, I can assure you that she divested herself of those responsibilities to dedicate herself — entirely, loyally, nobly and selflessly — to the Cuban Revolution and to the revolutionary, anti-imperialist struggle in Latin America.

Was the possibility of helping Che and the other comrades get out of Bolivia ever considered in Cuba?

Piñeiro: That's one of the "theories" that Benigno spread. He asked how it could have been possible that no escape plan was drawn up for Che and the other comrades, since Cuba had rescued other Cuban combatants in Venezuela. With that logic, the explanation seemed obvious: there was no political determination to rescue them; rather, a political decision had been made to abandon them.

Basing themselves on that fabrication, the writers of one of the latest biographies of Che took a comment that Benigno is supposed to have made to another comrade ("We're alone, and we have no future") and went on to say that Che heard them and, while criticizing them for their comments, insinuated that he agreed that our country had abandoned them. I repeat: all of these lies are told for the express purpose of subtly creating an atmosphere of doubt and speculation about the attitude that the Cuban Revolution had concerning Che's Bolivian experience.

As I've already pointed out to other interviewers, just imagine what would have happened if Fidel or other leaders of the Cuban Revolution had decided to send military reinforcements to the guerrilla area. It would have been equivalent to declaring war on the Bolivian Government. We would have given the United States an excuse for bringing the OAS and all the Latin American countries into a military crusade against Cuba.

Moreover, can you imagine how long it would have taken to train 50 or 60 Cubans, provide them with documents and weapons, move them through other countries, explain to them what the border and the Bolivian Army were like, form them into a column that could enter Bolivian territory without being detected and then infiltrate them into an area that was completely surrounded by the enemy army? It would have taken months...

Therefore, I repeat: all that was fantasy, nothing but fantasy, as was supposing that the Council of Ministers of Cuba would meet, declare war on the Bolivian Government and send in an airborne division — which would involve flying over several other Latin American countries — and land 1,000 or 2,000 men in the Bolivian jungle. Now, apart from all that speculation, I'm sure that Che would never have agreed to being taken out of there. He knew from experience, both in our war of liberation and in the Congo, that there's no going back in such battles. The revolutionary armed struggle is no picnic, no vacation in which you go for three months or so and come back whenever you want.

We know that the CIA worked together with the Bolivian Army. The Soviet Union seems not to have been in agreement with the Bolivian mission. Did it play any role in it?

Piñeiro: You have go to back to the historical situation and what foreign policy positions the Soviet Union had at that time. As you know, its foreign policy was expressed in the so-called peaceful coexistence among nations with different economic, social and political regimes. At that time, the Soviets considered that everybody who acted outside their strategy of peaceful coexistence caused problems for them. But there was no peaceful coexistence between the peoples that were struggling for their national and social liberation, on the one hand, and imperialism and its allies, on the other.

We acknowledge the economic and military help that the Soviet Union gave us so we could defend the revolution and build socialism in our country, but we didn't consult with the Soviet Union about Che's plans, either in the Congo or in Bolivia, or about the help that Cuba offered the revolutionary movements of other African countries (we also sent advisers and combatants to former Portuguese colonies), and the Soviet Union neither approved nor disapproved of them. Fidel and the rest of the Cuban revolutionary leaders made all of those decisions.

Of course, because of the relations they had, the two parties had exchanges of ideas and analyses on selected topics, and our country's representatives informed their counterparts about those things that they deemed advisable; but they always honored the need-to-know discretion required by our policy of assistance to and solidarity with the revolutionary movements in different countries in the world.

In the case of Bolivia, had the Soviet Union been informed of Che's mission?

Piñeiro: The Soviets were informed when practically everybody knew that Che was in Bolivia. But, I repeat: the political, economic and military assistance that the Soviet Union gave Cuba was never made conditional on our abandoning our independence in making political decisions concerning not only our domestic but also our foreign policy. Independently of some copycat mistakes that we made in later years, Cuba — an underdeveloped country just 90 miles from the strongest imperialist power on the face of the earth — always maintained its own concepts regarding the specifics of socialist development and foreign policy.

Is it true that the Soviet Union wasn't happy about Che's mission in Bolivia?

Piñeiro: I think that the top leaders of the Soviet Union would have liked Che to be victorious in Bolivia. It would have meant one more country that had freed itself from U.S. imperialism. Later, it would have been necessary to make another analysis of the possibilities of cooperation in the defense and consolidation of the revolutionary power... The Soviet Union already had many commitments to Eastern Europe, Africa and Cuba... However, I think there was disagreement among the Soviet leaders, between those who looked kindly on the active solidarity that the Cuban Revolution was giving the peoples fighting for their national and social liberation and those who viewed it as an element that could hamper and create obstacles for their strategy of peaceful coexistence with the United States.

Was Che's mission in Bolivia a threat to peaceful coexistence?

Piñeiro: I think that no revolutionary is opposed to peaceful coexistence, but this doesn't mean that the revolutionary struggle should be halted. We are not in favor of war. It is our enemies who impose war on us. We resort to it only when we have no alternative, when all possibilities for advancing along the path of democracy and for trying to achieve political power through peaceful means are closed to us. So far, with only a few exceptions, no revolutionary force has managed to gain political power without resorting to one form or another of revolutionary armed struggle. Those who have adopted peaceful means for obtaining political power may have held the reins of government or been represented in government, but they have never been able to achieve and hold on to political power.

The relations between the Bolivian Communist Party and the Soviet Union were very close. Is it conceivable that, as general secretary of the Bolivian Communist Party, Monje may have told the Communist Party of the Soviet Union about what was going to be done in Bolivia?

Piñeiro: Monje didn't know the details until Che — who was in charge of the operation — was in Ñacahuazú, in the guerrilla area. Monje may have deduced a lot, since he knew that objective elements existed, which, at that time, made Bolivia (within the situation in which the revolutionary struggle was developing in Latin America) the most logical option for beginning the struggle in the Southern Cone of Latin America. He also knew of the continental extent of that struggle. At our request, the Bolivian Communist Party and some of its structures had already supported other — Peruvian and Argentine — revolutionaries...

I don't know whether Monje informed the Communist Party of the Soviet Union or not. To express any opinion would be speculation on my part. I simply reiterate that Monje's decision to have nothing to do with the development of the guerrilla struggle meant that he broke the pledges he had made to the top leaders of the Cuban Revolution.

How did Che's diary reach Cuba?

Piñeiro: Antonio Arguedas Mendieta, Minister of the Interior of Bolivia, sent a copy of Che's diary to Cuba. As a student, he had been linked to the ranks of the Bolivian left. He sent a photocopy of the complete diary, including two pages that the CIA and the Bolivian Government left out when they distributed photocopies of the original diary — they took two pages with different page numbers out of every copy they distributed. Therefore, when the diary was published — Arguedas Mendieta was still Minister of the Interior at the time — the CIA and Barrientos knew that it was based on the copy given to Arguedas.

Apart from that, Arguedas gave us a lot of help in clearing up the CIA's and the Bolivian high command's opinions and comments about and analyses of the guerrilla column and each of its members. That's why I told you that further studies should be made of Debray's attitude. Some of his behavior while in prison isn't entirely clear.

Let's go on to another subject. What importance do you think Che's speech at the Algiers conference had within the Cuban Revolution and for the revolutionary movement in the Third World?[2]

Piñeiro: That speech has many interpretations. Obviously, it is critical, expressing the criticism that, for several months, Che had been making of all the Soviet leaders with whom he had contact as a minister and on all the trips he made to the socialist countries. If you read all the articles and interviews that are coming out now about Che's life, that is one of the most debated topics. This is logical.

In his Algiers speech, Che called for unity between the socialist camp and the anti-imperialist struggles in the Third World. He called for awareness of the links that exist between the struggles for national and social liberation in the underdeveloped world and the international construction of socialism. He made a constructive criticism of the attitude that the European socialist countries were adopting in their relations with the countries that had just become independent of colonial rule, etc.

I think that life has shown Che's criticism to have been correct. Now, you can debate whether or not he chose the right method and moment. But, unfortunately, the analysis that Che made has been borne out by subsequent events.

As you know, basing themselves on that speech (and on Benigno's questionable remarks), some biographers came up with a story that Che

---

[2] Che's speech in Algiers is published in *Che Guevara Reader* (Melbourne: Ocean Press, 1997).

had a terrible argument with Fidel and other comrades in the leadership when he returned to Cuba. They claimed that things heated up and Che was accused of being a Trotsky, of being pro-China, etc. What really happened was that Che and other comrades in the Cuban leadership tried to influence and convince both the Chinese and the Soviet leaders that their wrangling was harmful to the development of the anti-imperialist struggle throughout the world and caused splits in the revolutionary movement. He did that both on his trips to the Soviet Union and on his trips to China.

Just look: Starting with some objective facts (the content of Che's speech in Algiers and the Sino-Soviet conflict), they came up with the utter lie that, following that speech, Che was a square peg in a round hole in Cuba and was being isolated — that he was hurting the interests of the Cuban Revolution and that that was why he was given all the facilities for going off on his project in the Congo and for keeping his internationalist pledge in Bolivia — and, after he had gone, was abandoned to his fate.

Those who uphold that "thesis" forget that, as far back as when they were in Mexico, Fidel had pledged to Che that, when the conditions permitted, he would be freed of all responsibilities so he could go and do what he, Che, felt was his historic mission: to continue the revolutionary struggle in other countries in the continent, especially Argentina. They also forget that the top Cuban leaders have always had group discussions. But it's one thing to discuss, analyze, have different points of view and come to conclusions about what is best for the interests of the revolution at a given moment, and it's quite another to go to the heartless extreme of sacrificing a comrade — especially Che...

How do you interpret Che's speech in Algiers?

Piñeiro: As I've already said, I think that Che's criticisms were fair and that he didn't seek to divide or to exacerbate the contradictions between the Chinese and the Soviets or between the Cuban Revolution and any other socialist country. Rather, he sought to call the socialist countries' attention to the need to review those policies that didn't contribute to strengthening the socialist camp and the revolutionary movements in the Third World.

This is why I think that it was and is stupid to think that, with that speech, Che was aligning himself with the Chinese position, and it's even more stupid to try to use Che as a symbol for splitting the revolutionary movement. Now, this doesn't mean that those revolutionaries who were critical of "real socialism" and of its ideological-political deterioration couldn't see that Che was right and draw strength from his analysis that was critical of the so-called Soviet model.

Fidel has been very clear about this. Apart from the public discussion that took place in the 1960s — above all, during the October 1962 Missile Crisis — it has always been our political position that, although we might criticize the Soviet Union and other socialist countries, we would always acknowledge and express our gratitude for all the help they gave us, both in military terms and in the sphere of economic cooperation. That assistance to Cuba, a Third World country just 90 miles from the United States, allowed us to begin to build socialism and train cadres — especially military cadres. This is why I think you have to separate these two things.

Now, after the disappearance of the Soviet Union and of "real European socialism," it would be easy to say it was all a terrible disaster. Independently of any criticism of the Soviet Union and of the other socialist countries, you have to view the two things separately and differentiate between them objectively.

Ever since the triumph of the Cuban Revolution, U.S. imperialism has been drawing up plans for killing Cuban leaders. Che was not only one of those leaders but also an ambassador of the revolution. Did the Ministry of the Interior — you were one of its leaders — have reliable information about any of the plans for assassinating Che before his departure for Bolivia?

Piñeiro: Yes. Right from the first few years after the triumph of the revolution, the counterrevolutionary organizations that were operating clandestinely in Cuba under the direction of the United States carried out assassination attempts against the main leaders of the revolution.

The enemy kept a particularly close watch on Che. It considered that he had a lot of influence in the revolution, was a radical communist and a legendary figure and posed a threat to the interests of the United States, not only because of his positions in Cuba but also because of his influence in the revolutionary movement. It was public knowledge that, ever since the triumph of the revolution, in addition to carrying out his political and administrative tasks, Che spent a lot of time maintaining contacts with the Latin American revolutionary movement, and such things always filter through to the enemy's agencies. Therefore, Che was always a prime target for assassination.

Several assassination attempts were detected and neutralized. Che was very difficult to kill, for he took safety measures. He knew he was a target of the U.S. intelligence agencies, special services, the CIA and the extreme right throughout the Americas.

What did you admire most about Che? In your opinion, what were his main virtues and his main defects?

Piñeiro: First of all, you have to view Che as a human being, a man of flesh and blood, with many more virtues than defects. His defects were completely overshadowed by his virtues, which were always outstanding. He was very human, fraternal, and never solemn. He never used his high political position, his authority as a guerrilla leader and combatant or his cultural and political knowledge for personal gain. Far from being arrogant, overbearing or proud, he was a very modest man who always worked as part of a group. He had a great sense of humor. He was a truly extraordinary man. Convinced of the need for struggle, he committed himself to this struggle even though he knew it would mean risking his life, because he felt he had to support his ideas — not only in theory but also in practice.

What influence did Che have on you?

Piñeiro: He influenced me — and not only me, but all the Cuban people and all the people in Latin America and the rest of the Third World and the world as a whole — by setting a great example. He left us his thinking, which was not only military (others place a lot of emphasis on this aspect of it) but also economic, political and social. He left us his approach, his contribution, his critical analysis of a certain kind of socialist construction and his ideas about the transition from capitalism to socialism in the Third World. It is really tragic that he couldn't complete his reflections. He made great advances in drawing up ideas, proposals and analyses, but you have to remember the times in which he did so and the differences between those times and the present situation.

What would Che do now in Cuba?

Piñeiro: I think it would have been very unlikely for him to have remained in Cuba, because, ever since the triumph of the revolution and his participation in the construction of socialism during the first few years, his goal, his mission, was to continue the revolutionary struggle in other Latin American countries.

If he had remained in Cuba his thinking and his actions would have made a tremendous contribution now. First, because of his authority, his influence, the affection and respect in which the people and revolutionary combatants held him, his scientific pursuits, his constant searching for answers to problems in theory that either hadn't been solved at all or had been solved on the basis of the realities in European or Asian socialist countries, his constant searching for theoretical-practical answers to problems related to the construction of socialism in an underdeveloped country (such as ours, just 90 miles from the United States) and his steadfast refusal to make concessions in principles.

In short, together with Fidel, Raúl and the other comrades who have been the historic leaders of the revolution, he would have been a source of inspiration and an important factor in consolidating awareness of the need to build socialism by setting an example; by increasing the people's ideological and political knowledge; and by creating more and more examples of the new human being, of which he dreamed so much...

Tricontinental

Speech presenting the Special Issue of Tricontinental
Magazine Dedicated to Ernesto Che Guevara,
September 27, 1997

First of all, I would like to thank the Organization of Solidarity with the Peoples of Africa, Asia and Latin America [OSPAAAL] for having given me the great honor of presenting this special number of *Tricontinental* magazine, which marks both the 30th anniversary of Che's death and the 30th anniversary of the founding of this publication.

Frankly, at first, I had my doubts about accepting this generous offer. I am one of the people interviewed in this issue of *Tricontinental* — and, therefore, one of its authors — and was also, to some extent, a modest protagonist in some of the events described in it; therefore, it seemed to me that it wouldn't be correct for me to talk about a magazine issue to which I had contributed.

Later, however, on thinking it over, it occurred to me that the presentation of the magazine gave me an exceptional opportunity for sharing some very intimate, very personal ideas with you.

The first idea I would like to convey to you is related to how this magazine was created. I observed the efforts made by the comrades who directed, wrote, designed and produced this issue — they worked long hours, including weekends — so I know just how pleased they are that our modest tribute to Che (the subtitle of this issue) has been given such a warm welcome, both in Cuba and abroad.

The fact that there had to be a second printing in less than two months (the first one had come out just before the 14th World Festival of Youth and Students, which was held in August) testifies to the quality of the issue and the interest that Cubans and others have in its contents.

Now, let's give a big hand to Pez Ferro and the other comrades — especially Ana María Pellón, the young editor of *Tricontinental* — who put out this issue, which has unquestionably renewed this magazine's Guevarist, internationalist tradition of solidarity.

The issue that we are presenting today includes testimony and anecdotes by combatants who were linked to Che's African endeavor, documents, an address by Major Ernesto Che Guevara, articles, interviews that bring out little-known events in the trajectory of the Heroic Guerrilla and some essays that take a fresh and creative look at what Che's legacy means today.

All of those genres and authors (myself included) are linked by the admiration and love that we revolutionaries from various continents who had the privilege of knowing Che personally feel for him and his work — admiration and love that is shared by the members of successive generations who have studied Che's extensive, integral theoretical work since his death. Some of those authors are here with us today, and I'm sure that, in a little while, they will be willing to answer any questions you may wish to ask about their contributions.

As for myself, I think it was a very good idea for this issue of *Tricontinental* to combine history, recollections and anecdotes with profound reflection (surely polemical) on the applicability and timeliness of Che's legacy, both in the revolutionary peoples' struggles that are being waged all over the world (especially in Latin America) and in the construction of socialism.

It's a good way of thwarting those who want to bury Che's revolutionary legacy once and for all, or who, at best, want to relegate him to the museum of history. And, above all, this is an excellent occasion for confronting all those who are wasting enormous quantities of paper and ink trying to show that the political legacy left by the Heroic Guerrilla isn't valid for tackling the world's problems at the end of this century and in the coming millennium.

I understand that you have discussed these topics thoroughly, so I won't go into them. However, I'd like to give you my own view now: That, as long as there are any wrongs to be righted anywhere in the world and as long as there is any hope of bringing about revolutionary social change, Che, his example and his thinking, will live on as a powerful stimulus to all struggles by the oppressed.

In addition, without casting aspersions on any of the previous issues, I would say that the one we are presenting today marks the virtual relaunching of *Tricontinental*. Suffering — like many Cuban publications — from the rigors and shortages of the "special period," the magazine had almost gone out of circulation. Thanks to the efforts made by the members of the Secretariat of OSPAAAL and the editorial team and to generous international solidarity, *Tricontinental*, like a phoenix, has risen again with the renewed intention of being, as its founders and continuers have dreamed, one of the main voices speaking out for solidarity among all the oppressed and exploited in the world and especially for the cause of the peoples of Africa, Asia, Latin America and the Caribbean.

It isn't by chance that this occurred with an issue dedicated to Che, because he symbolizes historical continuity. When the first issue of this publication was being prepared, the secretariat of OSPAAAL, which was then headed by Comrade Osmany Cienfuegos and some other comrades, published Che's message to the peoples of the world — a document which, because of its great historical importance, became the Heroic Guerrilla's political testament.[1]

When that supplement appeared in April 1967, the first shots had already been fired in Che's Bolivian endeavor. Through that message, the world knew that Che, astride Rocinante and bearing his shield on his arm, was once again waging a new battle against imperialism in another part of the world. Little by little, subsequent reports of the epic feats that were being carried out in Bolivia confirmed that he was there, leading a small internationalist army, and that Che had decided to implement his catchcry of creating two, three, many Vietnams.

Lamentably, that supposition became certainty only when the world learned that, after having waged unequal battle and been taken prisoner after having been wounded and with his weapon put out of action, Che was murdered in cold blood by a cowardly hired assassin acting on the orders of the U.S. intelligence agencies and the military dictatorship that was ruling Bolivia at that time. The recent efforts by some of imperialism's hacks notwithstanding, no one can hide the fact that one of the worst crimes in history was committed at La Higuera.

Thirty years went by before Che's remains could be brought back to his second homeland, where, as you know, the people will pay him well-deserved tribute a few days from now. I am sure that that tribute will be enormous, for several reasons.

The first is that, as you have seen for yourselves, Che lives on; his memory is cherished in the hearts of the best of our people, in the hearts of Cuban children and young people. The poems, chants and optimistic smiles of our children and young people show me that the new man and new woman, as Che described them, have reappeared and are being constantly multiplied in revolutionary Cuba. These young people and those who follow them, with their struggles against the blockade and against imperialist aggression, give us reason to believe that the cause of the peoples' liberation to which Che gave his life will emerge victorious.

There is another reason for predicting that our people will give Che and all of the internationalists who were killed at his side a memorable tribute, and that is that the Cuban people know that they will not only be paying tribute to those killed in battle but will be taking up — with all the honor which they deserve — the new banners that will guide us

---

[1] See *Che Guevara Reader* (Melbourne: Ocean Press, 1997), 313.

in the difficult struggles of the present and of the foreseeable future for the construction of socialism.

The Cuban people also know that, through Che and his comrades, they will be paying tribute to all those who have given their lives on civilian and military missions to express our revolution's solidarity and internationalism.

Together with Fidel, I am convinced that being an internationalist is simply a way of paying our debt of gratitude to all humankind. Together with Che, I am convinced that internationalism is not only a duty but also a revolutionary necessity for the construction of socialism in Cuba and in any other part of the world.

The forms and content of internationalism have changed and must continue to change constantly, in accord with the circumstances of each historical moment, but the best of the Cuban people will always remember and cherish the internationalism set forth by Che:

"Socialism cannot exist if a change isn't wrought in the people's consciousness — a change that brings about a new, fraternal attitude toward humankind, both individually, in the society that is building socialism, and on the world scale, toward all the peoples still suffering from imperialist exploitation."

You — comrades from different continents who have joined us on this occasion — can be sure of this: our revolution will never make any concessions of principles to our historic and present enemies. We have many reasons for ratifying this pledge, but one of the most important ones is that Che — that exemplary internationalist, as Fidel described him — lives on in us and is just as powerful an enemy of imperialism as ever.

I am sure that *Tricontinental* will continue to play its part in the ideological and political struggles that lie ahead. I also hope that, after reading the contents of the magazine that is being presented today, you will make use of it and will be more determined than ever to join Che — the immortal commander of Latin America and legendary commander of the Third World peoples — in saying: Ever onward to victory!

The Immortality of Che

A new encounter between Tricontinental *and Comandante Manuel Piñeiro Losada* [1]

T hroughout 1997 international and Latin American public opinion was shaken, not without surprise, by what someone has called "Che's resurrection." There have been innumerable articles, books, biographies, radio and television programs, cassettes, videos, graphic productions, public events, concerts, exhibitions, conferences, as well as political and scientific events held surrounding the 30th anniversary of his death in combat. These testify to how, despite the systematic efforts to commercialize, annihilate or denigrate his example, the paradigmatic figure of the Heroic Guerrilla continues to call forth new battles around the world against imperialism, the oligarchies and revolutionary dogmas.

In our America, these events have included the 14th World Festival of Youth and Students, held in Cuba; the numerous, militant concerts in Santiago de Chile and Buenos Aires; the international seminar entitled "Che: 30 Years," sponsored by the magazine *América Libre* in Rosario, Argentina; the now traditional vigil held in La Higuera, sponsored by the Latin American and Caribbean Continental Organization of Students and the Félix Varela Foundation; the first "Che Guevara" International Meeting, organized by the Bolivian foundation that bears his name, in Vallegrande, the small Andean city where his immortal remains and those of his comrades in struggle were displayed. In addition, as the culmination of the Fifth Congress of the Communist Party of Cuba, there was the moving welcome that was given to these fallen combatants by hundreds of thousands of Cubans ready and willing to defend and carry out his socialist and communist ideals. These events have shown — with a view of the present as well as hope for the future — that Che's theoretical and practical legacy is still relevant for understanding and

---

[1] This originally appeared in *Tricontinental* No. 138. It was presented publicly on March 3, 1998. In fact, this was Manuel Piñeiro's last public intervention.

transforming the oppressive economic, political, informational, ideological and cultural "order" that prevails today.

Shortly before the international meeting entitled "The 21st Century: Legacy and Relevancy of Che's Work" was held in Havana — whose final declaration was acclaimed by hundreds of participants in the events in Rosario and Vallegrande — we published a special issue of *Tricontinental* devoted to Che (issue No. 137, July 1997). The success of this issue was of such magnitude that for the first time in recent years we were compelled to do a second printing after only two months.

Taking nothing away from the quality of the rest of the issue, including the design and graphic material that appear in it, a large part of this success stems from what was in fact a journalistic first: the exclusive interview granted to us by one of the Cuban revolutionary leaders closest to Che's internationalist efforts, Commander Manuel Piñeiro Losada. The impact of this interview was immediate. Giving greater or lesser credit to our publication, some of the major newspapers and magazines mentioned it in their pages, in some cases incorporating into it other questions and answers. And rigorously giving us credit, close to 10 alternative publications reproduced it in full or in part in various languages. There was no lack of publishers who asked us to expand it, with a view to larger publishing projects.

Because of this, and in recognition of his proverbial internationalism, Commander Piñeiro was asked to speak at a launching of issue No. 137 held in the context of the international event called by OSPAAAL and our magazine. He accepted what he called a "generous offer," an "exceptional opportunity" to share "some very intimate, very personal ideas" with dozens of representatives from all continents who attended this meeting, as well as with the journalists covering it.

This second tricontinental session was held September 27, 1997. After a few introductory remarks, our guest responded, in his charismatic style, to about 20 questions related to Che's revolutionary course of action. A large part of his statements were designed to respond to the fallacies spread by those interested in breaking the indestructible trilogy of Fidel, Che's internationalist efforts and the Cuban Revolution's consistent international and Latin American policy.

Given the importance of his new revelations, and once again as an exclusive, *Tricontinental* brings its readers a summary version — due to the space available in this issue — of his principal responses to the questions. In doing so, it offers apologies for the defects in the recording that made it difficult to identify each questioner.

—*Luis Suárez Salazar*

****

We have read with much interest what you said in issue No. 137 of Tricontinental[2] about how Che, at a certain moment, considered the possibility of going to fight in Nicaragua, Colombia or Venezuela. Could you elaborate on this?

Piñeiro: As early as the opening months of 1959, Che was in contact with a group of Nicaraguan exiles that had come from Mexico — among them Tomás Borge (who is here at this seminar) and the former lieutenant Somarriba. He offered them all possible support at a time when Cuba's security and solidarity apparatus was in its earliest stage.

One of the Cuban comrades who participated in that effort, Carlos Lugo, who is still living, took a message from Che to Somarriba in which Che said, more or less, that if Somarriba and his column managed to set themselves up in Nicaraguan territory, he would fulfill the commitment he had made. According to Lugo, this commitment — signed in a very friendly way, anonymously, as "He who helps you" — foresaw the incorporation of Che in the struggle of the Nicaraguan people against the Somoza dictatorship. That effort could not materialize because the Honduran army (with the participation of some of Somoza's officers) destroyed part of the expeditionary force. Two Cuban comrades — Onelio Hernández Taño and Marcelo Fernández Isla — died there along with a number of Nicaraguans. Notwithstanding, Che subsequently aided other groups of Nicaraguan revolutionaries, one of which was led by the brothers Harold and Alejandro Martínez, and another by Enrique Lacayo and Julio Alonso. On Che's instructions, the Cuban Renán Montero, who is still living, took part in the latter effort. Both groups sought to organize armed struggle in Nicaragua, from Honduran territory.

But regardless of the details, what I want to stress is that from the first days after the triumph of the Cuban Revolution, Che was already thinking about carrying out what he considered to be his historic commitment to participate in the liberation of other peoples of our continent. That's why he also committed himself, beginning in 1962, to participate in and lead, along with Jorge Ricardo Masetti, the effort to initiate a guerrilla struggle in Argentina.

These facts help refute the commonly told lie that Che left Cuba, first for the Congo and later Bolivia, due to his "irreconcilable differences with the revolutionary leadership of our country."

Venezuela and Colombia came later. In his frequent meetings with revolutionary leaders from those countries, Che explored the possibility of participating in guerrilla struggles that were developing there. In my opinion, I think he wanted to initiate and lead his own effort and, above all, guide it toward the Southern Cone, specifically to Argentina. He felt

---

[2] For the *Tricontinental* interview with Piñeiro see Chapter 1.

very anxious to carry out that commitment to his people and to our peoples. He could not stand to sit comfortably behind a desk while other *compañeros* fought and died trying to put some of his ideas into practice.

What can you tell us about Che's solidarity with the struggles of the peoples of Paraguay and Puerto Rico?

Piñeiro: He always paid very close attention to the revolutionary struggle of the Paraguayan people, so much so that in early 1959, with the help of other *compañeros* from "Ciro Redondo" Column No. 8,[3] he personally participated in combat exercises with a group of Paraguayan combatants who were then training in Cuba. Che also helped various Puerto Rican independence leaders. I can assure you that he — like Fidel and the Cuban Revolution — continually expressed his immense sympathy and solidarity toward the anti-colonial struggles that were taking place in the early 1960s on that sister Caribbean island. He especially admired the late *compañero* Pedro Albizu Campos.[4]

Some of Che's biographers have claimed that he lacked the most basic knowledge of the situation in Africa and in particular the Congo. What is your opinion on this?

Piñeiro: I have read some commentary in this regard. I don't wish to judge the intentions of the authors. But it must be remembered that before joining the struggle in the Congo, Che had traveled through a number of African countries, and he personally knew many leaders of revolutionary movements and several progressive heads of state in the region. Che was not unaware of what was happening in Africa, or of the difficulties created for the anti-imperialist struggle by the social, tribal, ethnic and cultural conflicts that characterize the majority of African countries — not to mention the negative qualities of some of the leaders of the so-called Supreme Council of the Revolution of the Congo.

His diary and his *Episodes of the Revolutionary War in the Congo*[5] make clear that Che sought to broaden his knowledge of the characteristics of the area where the Cuban contingent operated, of the features and capabilities of the Congolese and Rwandan leaders, as well as the best banner under which to advance the revolution in that central African country. Against his will, the abrupt interruption of that solidarity effort kept him from concluding his investigations.

I want to emphasize one point: Che had an anti-imperialist and tricontinental strategic conception that fully coincided with the policy of

---

[3] The Rebel Army column commanded by Guevara in 1958.
[4] Pedro Albizu Campos was a leader of the Puerto Rican Nationalist Party and imprisoned by the U.S. government for over 20 years for pro-independence activities.
[5] Major excerpts from Guevara's manuscript on the Congo are included in *Che in Africa* by William Gálvez (Melbourne: Ocean Press, 1999)

the Cuban Revolution, which, in turn, was the source of the decision that he would command the Cuban contingent that went to what is now known as the People's Republic of the Congo. Contrary to what some biographers have said, this was not an individual decision. This and other solidarity activities with the peoples of Africa were the product of the consistent policy toward that part of the world, developed from that period onward by Fidel and the revolutionary leadership of our country.

What role did you play in the preparation of Che's internationalist effort in Bolivia?

Piñeiro: As first deputy minister of the Ministry of the Interior, I was responsible for all activities aimed at determining the "operative situation" — to use the official term — in that country and neighboring countries: immigration controls, passports and the documents necessary to guarantee the clandestine transfer of the *compañeros* to Bolivian territory.

Likewise, we took responsibility for surreptitiously getting Che out of Tanzania, for attending to him and his security while he was living clandestinely in Czechoslovakia, as well as organizing the routes and details of his subsequent trip from Cuba to Bolivia.

As with other countries in Latin America, Asia or Africa, the team that I headed up took responsibility for reviewing the available information on the political, economic and social situation in Bolivia. We oversaw the initial contacts with leaders of the Bolivian revolutionary organizations (first of all with the members and leaders of the Communist Party) who had made a commitment to support the internationalist effort commanded by Che. We also organized the training of a number of Bolivian comrades in Cuba. I think that these were the basic things. Perhaps with the passage of time — at an appropriate political moment — other actions that we carried out in Latin America, Europe and other parts of the world aimed at supporting the revolutionary strategy of the Heroic Guerrilla can be made public.

What did the CIA and FBI know about Che's activities in Africa and Latin America? Did Che and the incipient Cuban solidarity apparatus you headed deceive the U.S. intelligence agencies?

Piñeiro: From what I have been able to read over all these years — including various statements by former high CIA officials, as well as information from sources friendly to our country — they lost Che's trail in Africa. Faced with that reality, they unleashed a systematic campaign to create a state of uncertainty about his whereabouts. In an operation very similar to the one they are currently waging, they began using all means at their disposal to spread slanders about how Fidel had jailed or murdered Che, or how Che had been expelled from Cuba due to disagreements with the top Cuban leadership. In addition to creating confusion in the revolutionary ranks during the 1960s, these actions were designed to learn Che's possible destination. Comrade Fidel maintained strict silence. The only thing he would ever say was that Che was in the right place and that he was making revolution. In that way he waited for the best moment to announce the exact place where Che was fighting.

Perhaps the CIA and the FBI had some clue as to Che's presence in Latin America. The facts, however, showed that they had no prior information on the plan, the sending of a number of Cuban comrades to Bolivia, much less the logistical resources that were sent there. If they did, then why didn't they stop any of these actions? Further proof that the CIA and the enemy's special services were deceived is that Comrades Renán and Tania were in Bolivia. In spite of the fact that Tania unfortunately was unable to accomplish the main task assigned to her, she lived there without her real identity being revealed, until unforeseen circumstances led to her joining the incipient guerrilla detachment.

Can you offer us an assessment of the quality of the logistical support assigned to Che's internationalist effort in Bolivia? As you know, some biographers accuse Cuba of failing to make available the necessary means of support.

Piñeiro: The logistical support had to be obtained in Bolivia itself; sending equipment from Cuba proved to be very difficult. The weapons of the guerrilla unit were the same as those used by the Bolivian Army. It is true — as has been said — that the communications equipment that the *compañeros* in Bolivia were able to obtain was inadequate for the needs at that initial stage of the struggle, when the mobility of the guerrilla unit demanded that each combatant prioritize the carrying of essential munitions and food. We must remember that one of the laws of guerrilla struggle is to seize and use the weapons, munitions, equipment and provisions of the enemy forces. Otherwise, the development of the guerrilla detachment will depend on the difficult, if not impossible, task of getting supplies from abroad. As was proven in the Cuban experience, what makes the guerrilla unit superior is the moral quality of its fighters combined with the appropriate strategy and tactics, including the use of surprise. With some exceptions, the quality of the weapons, equipment, or logistics of the insurgent forces will always be inferior to that of the enemy forces. Anyone who thinks or says otherwise knows nothing about irregular warfare.

The biography of Che written by U.S. journalist Jon Lee Anderson states that there is still a big mystery surrounding who decided to initiate the guerrilla struggle in Bolivia. Other biographers — such as Mexican intellectual Jorge G. Castañeda — claim that it was Commander Fidel Castro who "sold" that idea to Che, in order to solve the "ambiguous" situation he had been left in following the defeat in the Congo. What can you tell us?

Piñeiro: I repeat that the decision to undertake the guerrilla struggle in Bolivia and from there extend it to Peru, Argentina and other countries in the Southern Cone, was entirely Che's. He took into account and had full confidence in the information we sent him through various channels from Havana, which were passed on to him directly by the Cuban comrades (such as Martínez Tamayo, Harry Villegas, and Renán Montero), as well as the information sent to him by Tania. He had previously sent all of these compañeros to Bolivia on different missions. But each and every one of the decisions was made by Che: the plan, the strategy, the selection of the Cuban combatants who accompanied him, each of the preparatory steps, the Bolivian and Latin American political organizations — initially from Argentina and Peru — that were contacted, and so on.

Those of us who knew him were aware that he had a lot of experience, not only from the responsibilities he had assumed in building our socialist state, but also as a military leader and a guerrilla leader. That experience was enriched in the Congo. That's why everything was studied and discussed with him. He always asked for and listened respectfully to the opinions of others — even when he disagreed with them — and he liked to debate and give thought to each decision. He sought out different points of view. In spite of his desire to begin the struggle as soon as possible, and the fact that he was a man of strong temperament, passion and will, he was nevertheless very demanding, meticulous, and cold-blooded in his analysis... I would say that he was very objective, precise in all his thinking, particularly when it came time to make a decision.

That is why I have no doubt that apart from all the support we gave him as a state — on Comrade Fidel's orders — Che used his own methods and channels to verify the most important information we sent him. This is logical, since in examining the circumstances of any country there can be subtleties, discrepancies between different sources of information, different conclusions reached by various *compañeros*, etc. Che was very careful about that. As we say in Cuba, "He never swung at the first pitch; he would wait for the best one to hit."

Considering that Che was responsible for planning and organizing all the details of the development of the guerrilla struggle in Bolivia, what is your analysis of the mistakes he made and of the causes of the failure of the Bolivian experience?

Piñeiro: Much has been said and written about that. As for the causes of the defeat of the Bolivian guerrilla movement, I think there were several. First of all, the early discovery of the location of the rear guard and the premature beginning of guerrilla operations. We know that a movement of this type must first get itself established, create ties and explore the terrain. It has to enable the combatants to become seasoned. It has to determine their capacity to withstand and adapt, and their willingness to continue the struggle, above all to continue it in the initial stage, which is always the most difficult. Before these minimum conditions were met, and while Che was away on an exploratory journey, the fighting began in Ñacahuazú. As a result, the existence of the guerrilla camp was revealed, all the plans were prematurely set in motion, and they had to begin fighting in an area that lacked the social and political conditions for the development of guerrilla struggle. This facilitated the gradual tightening of the encirclement by the 10,000 Bolivian soldiers involved in the confrontation with Che's small detachment.

Second, Che tried to get Régis Debray and Ciro Bustos out of the zone of operations. He knew that the army was going to wage an intense effort to locate, confront and surround the guerrilla unit. For this purpose, and faced with the fact that some comrades were sick and others had little willingness to fight (he termed them "the dead weights"), he divided the detachment with the aim of reuniting in 15 or 20 days. That was not accomplished, reducing the firepower and combat capability of the column, which nevertheless obtained several military victories. Unfortunately, for six months, and with a reduced number of men, Che was circling around in an inhospitable area, making successive attempts to reunite with the group led by Comrade Vilo Acuña (Joaquín). Now it may be analyzed whether this was correct or not, but I am sure that it was a decision made, among other reasons, out of Che's humanism and comradeship, and not for military reasons. In his mind it was unthinkable to abandon any *compañero*. That excessively delayed his plan to move to northern Chapare, an area of operations closer to La Paz and with much better social, political and topographical conditions than those where the guerrilla unit operated.

Thirdly, not all the commitments previously made by the various Bolivian forces, both with Cuba and with Che, were fulfilled, either quantitatively or qualitatively. One of the causes of this, as is recognized today by the leadership of the Bolivian Communist Party, was the negative stance taken by Mario Monje, who was then its general secretary. This disoriented, disorganized and demobilized many members of the party and its youth group, who, as we saw later, were ready and willing to join the struggle. The urban network, which was being built in various cities of Bolivia on Che's orders, was hard hit before it was ready, and the channels of communication, both within Bolivia and with Cuba, were unable to function. Logistical support was interrupted, as was the possibility of obtaining Bolivian reinforcements. This included some 20 comrades from that country who had already received training but were unable to leave Cuba. Those of us who have participated in guerrilla struggle know that in the initial phase, the guerrilla unit is compelled to rely primarily on its own forces and resources. Nevertheless, the support of the urban network is always necessary.

This whole situation conspired against the possibilities for the Bolivian detachment to survive. In addition, no examination of this type can ignore the fact that elements of chance always come into play. Not everything occurs in a pre-established way. Sometimes accidents — even though they are not decisive in the end — condition the evolution of political or military events. There is more than one example of this in the history of the world, of Latin America and of Cuba.

Finally, I want to stress that I evaluate the Bolivian experience as a whole, and therefore I do not characterize it as a total failure. All of us would have wanted Che's Latin American undertaking to have achieved great triumphs. Had this been the case, the situation in Latin America, and perhaps the world, would be different today. But even though from an objective standpoint it turned out to be a defeat in military terms, it constituted without a doubt a great moral, political and ideological victory. It has put Che, the internationalist, forward as an example to millions of men and women in the world who raise the revolutionary banner.

It has been asserted very strongly that conditions did not exist in Bolivia for the development of the guerrilla struggle. What is your opinion 30 years later?

Piñeiro: Based on what is known about the way events unfolded, I'm aware that some "historians" believe that Che, or the leadership of the Cuban Revolution, did not take into account the objective and subjective situation and the relationship of forces that existed in Bolivia at the time. Others term that effort "voluntaristic," "*foquista*," and "militaristic." I disagree with these opinions. I sometimes ask myself, what would these same "historians" have said if Fidel had been killed in the [July 1953] Moncada attack or at Alegría de Pío,[6] and had been unable to continue the insurrectional effort right then? I'm sure they would also have said that the Cuban Revolution was impossible, that the objective and subjective conditions did not exist, or that Fidel was a "putschist," a "vanguardist," or an "adventurer."

Historical analysis cannot be reduced to a few epithets and insults... Think about the subsequent course of Bolivia's political situation, for example. There was an upsurge of struggle against the dictatorship that was already under way among the miners and students beginning in

---

[6] Alegría de Pío was the first battle of the Cuban revolutionary war in December 1956, in which the revolutionary forces were taken by surprise and almost eliminated.

1967 (I spoke about this in the interview that appeared in issue No. 137 of *Tricontinental*). Furthermore, barely three or four years later a broad nationalist, anti-dictatorial and popular movement unfolded, headed by the late general Juan José Torres and other important political figures of the Bolivian left. Leaving aside its own errors, this effort could only be crushed by a merciless attack by the political and military right wing, supported by the United States.

This demonstrates that beginning in the second half of the 1960s, major economic, social and political contradictions were ripening in Bolivia, including within the ranks of the military itself and in the high command of the army. In addition, a will to struggle against the traitors of the 1952 revolution was being created.[7] All these forces needed to be organized and forged into a vanguard. Had the guerrilla movement led by Che been able to survive the difficulties of its initial stage, it had the potential to play such a role. I believe that Che grasped this situation like few others, and he concluded that the minimum conditions existed to begin the guerrilla struggle. As he conceived it, the remaining objective and subjective conditions would mature as the revolutionary armed struggle unfolded, including as a result of it.

The same could be said about the political situation in Peru and Argentina. Less than a year after Che's death, a movement of nationalist officers broke out in Peru, with important backing from progressive sectors.[8] Despite its limitations, this movement shook the traditional forms of domination by the oligarchy and imperialism. In Argentina, a few years later various powerful popular movements were born (the *cordobazo* and *rosariazo*)[9] as well as dynamic political-military organizations (such as the Revolutionary Army of the People [ERP] and the Montoneros), which could be destroyed only by one of the most brutal campaigns of repression ever seen by that country and the entire

---

[7] A revolutionary mass upsurge in Bolivia in 1952 resulted in nationalization of the largest tin mines, legalization of the trade unions, initiation of land reform, and the elimination of the literacy requirement that had effectively disenfranchised the majority of Bolivia's people, the Aymará- and Quechua-speaking population. But Bolivia remained one of the most impoverished countries of the Americas. The increasingly corrupt and fractured government of the Revolutionary Nationalist Movement (MNR), a bourgeois party that initially had strong support from Bolivia's superexploited tin miners, was overthrown by a military coup in 1964.

[8] General Juan Velasco Alvarado led a military coup in Peru in 1968. The Velasco regime nationalized the country's oil fields and began a program of land reform.

[9] In May 1969 a general strike erupted in Rosario, Argentina's second-largest city, followed by a massive uprising in Córdoba, the third-largest city. The *cordobazo* ushered in a period of rapidly sharpening class struggle in Argentina. Only after the workers movement failed repeatedly to resolve the conflict in its interests did the struggle culminate in a 1976 military coup, followed by years of the infamous "dirty war" waged by the dictatorship of Gen. Jorge Rafael Videla, in which tens of thousands of Argentines were killed or "disappeared."

continent. No less than 30,000 persons and hundreds of fighters from among the people were murdered or disappeared. If Che had been able to continue developing his strategic plan, I am sure that many of these *compañeros* would have joined his struggle. Remember that his was not a short-term strategy. It assumed that the struggle for national and social liberation of these countries would last 10, 15, or perhaps 20 years, above all because he always foresaw the probable intervention by imperialism.

What role did Régis Debray play? Was he the "beginning of the thread" that led to pinpointing the location of the guerrilla unit?

Piñeiro: There are various versions. Some *compañeros* allege that Debray revealed Che's presence in Bolivia. However, the information we possess — which is quite extensive, even if there are still some facts to verify — indicates that what Régis did, in the difficult situation he found himself in, was to confirm the information already supplied to the Bolivian army by some lower-level deserters and, above all, by everything given them by the Argentine Ciro Roberto Bustos. The latter made drawings of each of the members of the guerrilla unit, and gave an immense quantity of facts, providing the enemy with very precise information on the guerrilla unit's camp, its composition, and its weaponry. What Debray does seem to have revealed for the first time, was Che's strategic plan of extending the guerrilla struggle from Bolivia to other South American countries, that is, the continental character of the movement undertaken in Bolivia.

The negative positions taken by Debray in recent years, his "repentance" of the revolutionary struggle, his direct or indirect connections with persons today who want to throw mud on the figure of Fidel, on Cuban socialism, and on our revolution's support to Che's internationalist efforts, cannot lead us to ignore the facts I have mentioned. It would not be ethical on my part, without proof, to assign Debray responsibility for pinpointing the guerrillas' location, much less for Che's death. As the saying goes, "Render unto Caesar the things that are Caesar's; and unto God the things that are God's."

According to the biography written by Jorge G. Castañeda, Che had a martyr complex. What is your opinion of such a statement?

Piñeiro: I have read it. He also says Che had a mystical affinity, and he tries to explain all of Che's acts by what he calls a *"fuite en avant."*[10] I don't know if this is a literary term or a psychological concept, but all of us who were acquainted with Che know that he did not seek death, but rather victory of the revolutionary cause. He was very altruistic and daring, so much so that Comrade Fidel termed his audacity his

---

[10] A surge forward, no matter what the obstacles.

"Achilles' heel."

In my opinion — and this is shared by other *compañeros* who were with him in the guerrilla effort in Bolivia — these were personality traits that led him to play an active role in the battle of the Yuro ravine. In this, as on many previous occasions in the Sierra Maestra and the Las Villas campaign — Che, rather than pull back, remained in the front line to slow up the attack of a Bolivian unit and thus facilitate the retreat of the other *compañeros*, in particular those who were ill. One can ask oneself today whether or not this was correct, but for him it was very difficult to abandon *compañeros* in such a state. This does not mean that he went around seeking death. What he certainly was seeking was to preserve the maximum guerrilla forces in order to reorganize them and continue the struggle.

Something else that disproves this "psychoanalysis" is that even when he was wounded, with his carbine put out of action, and with no bullets for his pistol, Che tried, with the help of a Bolivian *compañero*, Willy Cuba, to break out of the encirclement and meet up again with the other *compañeros* at a prearranged site. Che was someone who defended his life, conscious of what it signified for the revolutionary plan of action, and he was determined to sell it very dearly to our enemies. It's true that he did not fear death and that he was prepared like few others to face it. But that is different from stating that Che had a propensity to martyrdom.

Was an escape route or a plan to rescue Che envisioned ahead of time? If so, what prevented such a plan from being carried out?

Piñeiro: The idea of a supposed "rescue plan" for Che in Bolivia that was not implemented because *compañero* Fidel did not authorize it, is one of the many lies propagated — with the clear support of our enemies — by Dariel Alarcón, alias Benigno. He raised this [in 1996] after betraying the Cuban Revolution and the ideals he fought for together with Che. These arguments reveal his frustrations and resentments, and the way he is being manipulated by the enemies of the revolution. We note his trips to the United States to offer his services to the CIA and to the imperialist campaign against Fidel and the Cuban Revolution.

What Benigno and the authors of these fallacies suggest is that Cuba should have declared war on Bolivia, that it should have sent a unit or a commando squad, thousands of kilometers away, to a landlocked country, transporting tens or hundreds of thousands of soldiers by air to rescue Che. Such a thing is seen only in adventure movies…

Furthermore, I think that those who have spread such a hoax forget one basic thing: no one who is fully and consciously involved, as was Che, in guerrilla struggle or in revolutionary combat, maps out a rescue plan in the eventuality of failure. For this reason neither Che in Bolivia nor Fidel in Cuba ever envisioned ahead of time any rescue plan. Che went to Bolivia with the determination to fight, to win or to die. As I stressed in the interview already mentioned, he was optimistic about the possibility of carrying out the revolutionary plan of action, given the conditions of Bolivia and the Southern Cone of Latin America. And he believed that as the project grew, it would receive the solidarity of all progressive sectors of Latin America and the world.

As I already said, the only thing approximating a plan or an "escape route" foreseen by Che was to head toward another region of Bolivia where there were better conditions to develop the guerrilla struggle. He certainly would have done this, even if all he had left was a handful of combatants. I'm convinced that regardless of the circumstances, Che would have made all efforts to reorganize and reinitiate the struggle, just as Fidel did in Cuba after the "shipwreck" of the *Granma*, and above all, the disaster of Alegría de Pío. Remember that when it appeared he had only seven men and five rifles, Fidel said, "Now we've really won the war!" Che had this same spirit, this same strategic optimism.

Those who believe in "escape routes" and "rescue plans" mapped out ahead of time, apparently project onto others — as the psychologists would say — their own cowardice, inadequacy and pragmatism. But fortunately we revolutionaries are not so pragmatic. We are inspired by different values and principles. We have confidence in victory. We try to make great ventures possible at all costs. The more difficulties they entail, the more interesting and attractive they look to us. This is what Fidel and the Cuban Revolution have demonstrated each and every day. And it is proved by the life of all men and women who, like Che, know how to conquer immortality.

Speeches and Essays on the Latin American Revolutionary Movements

1972-90

The Cuban Revolution and Latin America

Speeches to the
General National Liberation Department [1]

August 5, 1972 [2]

C omrades, it gave me great satisfaction today to recognize the merits that these comrades have attained in their revolutionary work. It made me feel optimistic. Here, we see a reflection of the development and advances that our revolution, our people and — as an

---

[1] The General National Liberation Department (DGLN) of the Ministry of the Interior (Ministerio del Interior, MININT) of the Republic of Cuba was founded in 1970. The Political Bureau of the Central Committee of the Communist Party of Cuba decided to separate the functions of the intelligence bodies from those tasks directly linked with the Cuban Revolution's solidarity toward popular, revolutionary, anti-colonial and anti-imperialist struggles in diverse countries in the world. This work had been coordinated from the beginning of the 1960s by the Technical Deputy Ministry (VMT) of the Ministry of the Interior.

The DGLN had among its essential objectives the implementation in various forms of Cuba's solidarity and internationalism toward Latin America and the Caribbean. This organ of MININT disappeared at the end of 1974. In the months prior to the First Congress of the Communist Party of Cuba (December 13-18, 1975), the principal tasks of the DGLN in international political relations were assumed by the Auxiliary Office of the Central Committee of the Communist Party. As a result of this, in February 1975 the Americas Department of the Central Committee was established. Maintaining its functions, this Department became the Americas Area of the International Relations Department of the Central Committee following the Fourth Congress of the Communist Party in 1991.

These speeches were given to the National Liberation Department in the period 1972-74. The speeches have been excerpted for this volume.

[2] Address given at the ceremony held on August 5, 1972, to assign ranks to combatants in the General National Liberation Department (DGLN) of the Ministry of Interior.

inseparable part of them — our Ministry have achieved in the course of these hard, intensive, demanding years. If we look back, we can see how much we have done, but it is our duty to look forward, not back. We must look to the future to understand that our revolutionary duties and obligations have just begun.

No one should rest on their laurels. We have a long, hard, complex struggle ahead. Internally, we must continue to promote the economic, cultural and social development of the revolution with maximum efficiency. This is not an easy task, because imperialism will continue to threaten us as much as it can.

Imperialism isn't as strong as it was some years ago, but it is still powerful and will continue to use its entire arsenal of reactionary weapons — aggression, subversion, corruption, intrigues and ideological penetration — against the peoples of Latin America and other parts of the world.

Our problem, as you know full well, isn't just one of struggling selfishly to ensure Cuba's safety. We are communists, internationalists. Our cause will be achieved only with the definitive defeat of imperialism and with the full liberation of all oppressed peoples, especially those with whom we have geographic, cultural, historic and blood ties.

Our people — and all of us, as part of our people — are ready to defend the Cuban Revolution to the death, because Cuba's flag doesn't stand for any narrow nationalism. Rather, it represents an internationalist principle and cause, the future of an entire continent.

Fidel has taught us that we are an integral part of Latin America and that, in this age of the scientific-technical revolution and of great human communities, our homeland must ensure its future by strengthening its links with the other Latin American countries, with political and economic unity based on the revolution and socialism.

Naturally, this can't be achieved overnight. The prospects for Latin American liberation now appear to be medium- or long-term. We must prepare ourselves to wait — to wait as long as necessary: 10, 15, 20 or even 30 years. We must prepare to repulse the enemy in all fields, no matter what means he may use to attack us. And, of course, we must prepare to help to speed this process of revolutionary transformation as much as possible.

Our Commander in Chief has emphasized that internationalism is the supreme test of Marxism and socialism. Communism cannot exist without internationalism. Solidarity among our people cannot exist without solidarity among the peoples.

These words have special applicability for all of us, for our party and for our commanding officers. We must constantly prepare and strengthen ourselves, not only increasing our capacities for doing the specific work entrusted to us by the revolution but also keeping in mind that the struggle will be a particularly long one in the ideological field and that imperialism is giving ever greater importance to the subtle weapons of penetration and domination. This means that we must continue delving into the principles of Marxism-Leninism, revolutionary ideas, the study of the great problems of history and political problems of the present day.

It means that we must strengthen this area much more, that we must go as deeply into it as is humanly possible and that we must defeat all of the reaction's maneuvers in this field.

It means that we must be more tenacious and systematic in our studies. We must make our analysis of the works of Marx, Engels and Lenin, our study of Comrade Fidel's speeches, and our efforts to put revolutionary principles into practice a substantial part of our daily work.

Our tiny country has the historic privilege of heading an entire continent's struggle against exploitation and for its definitive liberation. Our people are capable of carrying out that mission, for they are armored against wishy-washiness, opportunism, selfish nationalism and the infiltration of imperialist ideology.

Moreover, we are not alone. We have the solidarity of the rest of the socialist camp, the revolutionary movement and especially the Soviet Union, whose contributions to our economic development, strengthening of our defense capacity, and political and moral support constitute a clear example of proletarian internationalism and loyalty to Leninist principles.

As Fidel said during his visits to several African and socialist European countries,[3] our homeland, like the other revolutionary countries, is faced with the double challenge of continuing to struggle to consolidate and improve socialism and its institutions and of helping the rest of the world that is still fighting for liberation against imperialism. This is why, when speaking of revolutionary work of all kinds, our party upholds the banners of solidarity — especially militant solidarity with the heroic people of Vietnam, whose feat against imperialist aggression is now and will always be a source of inspiration for all revolutionary combatants in the world.

This is our path. Now, more than ever before, we have cause for viewing the future with confidence. Thanks to the selfless efforts and work of the people, our revolution is making sure progress. Revolutionary ideas are gaining ground in Latin America and the rest of the world, and the balance of power is ever more favorable to the revolutionary countries and unfavorable to the reaction and

---

[3] The reference is to Fidel Castro's visits to Guinea, Sierra Leone, Algeria and eight Eastern European countries, including the Soviet Union, between May 3 and July 5, 1972.

imperialism. Nothing can save imperialism from definitive defeat if each of us does everything they can at their workplace every day, with more creative, self-sacrificing work. With more communist conscientiousness and more internationalist solidarity, we can shorten this road and make our modest contribution to the cause of the liberation of humankind.

In our work, communist conscientiousness and internationalism, let us be inspired now and forever by that exemplary soldier of the Cuban Revolution; that model of combativity, firmness, staunch loyalty to principles, selflessness, austerity and lack of pretentiousness; that man whose heart contained no frontiers and who fought and died for other peoples, unconditionally; that man who was the supreme example of the proletarian internationalist spirit and whose ideas, name and heroic struggle will live on forever in the awareness of the peoples of the Americas and the world: Major Ernesto Che Guevara.

Comrades, let us set ourselves the task of humbly following his example. Let us struggle as tenaciously as Che against errors and deficiencies. Let us be as demanding and disciplined in carrying out our duty as he was. Let us, like the Heroic Guerrilla, dedicate all of our efforts and intelligence to the cause of socialism and communism. Let us pledge to do this now, in this meeting in which we have given deserved recognition to revolutionary merits. Let us be inspired by Che's merits to continue advancing and to make this commitment our revolutionary response to our Communist Party; its Central Committee; and its beloved First Secretary, Commander Fidel Castro.

Homeland or death!

We will win!

******

June 8, 1973[4]

As part of the activities held to mark the 12th anniversary of the creation of our Ministry, we are meeting this afternoon to award 10 Years' Service Orders to the comrades in the Ministry of the Interior who have just earned this honor.

This ceremony, which is being held in the year of the 20th anniversary of the attack on the Moncada Garrison, has special meaning for me — first of all, because it gives me an opportunity to note with satisfaction that our Department's work is being carried out successfully, though with some deficiencies and difficulties and in the midst of the

---

[4] Remarks at the ceremony held on June 8, 1973, to present 10 Years' Service Orders to combatants and officers of the General National Liberation Department of the Ministry of the Interior.

necessary definitions that will determine our future prospects. I also note that the comrades who work in it are doing an ever better job in revolutionary work, even though there is still much to be done before we can feel completely satisfied.

Secondly, this ceremony is meaningful because it tests our mettle and leads us to be more eager to get more things done and more demanding in carrying out the tasks that the revolution has assigned to us, so as to be worthy of the example of and sacrifices made by those who, 20 years ago, following Fidel's lead, launched themselves courageously into an effort to achieve freedom and happiness for our people.

The attack on the Moncada Garrison blazed a decisive path in the history of Cuba and of Latin America as a whole. These last two decades have witnessed not only the most radical, history-making transformation ever seen in the life of our homeland but also unprecedented events in the rest of Latin America. In this period, the land which Martí called "Our America" — to differentiate it from the other America, which wasn't ours — has been the scene of revolutionary upheavals, heroic searches, unstoppable peoples' movements, a desire for change and tremendous advances in anti-imperialist awareness, which irreversibly show the peoples' advances toward their complete and definitive liberation.

Our people, who fell behind the rest of Latin America in the process of emancipation from the colonial yoke in the past century, have had the historic honor and privilege of serving as a catalyst and of heading a revolutionary feat in this part of the world that will save hundreds of millions of men, women and children from exploitation and poverty; unleash the thus-far repressed and alienated forces of a continent; and, in response to history, achieve close unity in a great family of peoples with the same historic and cultural roots, peoples who have been artificially separated and divided for centuries by their common enemies. This revolutionary feat, that is now under way and cannot be stopped, will deal U.S. imperialism a mortal blow.

The feat of the heroic young people of the generation of the centennial[5] not only started up the "big motor" of the class struggle in our homeland — which led to the triumph of the socialist revolution — but also unleashed and gave impetus to the struggle of the exploited and

---

[5] In Cuban political and historical terms, the generation of the centennial consisted of those young people on the island who entered the country's political life in the year of the 100th anniversary of the birth of José Martí (1853-95), Cuba's apostle of independence. The best representatives of that generation, headed by Fidel Castro Ruz, attacked the Guillermón Moncada and Carlos Manuel de Céspedes Garrisons on July 26, 1953. Thus, they were the founding nucleus of the July 26 Movement (M-26-7) and, later, of the Rebel Army, which headed the political-military struggle against Fulgencio Batista's dictatorship.

all honest patriots throughout Latin America against the exploiters in their own countries and against omnipresent U.S. imperialism.

We have all experienced, and been participants in, this class struggle. In it, we have learned something that Martí foresaw as far back as the last century, when he said that a mistake in Cuba would be a mistake in Latin America and for all humankind. That is, Cuba's revolutionary struggle could not be confined within its territorial limits; its success or failure would have repercussions that would affect the life of all Latin America.

During the past 20 years, the main lesson we have learned is this: we are an inseparable part of Latin America. Our revolution is a part of the Latin American revolution. Each of our triumphs makes the fraternal Latin American peoples stronger. Every Latin American victory strengthens our revolution. Our battle won't have ended until all of the peoples of Our America have freed themselves of the neocolonial yoke. This is the path our revolution has shown us. This is the path Fidel has set forth. This is the duty exemplified for us by the Heroic Guerrilla and the internationalist combatants who fought and died at his side.

At the same time, comrades, we should draw the pertinent conclusions from that reality. The class struggle continues and will continue to do so as long as imperialism exists. We shouldn't deceive ourselves with the idea of a sweeping victory throughout Latin America. The revolutionary process inevitably advances, taking the most diverse forms, but it must confront very complex situations and powerful enemies.

Imperialism is still strong. Imperialism is egging on the counterrevolutionary struggle and mobilizing all its resources to try to contain, weaken and hold back the peoples' advance as much as possible. Imperialism still has considerable strength; it is capable of resorting to violence when the conditions so permit; and, at the same time, it is testing the most refined and immobilizing weapons of ideological diversionism, cultural penetration, divisionism, pseudo-revolution and the undermining of revolutionary movements from within.

As Fidel has said, we are soldiers of the Latin American revolution. Therefore, we should prepare ourselves for that long and hard struggle, which will, necessarily, become ever more complex. We must be prepared to struggle as long as necessary and oppose the enemy on any terrain — both political-military and ideological — no matter what tactics it may adopt.

We must derive our duties, obligations and manner of work from that concept. Therefore, I reiterate that it is necessary to establish constant, systematic study and self-improvement as the main principle guiding the lives of all combatants in our Department.

In its uncontainable crisis, imperialism is trying to use the resources of diversionism and ideological struggle to the utmost. Nowadays, the imperialists often make use of pseudo-leftist writers and intellectuals, trying to attack the revolution from socialist, seemingly Marxist positions and even invoking the need for a "humanization" of socialism. From those positions, they attack the Soviet Union, Cuba and the rest of the socialist community and revolutionary movement, trying to split it and thus undermine the ranks of the revolutionary movement, whose strongest bulwark of solidarity and internationalism consists of the socialist countries.

There's something else in this regard that I should emphasize. As Lenin said, anyone who aspires to see a "pure" revolution — one produced in a laboratory — will be wasting their time. Life teaches us that revolutions don't go along beaten paths. We see this now in Latin America. Chile, Peru, Argentina and Panama[6] are expressions of extremely varied, complex and convulsive political situations. As Marxists and Leninists, we should pay particular attention to the main, anti-imperialist direction that is expressed in those movements, to the pressure exerted from below by the masses, which seek definitive change and are the motor force of history.

To be Leninists, like Fidel and the rest of our revolutionary leaders, is to abandon all dogmatism and schematism. It is to learn from life and from the struggle. It is to interpret reality as it really is, so as to hasten its transformation. Therefore, without mechanistic theories of any kind, we support and will always support all of the Latin American movements that express the peoples' determination to break with oligarchic and imperialist rule and to achieve true liberation.

This struggle also requires that we make an ongoing effort to improve ourselves, to maintain vigilance and to struggle consciously

---

[6] Readers should recall that peoples' nationalist and anti-imperialist processes developed in Peru and Panama starting in October 1968, led by the sectors of the Armed Forces headed by General Juan Velazco Alvarado, in the case of Peru, and by General Omar Torrijos, in the case of Panama. Up until his mystery-shrouded death in a plane crash on July 31, 1981, General Torrijos led the Panamanian people's history-making struggle to recover their sovereignty over the Panama Canal. Up until 1975, General Velazco Alvarado headed an important program of structural transformation in Peru's economy, society and international political and economic relations. Coinciding with those nationalist-military processes, Popular Unity (Unidad Popular, UP), headed by Salvador Allende Gossens, governed Chile between November 1970 and September 1973 — up to the fascist military coup. Moreover, the Cámpora-Perón Administration took office in Argentina on May 20, 1973. After Perón's death in July 1974, the most reactionary sectors of the heterogeneous Peronist movement began a bloody repression which led to the March 24, 1976, coup. Like Chilean military fascism, the successive military Presidents who took office after the coup engaged in state terrorism as a means for ruling Argentine society.

and tenaciously against all of the deficiencies and mistakes that we may bring with us in our conduct as revolutionaries.

Therefore, comrades, let us increase our vigilance against liberalism and always oppose it with the communist principles of stating things at the right time, in the right place and in the right way. Let us increase our vigilance against self-sufficiency and arrogance — which may appear like weeds in our work and, if we don't uproot them in time, wind up by invading everything. Let us oppose them with revolutionary unpretentiousness and with simplicity and austerity in our personal lives. Let us increase our vigilance against waste, against disorganization and against uneven, erratic work. Let us oppose them with the careful administration of resources, systematization, planning and the most intelligent use of all the human and technical resources we have.

In closing, comrades, let us remember our watchword for this 20th anniversary: "Our strength is that of the people." It expresses a profound revolutionary reality that has enabled us to defeat and made us invincible against a powerful, unscrupulous enemy. It also expresses the path we should continue along to obtain new victories. We are a part of the people. We are a part of the combatant arm of our workers and farmers. We are an expression of the uncompromising revolutionary, internationalist spirit of our revolution.

Homeland or death!

We will win!

******

March 2, 1974[7]

Today, we are meeting here in this unit to pay well-deserved tribute to a group of comrades who have just been promoted to different military ranks — up to and including that of first lieutenant. Unfortunately, not all of the comrades being promoted are here today, for a very specific and understandable reason...

Many of those who were killed in the struggle didn't even witness a ceremony such as this; the only incentive they received was that of the incomparable satisfaction of having done their revolutionary duty.

This doesn't mean that the incentive you are receiving here today is not praiseworthy, but the incentive of those who heroically gave their lives certainly constitutes a shining example for us. Thanks to them, we have managed to come this far and are staunch, determined and ready

---

[7] Excerpts from the address given in the ceremony held on March 2, 1974, to assign ranks to officers of the General National Liberation Department of the Ministry of the Interior.

to give our all for socialism, for the national liberation of the peoples, for the man of the future and for communism.

We think this because our ideology, our party, Fidel and Che have taught us that, rather than being a virtue, heroism is a duty, a daily task, of revolutionaries and that the best credentials a revolutionary can have consist of our attitude toward life, as expressed in social practice.

We have just observed the 100th anniversary of the death in combat of Carlos Manuel de Céspedes, the Father of his Country. In the midst of the difficulties with which Cuban revolutionaries were faced in 1869, Céspedes described what he expected of each person, what he himself would do and what all those who loved their homeland should do when he said, "Cubans, I am counting on your heroism to consolidate the Republic. You can count on my selflessness."

Let us follow his example, comrades, and steadily increase our heroism, our virtues and our revolutionary selflessness. By so doing, we will continue to be standard-bearers of our homeland and of proletarian internationalism...

Latin America today is not the same as it was at the time of the Tricontinental Conference.[8] The balance of power in the world has changed...

It's hardly necessary to tell you about the role that the socialist community and the national liberation movement have assigned to our revolution. It's no secret to anyone that the Cuban Revolution is an irreversible fact with which all the enemies of revolutionary ideas must reckon when analyzing the balance of power in Latin America and the powerful role that our homeland — under the firm, sure guidance of our party and Comrade Fidel, our Commander in Chief — plays as a catalyst of the most consistent revolutionary ideas.

The Latin American and international situations are very complex and dialectically changing, however. Today's Latin America doesn't have the same panorama as Latin America had in the past, when revolutionary combatants from its different countries and the heroic representatives of our people — whose best example is unquestionably Major Ernesto Che Guevara, the Heroic Guerrilla — risked their lives for its freedom.

Therefore, even though the liberating, internationalist ideas handed

---

[8] The First Tricontinental Conference was held in Havana, Cuba, in early January 1966. Its resolutions included founding the Organization of Solidarity with the Peoples of Africa, Asia and Latin America (OSPAAAL), whose Permanent Secretariat was established in Havana. At the request of Salvador Allende, a Senator and leader of the Chilean Socialist Party (Partido Socialista, PS) at the time, the Tricontinental Conference also resolved to create the Latin American Solidarity Organization (Organización Latinoamericana de Solidaridad, OLAS), which held its first and only conference in Havana in August 1967.

down to us by those 20th century Latin American patriots are still valid, our party members and combatants who have played a modest part in the complex international situation, especially in Latin America, must make an in-depth study of the new situation, the new shape taken by the confrontation of our peoples' common enemy, U.S. imperialism — the enemy which we must confront, fight against and defeat on all terrains, both directly, with arms in hand (which we are always ready to do), and in the political-ideological or diplomatic struggle.

In short, comrades, the changing international situation is not the product of any greater understanding of U.S. imperialism and its diverse followers. Rather, it is the result of the present balance of power, which is favorable to the peoples' struggle headed by the socialist community — mainly Lenin's homeland, the great Soviet Union — and the upsurge of the nonaligned countries' and peoples' liberation movement. That is what determines U.S. imperialism's and the other capitalist powers' present policy.

The situation in the Middle East, which is unquestionably favorable to the Arab peoples; the U.S. failure in and consequent departure from Vietnam; and the new U.S. policy against the patriotic nationalist processes that are developing in Peru, Panama and other Latin American countries are examples of this.

However, we shouldn't deceive ourselves by thinking that imperialism's positions will be defeated soon. Even though it isn't as all-powerful as it once was, imperialism is still strong and can impose its policy of force when the historic, socioeconomic and political conditions permit this. The Brazilian monster, which has been assigned the sorry role of sub-imperialism in Latin America,[9] is proof of this, as are the guerrilla-civilian dictatorship of Bordaberry and company, which has grossly abandoned the institutional democratic tradition of the Uruguayan people,[10] and, more recently, the criminal dictatorship that

---

[9] In March 1972, U.S. President Richard Nixon publicly stated that, as Brazil went, so would go the rest of South America. From then on, the hypothesis that U.S. policy sought to turn Brazil into a sub-imperialism that would cooperate with the United States in sustaining its policy of domination over Latin America, the Caribbean and — eventually — other parts of the South Atlantic gained strength. That supposed U.S. strategy was linked to actions that the Nixon-Kissinger duo took to strengthen the role of its regional allies in the acute political-military confrontation that was developing in different parts of the underdeveloped world — especially Southeast Asia — at the time.

[10] With the support of the United States, breaking the democratic-liberal precedents of Uruguayan policy and coinciding with the fascist coup in Chile, an intensive wave of repression took place in Uruguay that culminated in the installation of a military dictatorship in December 1973. After intensive political and social struggles — both armed and peaceful — the Naval Club Civilian-Military Pact was signed in July-August 1984, as a result of which an election was held in November 1984, in which

has imposed fascist genocide on the Chilean people, trampling on all international norms of respect for human dignity.[11]

The heroic example set by Salvador Allende is growing ever greater in Latin America. The triumph of the Popular Unity government was a result of the heroic struggle that was waged in Latin America in the 1960s; the overthrow of Salvador Allende's popular government led to a new experience in the 1970s. Allende wanted to use bourgeois legality to make a revolution, help his people and advance toward socialism, respecting the Constitution and the laws inherited from his Christian Democratic (DC) predecessor, Eduardo Frei, who represented the Chilean national bourgeoisie.

In response to this, imperialism resorted to fascism. Fidel said of the resistance that Allende headed, "Never before had brute strength come up against such resistance, carried out in the military sphere by a man of ideas, whose weapons were always the spoken and written word. Allende died as a true combatant." Allende's death and the overthrow of the Popular Unity government showed, as our Commander in Chief put it, "the validity of the Marxist principle of the dictatorship of the proletariat: revolution and social change require a revolutionary dictatorship."

The development of the revolutionary struggle shows that we must strengthen ourselves more than ever in Marxist-Leninist theory and practice.

Yesterday, many of you took a test of your Marxist knowledge. I can't congratulate you, because you still have a lot to learn; we can never congratulate ourselves in this regard, because we will always have to keep on learning...

Moreover, to confront the ideological struggle and embrace the theory and practice of Marxism-Leninism, we must also struggle to improve ourselves in general; increase our cultural and technical knowledge; maintain exemplary lives as communists; uphold the policy of our party and its leaders; and form part of the history-making revolutionary vanguard, following the examples of Fidel and Che.

We should consider ourselves revolutionaries — communists — not only because certain of our merits are recognized and we carry out our tasks and participate in study circles and minibrigade construction work

---

Julio María Sanguinetti became President.

[11] As already mentioned, a fascist-type military dictatorship began to rule Chile on September 11, 1973. It remained in power until early 1990. At that time, after a Constitutional reform and a plebiscite that overwhelmingly opposed August Pinochet's remaining at the head of the government and approved the holding of a general election, Patricio Aylwin (a Christian-Democrat) headed a "transition government." He was replaced when Eduardo Frei Ruiz-Tagle (another Christian Democrat) was elected President.

but also because we test ourselves every day, in all our actions, in our daily life, at work, at home, in our relations with our fellow citizens and in our internationalist determination. Only in this way, convinced that we still have many deficiencies to remedy, can we struggle to be ever better revolutionaries.

No setbacks should intimidate or difficulties frighten us. Let us be constant in the struggle, confident in the party and alert to carry out our Commander in Chief's orders — wherever, however and whatever they may be.

That is the path that lies ahead.

Eternal glory to our comrades who have died in the struggle!

Long live proletarian internationalism!

Long live the national liberation struggle!

Long live our Commander in Chief!

Long live our Communist Party of Cuba and its First Congress!

Homeland or death!

We will win!

******

April 28, 1974[12]

As in the ceremony held on March 2, I would like to emphasize that these promotions are simply recognition of the conduct, efforts, loyalty, self-sacrificing revolutionary spirit and discipline shown in your daily activities.

This promotion is cause for satisfaction, but, at the same time, you are making a new commitment. The Revolutionary Government recognizes your virtues; you know your deficiencies. The revolution encourages you, and you pledge to become better, more selfless and self-sacrificing, and more useful by raising your cultural, political and technical levels; by working more efficiently; and by studying with more dedication and better results.

On receiving this deserved recognition, you are making another pledge to the revolution and ratifying your pledges to the people, to whom we owe everything. Always remember that we are an integral part of the hard-working, selfless, unassuming people, who are always alert and ready to make greater sacrifices to promote the advance of our

---

12 Excerpts from the address given in the closing session of the ceremony held on April 28, 1974, to assign the ranks of noncommissioned officers and officers to combatants in the General National Liberation Department of the Ministry of the Interior.

socialist revolution and to defend one of its most inspiring principles: proletarian internationalism.

Promotion obliges you to be more unassuming with your comrades and fellow citizens, to be more disciplined and consistent — in short, to act as leaders at the various levels.

The missions that many of you have carried out in the course of over a decade have had great political meaning. They have embodied the principles of proletarian internationalism, which break through frontiers, draw human beings closer to one another and urge you to work for others; they make society one great brotherhood in which everyone works together to create the future.

The missions we have ahead of us have this purpose, too. Describing how to carry them out — how to be a political cadre, an internationalist, a revolutionary, a communist — Che wrote, "The common denominator is political clarity. This doesn't mean blind support for the postulates of the revolution; rather, it demands reasoned support, a great capacity for self-sacrifice and a dialectical capacity of analysis that makes it possible to make continuous contributions at all levels to the rich theory and practice of the revolution."[13]

To fully assimilate that rich theory and practice of our Marxist-Leninist revolution to which Che referred, we must strengthen ourselves in theory and apply it in our daily lives. A revolutionary doesn't have the duty to engage in a heroic action or to make the supreme sacrifice on a single day. What distinguishes him or her from a bourgeois is that all of a revolutionary's daily actions are consistent with their philosophy. The crux of the matter doesn't lie in believing yourself to be a revolutionary; it lies in being uncompromisingly revolutionary...

Comrades, we must do more than simply maintain an attitude, an internal position. We can never separate our lives and actions from what is going on in Latin America. Each of us must delve deeper and develop the immense prestige and great firmness of principles that the actions of the Cuban Revolution have gained in 15 years of tenacious, indefatigable struggle against all of the acts of aggression launched by U.S. imperialism, the worst enemy of humankind and of our people.

We have experienced difficult times in the recent past. Even harder times await us in the immediate future. Now, it is clearer than ever that imperialism is moving, changing its facade and maintaining a strategic offensive in Latin America that is sometimes called a fascist coup and at other times called the New Dialogue.[14] Unquestionably, the Cuban

---

[13] See Ernesto Che Guevara: "El cuadro, columna vertebral de la Revolución" (The Cadre, Backbone of the Revolution), *Obras 1957-1967* (Havana: Casa de las Américas, 1970), Vol. II, 158. See *Che Guevara Reader* (Melbourne: Ocean Press, 1997)

[14] Starting in the first half of the 1970s, new tactics were adopted in the U.S. strategy toward Latin America and the Caribbean. In addition to its policy of destabilizing the

Revolution is the only revolution in this hemisphere that has been consolidated and is invincible, and imperialism is seeking and will continue to seek new forms of alliance with the national bourgeoisie in an offensive aimed against the peoples' movements and against their main support: the example of the Cuban Revolution.

First, there was the 1964 coup in Brazil, after which that country was turned into an accomplice of fascism and expansionism. Then came the coup in Bolivia.[15] It was soon followed by the coup in Uruguay and, now, the coup in Chile, which has had great repercussions throughout the world and will constitute — directly — an example threatening the people's movement in Argentina and that of the Armed Forces in Peru.

Imperialism couldn't accept — nor can it accept — a new Cuba and has adopted a counterrevolutionary policy in all its forms, aimed at preventing the coming of a true Latin American revolution.

You should always remember that, starting just a few days after the triumph of our revolution, campaigns for isolating the focal point called Cuba alternated between outright aggression: maneuvers in the OAS; the Bay of Pigs attack; the economic blockade; infiltration and acts of sabotage by the CIA; the Alliance for Progress; and the refinement of the tools, weapons and methods for suffocating all attempts at rebellion in Latin America.

We shouldn't forget that, far from weakening the Cuban Revolution,

---

nationalist, progressive and revolutionary governments (in Peru, Panama and Ecuador) that existed in the region at the time and of supporting the military dictatorships that had existed earlier (as in the cases of Brazil, Guatemala, Nicaragua, Honduras and El Salvador), the Nixon Administration promoted fascist coups in Bolivia (1971), Chile and Uruguay (1973) and the state terrorism that was unleashed in Argentina after the death of Juan Domingo Perón. Prior to those events, in May 1973, William Rogers, then Secretary of State of the United States, began an extensive tour of Latin American and Caribbean countries. In his contacts with the leaders of Mexico, Nicaragua, Colombia, Venezuela, Peru, Argentina, Brazil and Jamaica, he promised generalized trade preferences to the countries of the region and also promised that changes would be made in the worm-eaten inter-American system. Later on, the Republican Administration called that "carrot and stick" policy the New Dialogue with its southern neighbors. As was brought out at the time, those new tactics sought to destroy the many forms of growing resistance to imperialist rule over the Latin American and Caribbean peoples.

[15] In July 1970, after an uprising that had the people's support, General Juan José Torres became President of Bolivia. Inspired by the nationalist military governments in Peru, Panama and Ecuador, the former Chief of Staff of the Bolivian Armed Forces initiated a progressive program of economic, social and political transformations both inside Bolivia and in its international relations. After intensive plotting supported by the United States, the Torres Administration was overthrown on August 21, 1971, by a bloody coup headed by Colonel Hugo Bánzer Suárez. General Juan José Torres went into exile in Buenos Aires, Argentina, but was kidnapped and murdered with the collaboration of the military and paramilitary forces of that country's government. His body was found on November 2, 1976.

each of those actions strengthened it and that the revolutionary flame of socialist Cuba extended throughout Latin America. In one way or another, those revolutionary actions and cries of "Independence or Death" spread from the Río Grande to Patagonia, strengthening the Latin American peoples' awareness, and created the conditions for the nonworking sectors to participate in diverse protests — and, by so doing, join in supporting the struggle that the exploited were waging for redemption — and made socialist Cuba's historic destiny and its ideological influence integral parts of the Latin American revolutionary movement.

Students, Catholics (including priests) and even military men joined Latin America's struggle against imperialism. The Tricontinental Conference and the Latin American Solidarity Organization showed the unity that had been created between the workers and other radicalized sectors in Latin America that, up until then, had remained indifferent to — and, in some cases, had been unwitting collaborators of — imperialism.

We should remember that, with its firm principles and revolutionary ethic, the cause of revolution won over men of such different backgrounds as Fabricio Ojeda, Augusto Turcios Lima, Luis de la Puente Uceda, Camilo Torres and Francisco Caamaño.[16] However, the history of

---

[16] Fabricio Ojeda was a prominent Venezuelan political leader who had been outstanding in the struggle against the pro-imperialist dictatorship of Marcos Pérez Jiménez. Early in the 1960s he renounced his membership in Parliament as a representative of the Democratic Republican Union (Unión Republicana Democrática, URD) and joined the guerrilla struggle. He became commander of the National Liberation Armed Forces (FALN) and of the United Liberation Front (FUL) of Venezuela, was taken prisoner and was murdered in the garrison of the Intelligence Service of the Venezuelan Armed Forces in 1966. Luis de la Puente Uceda founded the Rebellious American Peoples' Revolutionary Alliance (APRA Rebelde). Then, from that splinter group of the conservative and traditional APRA party, he founded the Movement of the Revolutionary Left (MIR) of Peru and was the top leader of that guerrilla organization at the time of his death. Inspired by the social doctrine of the Church, the guerrilla priest Camilo Torres Restrepo took part in many acts of resistance against the oligarchic, authoritarian, repressive governments installed by the National Front of Colombia (FNC). Then he joined the nascent National Liberation Army (ELN). He was killed in combat on February 15, 1966. Colonel Francisco Alberto Caamaño Deñó, of the Dominican Armed Forces, became the leader of the Constitutionalist revolution of April 1965. While he was fighting to allow Juan Bosch, the Constitutional President, to return to the country, Congress named Caamaño Head of Government. He headed the resistance to the April 1965 invasion of the Dominican Republic by the United States. After that, he was sent abroad on a diplomatic mission. He left those functions to organize a guerrilla expedition against the pro-imperialist civilian-military administration of José Joaquín Balaguer. The members of the expedition landed in the Dominican Republic on February 2, 1973. A few days later, Caamaño was wounded in battle and taken prisoner. He was murdered on February 16, 1973.

the revolutionary flame that swept through Latin America can be summed up in the name of a single man — Che — for he showed the way, advanced along it impressively and gave us the eternal example of his life.

As Commander in Chief Fidel Castro said during the meeting of solidarity with Chile, "Revolutions don't come about because of somebody's whim. They are results of the course of history." That lesson, that inexorable law, cannot be erased by torture or other crimes; by the anachronistic regimes in Brazil, Uruguay and Chile; or by reformist formulas, such as "bloodless revolutions" and the "New Dialogue."

The victorious existence of our revolution and of its principles is proof of this. The blockade, which was imposed in an attempt to bring us to our knees, is collapsing. The isolation that the OAS sought to impose on us is isolating that organization and exposing its rottenness and obsolescence. Cuba already has relations of friendship and diplomatic relations with eight countries in this hemisphere, and other nations have expressed their desire to renew their relations with our country. Meanwhile, in recent Latin American meetings, the most backward positions have lacked supporters, and imperialism has been called on the carpet to a greater or lesser degree.

While this has been going on, some of those Latin American peoples have been striving to attain their full political and economic independence and have been advancing toward progressive policies. Peru is developing a nationalist policy for controlling its national wealth and an independent foreign policy; Panama is involved in a struggle to legitimately recover its national territory; and Argentina, in the midst of an intensive process of ideological struggle, is playing an important role within the framework of Latin American foreign policy.

The way is being paved for new hopes in Venezuela and Colombia,[17]

---

[17] Carlos Andrés Pérez, a Social Democrat, became President of Venezuela in March 1974. In his inaugural address, he announced the nationalization of Venezuela's iron and oil and the development of a policy of cooperation with all Latin American and Caribbean countries, including Cuba. A few months later, Alfonso López Michelsen, the leader of what had been called the Liberal Revolutionary Movement (Movimiento Revolucionario Liberal, MRL), became president of Colombia, representing the Liberal Party (Partido Liberal, PL). His platform called for seeking a negotiated, political solution to the long civil war that was going on (and still continues) in his country; supporting the Panamanian people's struggle to recover their sovereignty over the Panama Canal; and normalizing Colombia's relations with Cuba. This last point was fulfilled in 1975. Before then, together with other Latin American governments, the Colombian Government successfully pushed through a modification of the 1964 OAS resolutions that had pressured the OAS member countries to break off their diplomatic and consular relations with the Revolutionary Government of Cuba.

and efforts are being made to achieve political and economic independence in the Caribbean, going counter to the line that imperialism had always drawn up for that area. Apart from the governments of Venezuela and Colombia, there are others that, though far from progressive, recognize the need to adopt certain independent positions that will enable their countries to develop, seek markets, place their raw materials on them and obtain greater advantages from their natural resources.

These are clear contradictions with imperialism, and they are mounting. They led to the meetings of Tlatelolco and Washington[18] — where, in fact, the precarious situation of the OAS and its uselessness and inability to solve the serious socioeconomic problems with which the Latin American peoples are faced were recognized. In that confrontation, many of those governments that have, traditionally, been declared enemies of our revolution are now speaking — or whispering, as the case may be — of the need for Cuba to rejoin the regional system. Some of those governments are already willing to accept Cuba in the new mechanism of the Conferences of Foreign Ministers.

It goes without saying that the puppets and their U.S. master don't support this.

Cuba has clearly reiterated that it will not rejoin the OAS and that no discussions can be held between the United States and the Revolutionary Government of Cuba until the blockade against our country has been unconditionally lifted.

The situation in our region is also part of the balance of power on the international scene — a balance that has been considerably changed by the energy of the Soviet Union and the rest of the socialist camp. As our Commander in Chief said in the nonaligned conference in Algeria, "The fact that the Soviet Union exists holds the aggressive forces of the imperialist world back from going out on military adventures." This balance of power has helped the Cuban Revolution to grow stronger,

---

[18] In the first half of the 1970s, the governments of Mexico, Colombia, Venezuela, Peru, Panama, Argentina and Chile (prior to the September 11, 1973, coup), among others, sharply criticized the inefficient functioning of the Organization of American States. As part of that process, several OAS conferences were held, including the ones mentioned in the text of this address. All took note of the profound crisis affecting the so-called inter-American system. Special Conferences of Foreign Ministers were held to make a thorough reform of the OAS and try to solve the crisis. U.S. resistance to that effort frustrated it, however. Linked to the discussion of that reform, there was talk of the possibility of Cuba's returning to the OAS. Even though the veto power which the United States and its closest allies in the region had (and still have) in that organization made it impossible to change the 1962 OAS resolution that had excluded the Cuban Revolutionary Government, it couldn't keep the other OAS members from modifying the 1964 resolution, which pressured the member governments to break off their relations — of all kinds — with Cuba.

especially because of the Soviet Union's incalculable support and solidarity.

Moreover, this balance — together with the daring, heroism and determination of the Vietnamese people led by the faithful followers of Ho Chi Minh — dealt U.S. imperialism a great defeat in Vietnam, a defeat that is spreading throughout Southeast Asia with the selfless struggles waged by patriots in Laos and Cambodia.

The strength of the socialist countries can also be seen in the complex situation in the Middle East and in the struggles that the peoples of Guinea-Bissau, Mozambique and Angola are waging against Portuguese colonialism — which is already in decline and entered a new phase of internal crisis[19] only a few hours ago — for their national liberation in Africa.

In spite of these undeniable triumphs of the revolutionary movement — which express and strengthen proletarian internationalism by awakening a new awareness in Latin America — and the irreversibility of the Cuban Revolution, new and perhaps worse dangers threaten the revolutionary forces.

Within the framework of world détente and of the Latin American problem we have analyzed, U.S. imperialism is refining ideological diversionism, its favorite weapon in the new version of the Cold War. The framework of world détente doesn't imply a situation of peace; it doesn't mean that we should renounce revolutionary struggle now that imperialism — which, by its very nature, is warlike — is talking of peace, because, in fact, it is preparing for war and for intervention of one kind or another in the revolutionary processes and in the struggles for national liberation.

In this situation, our Department plays a small but important role in the ideological and other confrontations with our class enemy. This is why we must be more alert and aware now than ever before and why we must continue to strengthen and increase our political knowledge; channel any doubts we may have through the party; and declare an open war on liberalism, using the Marxist-Leninist principle of criticism and self-criticism to cleanse our ranks and raising high the banners of internationalism among all the peoples on Earth and of the struggle against the imperialists and their lackeys.

In just a few days, we will be celebrating May Day — a special, historically meaningful day for workers all over the world and one on which our people will be expressing their joy. There is no anti-

---

[19] This reference is to the April 1974 "Carnation Revolution," which put an end to the military dictatorship that had ruled Portugal for more than 40 years and whose overthrow — the result of a civilian-military uprising — interacted positively with the struggles being waged for independence in the Portuguese colonies of Guinea-Bissau, Mozambique and Angola.

communism and no repression in Cuba, so there will be no protests here about such things. Our proletariat is not oppressed, hungry and deceived. No children in Cuba are starving, so no mothers here will carry signs and shout protests against such a situation. There is no unemployment, inequality or injustice in Cuba, so no workers will be protesting against those things. There are enough schools, doctors and hospitals in our country, so no one will be protesting their lack. Our labor leaders don't sell out the workers.

Our workers will honor the martyrs of Chicago by raising productivity and efficiency, becoming better organized and doing voluntary work as a spontaneous contribution to their political and ideological training. In Cuba, a proletarian party is in power. Our country is gradually overcoming all of the difficulties that imperialism keeps placing in our path. Our country is advancing firmly and resolutely toward socialism.

Long live our Communist Party!
Long live the working class!
Long live proletarian internationalism!
Eternal glory to the heroes of the Bay of Pigs!
Long live our Commander in Chief!
Homeland or death!
We will win!

******

July 25, 1974[20]

Twenty-one years have passed since the day when a vanguard group of Cuban young people led by Comrade Fidel attacked the Moncada Garrison in a revolutionary action that blazed the way in the struggle against the tyrant Batista, marking the path of open, direct, continuous and definitive armed struggle.

That action wasn't just an isolated occurrence within the revolutionary context of Cuba of that era. It was organized patiently and consistently. It sought not to give the enemy a slap on the wrist but rather to be a tactical blow that would serve as the first action in a prolonged war. Our working class, farmers, young students, professionals and intellectuals were included in that group of heroic

---

[20] Address given in the closing session of the ceremony held in the General National Liberation Department of the Ministry of the Interior on July 25, 1974, to mark the 21st anniversary of the attack on the Moncada Garrison.

Cubans, true representatives of the people — who were eager to find a revolutionary vanguard that would blaze the way to struggle for national and social liberation.

The young people who attacked the Moncada Garrison were true representatives of our people's legitimate aspirations. They represented the farmers' rebelliousness against the big landowners, the middlemen who exploited them and the Rural Guard; the workers' rebelliousness against being exploited and against the labor leaders who sold them out; the young people's desire to be educated, to have schools and equal possibilities, and to wipe out the privileges enjoyed by technicians, professionals and even those who simply knew how to read and write; the pain of mothers who couldn't find hospitals that would take care of their sick children; and the blacks' and women's rebelliousness against racial and social discrimination.

In addition, the young people who attacked the Moncada were standard-bearers of the people's rebelliousness against and hatred of U.S. citizens who took possession of our wealth and trampled on our national dignity. On July 26, 1953, those feelings inspired the young people who attacked the Moncada Garrison, uniting them in a single battle cry of freedom or death. Those same feelings inspired the heroic militiamen led by Frank País to take control of the streets of Santiago de Cuba on November 30, 1956, and inspired Fidel and the other guerrillas aboard the *Granma* when they landed on the eastern coast of Cuba on December 2, 1956, keeping the pledge that Fidel had made to the people — to be free or die in the attempt.

Those same feelings inspired all the other actions that were carried out throughout the island — in the eastern mountains, in the Escambray and in our cities and towns; they inspired the attacks on the Presidential Palace and on the Goicuría Garrison...[21] All of the martyrs in our struggle for national liberation were inspired by those feelings, as were the Cuban, Peruvian and Bolivian internationalists who went to Bolivia with Che and fought selflessly, sacrificing their lives heroically for the cause of the Bolivian people.

The feelings that inspired the July 26 attack on the Moncada Garrison, an attack symbolizing rebelliousness and expressing a cry of independence or death, also inspired many other actions in Latin America — in Bolivia, Argentina, Peru, Colombia, Guatemala, the Dominican Republic, Haiti, Nicaragua, Venezuela and Panama — and many other parts of the world where the exploited have taken up battle cries against their exploiters. They are also found whenever the people

---

[21] The attack on the Goicuría Garrison, in the city of Matanzas, took place on April 29, 1956. That attack — during which the Army murdered most of the attackers without running any risk at all — helped to create a political atmosphere conducive to the overthrow of Fulgencio Batista's dictatorship (1952-58).

have applied revolutionary justice. Those feelings inspired us when we nationalized U.S. companies; implemented the Agrarian Reform; built schools, hospitals, roads, dams and dairies; and developed our economy, diversifying it during the past 15 years.

They inspired us when we defeated imperialism at the Bay of Pigs and when we defeated the mercenaries paid by the United States in the Escambray mountains, in the Sierra Maestra mountains and in our cities.

The feelings that inspired the July 26, 1953, attack on the Moncada Garrison live on in revolutionary Cuba — in the Cuba of José Martí, whose ideas inspired that attack; in the Cuba of Antonio Maceo, who foresaw the traitorous intentions of the United States toward our country; in the Cuba of Máximo Gómez, Ignacio Agramonte and all the other Mambí fighters against Spanish colonialism in the last century; in the Cuba of Julio Antonio Mella, José Ramón Trejo, Antonio Guiteras, Frank País, Abel Santamaría, José Antonio Echeverría and the many thousands of other Cubans who gave their lives to help achieve Cuba's true national independence and whose actions, sacrifices, determination, honesty and courage can be summed up now in two of our greatest leaders: Che Guevara and Camilo Cienfuegos.

The attack on the Moncada Garrison was a revolutionary action carried out by a handful of individuals who represented the people's interests. Now, it's not just a handful of people who are inspired by those feelings; now, those feelings inspire all of our workers, who are willing to make great sacrifices for them; they inspire our revolutionary, internationalist people, who are advancing quickly and decisively, defeating all attacks by imperialism and, led by the Communist Party of Cuba and with the wise leadership of Comrade Fidel, delving ever more deeply into socialism, exploring the possibilities it offers.

Therefore, comrades, let us prepare ourselves with determination and optimism for all of the alternatives that our revolutionary future may offer. Let us constantly strengthen our political-cultural and technical-operational training. Let us make our beloved Communist Party of Cuba, the vanguard of our working class, stronger, more united and better prepared ideologically.

Everyone should help to build the new society that the party is called upon to create. The party has had an important role in the tasks that we have been carrying out so far, but the party's work will be a prerequisite for ensuring the successful completion of our future activities. Therefore, the party's work will be vital for our sustained, increased training in all fields, especially ideological.

The attack on the Moncada Garrison was both a milestone in Latin America's past and an indication of its future. Martí, the most radical and deepest political thinker in the Americas in the past century, was the moving spirit behind that attack. As Fidel has pointed out, his revolutionary thinking contained the moral basis and historic legitimacy of that armed action. The heroic effort of that Saint Ann's Day morning was deeply rooted in Cuban, Latin American and world revolutionary values, and it set an example in the hearts and consciousness of the masses of the people from the Río Grande to Tierra del Fuego.

The military setback that the incipient embryo of our revolutionary army was dealt galvanized our people's support and attracted growing fellow-feeling, becoming first a moral victory and then a political and military triumph that paved the way for the first socialist revolution in what had, up until then, been U.S. imperialism's back yard. Therefore, every anniversary of the attack on the Moncada Garrison is not only a day of celebration for Cuban and other Latin American revolutionaries but also an opportunity for analysis and taking stock.

Now, more than 15 years since the Rebel Army — our people's political and military vanguard, which was supported in its firm advance by the revolutionary general strike — entered Havana in triumph, the combatants in the Ministry of the Interior feel the satisfaction of those who, following where Martí and our Commander in Chief have led, have, along with the rest of our people, taken part in 15 years of strategic victories by the Cuban Revolution.

In accord with the laws of history, there have been tactical setbacks. Such setbacks occurred in Cuba and the rest of Latin America both in our wars for independence during the last century and in the struggles waged in this one. Martí, Maceo, Mella and Guiteras lost their lives. So did Abel Santamaría, Camilo Cienfuegos, Turcios, Camilo Torres, Masetti, Coco and Inti Peredo,[22] and Che.

But here is the Cuban Revolution, more solid and united than ever. Here is our Marxist-Leninist Party, the heir to Martí's Cuban Revolutionary Party (Partido Revolucionario Cubano, PRC), which is

---

[22] The reference is to José Martí, the apostle of Cuba's independence; General Antonio Maceo, who was killed in combat on December 7, 1896; Julio Antonio Mella, founder of the Federation of University Students (FEU) and of the first Communist Party of Cuba; Antonio Guiteras, a founder of Young Cuba (JC), a political-military organization, and a minister in the provisional government that was formed after Gerardo Machado's dictatorship was overthrown in 1933; and Abel Santamaría, second in command of the group of young people who attacked the Moncada Garrison, who was murdered by Fulgencio Batista's dictatorship. Mention is also made of Major Camilo Cienfuegos, who disappeared when his plane was lost on October 28, 1959; Guatemalan guerrilla commander Luis Augusto Turcios Lima, who was killed in an accident in Guatemala City on October 2, 1966; guerrilla priest Camilo Torres; Jorge Ricardo Masetti, who disappeared in early 1964 while preparing the conditions for beginning a rural guerrilla struggle in Argentina; and the brothers Coco and Inti Peredo. The former was killed in combat on September 25, 1967, when he was a member of the vanguard of Che's guerrilla column. Inti Peredo survived the Heroic Guerrilla but was killed in combat on September 9, 1969, while leading the National Liberation Army (Ejército de Liberación Nacional, ELN) of Bolivia.

forged in the Leninist ideas of a working-class party and of proletarian internationalism. And here are the Latin American peoples, who are becoming more and more aware that their only salvation is to free themselves of imperialist rule, make a revolution and unite. In the long run, nobody can stop this process.

Twenty-one years after the temporary setback of the attack on the Moncada Garrison, socialist Cuba stands tall, an example and incentive for the other Latin American and Caribbean peoples. It is growing ever stronger and more secure as the irreversible presence of socialism in this part of the world. Our people's battle to achieve and protect each of its advances has been long and hard, a never-ending struggle. Every achievement has had to be won through sustained combat.

Throughout these years, our people have learned how to fight and to win. Never bowing their heads or lowering their banners, they have turned setbacks into victories, and the hearts of Cuban men, women and children have been filled with the inspiring feelings of solidarity and revolutionary internationalism.

The Cuban Revolution marked a historic turning point for the Latin American peoples. Led by Fidel and the party, the Cuban people proved that it was possible to defeat even such a powerful enemy as U.S. imperialism. The courage, intelligence and determination of an entire people, together with international solidarity — mainly from the socialist camp, and especially from the Soviet Union — made it possible to attain what is now part of the patrimony of all revolutionaries. The victorious presence of the Cuban Revolution gave the other Latin American peoples renewed spirit; the exhausting revolutionary efforts and struggles for Cuba's full and definitive independence have had a lasting effect on the future of all Latin America.

The triumph of the armed movement in Cuba took place just when the world balance of power began to shift in favor of socialism. Since then, the forces of imperialism have been considerably weakened and have been forced to change their methods, making them more subtle — without becoming any less aggressive or interventionist. The economic, political and military power of the socialist forces and the worldwide revolutionary struggle has limited imperialism's possibilities, but it is still strong and powerful.

While, on the one hand, it cannot crush such realities as those of Peru, Panama and Argentina rapidly and with impunity, as it used to do, on the other hand, it is making Chile, Uruguay and Bolivia more fascist. It maintains puppet governments in Nicaragua, Guatemala, Haiti and Paraguay; is creating a sub-gendarme government in Brazil; and has and is developing ever more sophisticated mechanisms of diversionist penetration. Moreover, it is drawing up more and more formulas for holding back the revolution in Latin America.

Now, no one can keep communists, socialists, Christians, military men, workers, farmers, students and other patriots from viewing revolutionary, tactical and strategic unity as a prerequisite for overthrowing the rule of imperialism and its class allies in our countries. Imperialism cannot prevent socialist revolutions, which are the only valid alternative for solving the serious problems of our underdeveloped nations.

The revolutionary struggle has generated complex new situations in Latin America's political panorama that force us to analyze the new phenomena with increasing depth. Never before have we had to delve so deeply into revolutionary theory and its expression in the documents of the Cuban Revolution to understand and guide ourselves in current conditions. Never before has it been so important to arm ourselves with the ideas of Marx and Engels — developed and applied by Vladimir Ilyich Lenin, the leader of the October Revolution, and brilliantly implemented in Latin America by Fidel.

In this complex situation, our strategic allies and we are employing flexible tactics. There are sectors of some national bourgeoisie that, because of their secondary economic contradictions with imperialism, are adopting attitudes that clash objectively with U.S. policy. It would be a childish mistake to fail to use this situation (which was evidently created by the current revolutionary struggle) to enter into agreements with those sectors. This favors the development of the revolutionary movement and promotes its organization, strengthening and preparation for the final battle to seize political power.

All this forces us to delve more deeply into the forms of ideological struggle against imperialism and capitalism and into ways and means of defending the ideas of socialism. We must make an active contribution to the defeat of imperialism and the bourgeois order and to the victory of the socialist revolution in Latin America. That is our strategic objective. In *Left-Wing Communism: An Infantile Disorder*, Lenin stated with his characteristic acuity:

> The Russian revolutionary Social-Democrats repeatedly utilized the services of the bourgeois liberals prior to the downfall of tsardom, that is, they concluded numerous practical compromises with them; and in 1901-02, even prior to the appearance of Bolshevism, the old editorial board of *Iskra* (consisting of Plekhanov, Axelrod, Zasulich, Martov, Potresov and myself) concluded (not for long, it is true) a formal political alliance with Struve, the political leader of bourgeois liberalism, while at the same time it was able to wage an unremitting and most merciless ideological and political struggle against bourgeois liberalism and against the slightest manifestation of its influence in the working-class movement.

For 15 years, socialist Cuba has stood firm against, repulsed and defeated every attempt that U.S. imperialism, with the support of nearly all the Latin American governments, has made to destroy it. The firmness of our convictions, the justice of our positions and the maintenance of our principles have frustrated imperialism's counterrevolutionary actions and, slowly but surely, are wrecking the policy of blockade and isolation which it has imposed against our country.

Cuba has reaffirmed an experience for all Latin American revolutionaries. Sooner or later, in the process leading to the seizure of political power by the workers, farmers and people as a whole, they must be prepared to wage bloody battles, arms in hand, against counterrevolutionary and fascist violence, using revolutionary war — the highest, most definitive expression of the class struggle — to oppose the terrorist resistance of the bourgeoisie and imperialism.

Cuba has been and will continue to be an incentive, a spur and a support for all consistent revolutionaries in the world, and especially in Latin America. Cubans have already risked their lives in other parts of the world, and we will continue to do so wherever our modest contribution is sought, either as combatants or as builders.

Comrades, you have been active standard-bearers of our party's internationalist policy. With today's ceremony, you are assuming greater responsibilities in the intelligent, mature and systematic implementation of this line of principles. We, the heirs of Yara, the Protest of Baraguá, Baire, the attack on the Moncada Garrison, the *Granma*, El Jigüe, Guisa, the Bay of Pigs and Quebrada del Yuro,[23] pledge today to those martyred in the attack on the Moncada Garrison that we will hold high their banners and carry them forward until final victory is won. The spirit of July 26 will be with us now and always.

Eternal glory to those martyred in the attack on the Moncada Garrison!

Eternal glory to those martyred in the revolutionary struggles in Africa, Asia and Latin America!

---

[23] He is referring to the Cry of Yara (October 10, 1868), when Cuba's independence from Spanish colonialism was proclaimed; the Protest of Baraguá (1878), in which General Antonio Maceo rejected the despicable peace treaty which a part of the Liberation Army had signed with representatives of the Spanish colonial government; the Cry of Baire (February 24, 1895), which began the War of 1895 (that, in 1898, put an end to Spanish colonial rule over Cuba); and the July 26, 1953, attack on the Moncada Garrison. The battles of El Jigüe and Guisa, both fought in 1958, were important victories for the Rebel Army. Between April 17 and 19, 1961, at the Bay of Pigs, the United States was dealt its first great defeat in Latin America. The Quebrado del Yuro was the place in Bolivia where, after a hard-fought, unequal battle, Major Ernesto Che Guevara was wounded, captured and divested of his weapons on October 8, 1967.

Long live the 21st anniversary of the attack on the Moncada Garrison!

Long live the Communist Party of Cuba!

Long live our Commander in Chief!

Homeland or death!

We will win!

Chile

Excerpts from the address given on April 19, 1975, the 42nd anniversary of the founding of the Socialist Party of Chile.

T his beautiful display of solidarity by the workers here, representing our working class and our people, is an expression of the strong ties of solidarity that link us to Chile, its parties and its goals of struggle.

The Narciso López Roselló Bus Plant has 600 workers who, with their efforts, have met their ambitious production goals for five consecutive years. Its workers are responsible for the fact that a Moncada Heroic Tradition Center banner is flown over this workplace. Its 194 vanguard workers had the great honor of presenting our Commander in Chief with the first Girón 11 bus during the history-making 13th Congress of the Central Organization of Cuban Trade Unions. Therefore, we have chosen it as the site for this ceremony.

Here, in this arena of hard, self-sacrificing creative efforts, we are marking the 42nd anniversary of the founding of the Socialist Party of Chile. Our workers have gathered here — some in person and others represented by their political organizations — to express a fraternal greeting on behalf of our Communist Party and the Cuban people to the heroic Socialist Party of Chile.

In paying this deserved homage by our workers and people as a whole and by our party to the Socialist Party of Chile, I would like to make special mention of one of its members, a man who always strove to promote unity, a leader and fighter killed in heroic, unequal combat on the tragic day of September 11, 1973: the Comrade President of Chile, Salvador Allende Gossens.

Since the founding of the Socialist Party of Chile, it has advanced along a long, hard path filled with the fraternal Chilean people's self-sacrifice, struggles, defeats and victories. Now, those events don't mean a mere recital of history. They constitute a challenge. Without being categorical, I may, perhaps, say that today's circumstances constitute the greatest challenge with which the Chilean revolutionary forces have ever been faced.

This is because the Chilean people are struggling against one of the most criminal, brutal and bestial regimes ever known in Latin America, a regime whose barbaric methods are seeking to equal the genocide and the most abominable excesses known to history, whether in Southeast Asia or Hitler's Nazi fascism in Europe.

Two experiences have been essayed in Chile, which, in different forms, seek the same goal: that of overthrowing our peoples' legitimate aspirations and preventing revolution — now through military fascism and earlier with the reformist experience inspired by the so-called Alliance for Progress. The Chilean right supported that experiment, and the Christian Democratic Party won a majority in the National Congress.

In reply, in its 1965 Congress, held in Linares, the Socialist Party set forth the duty of "working resolutely to promote a process of liaison, coordination and integration among all the Latin American revolutionary movements as the best way to help free ourselves of imperialism and to pave the way for the implantation of socialism in Latin America." The document also reiterated the party's "unalterable position of defending and expressing solidarity with the Cuban Government and people."

Based on that, the Socialist Party, like other revolutionary forces in Chile and the rest of Latin America, made the defense of our revolution one of the keystones of its political platform. And it did that in one of the most difficult and complex periods our revolution has had to traverse — that is, in the years when imperialism was making all kinds of attacks against our homeland.

Comrade Salvador Allende reaffirmed that position in January 1966, in the Conference of Solidarity with the Peoples of Asia, Africa and Latin America — the Tricontinental Conference. During that Conference, he also called for holding a new conference: the Latin American Conference of Solidarity, which led to the creation of the Latin American Solidarity Organization (OLAS) in August 1967.

On that occasion, the delegation from the Socialist Party of Chile contained some of the comrades who are honoring us today with their visit to this workplace. They include Comrade Carlos Altamirano,[1] present general secretary of that political organization.

As I already said, a reformist experiment inspired by the so-called Alliance for Progress was tried out in Chile. It failed, as did the imperial policy that had given rise to it. Now, the other experience is being

---

[1] Carlos Altamirano was general secretary of the Socialist Party of Chile during the Presidency of Salvador Allende. After the coup, he left his homeland clandestinely, stayed in Cuba for a while and then, retaining his post, took up residence in the German Democratic Republic. He now lives in Chile.

developed: that of a military junta that is trying to drown the Chilean people's aspirations in blood. I am sure that, just like the Christian Democratic reformist experiment, this will also be a resounding failure. In both cases, the working class, the Chilean people, will bury them.

It is clear that the present process has a more brutal, bloodier nature than any other imposed on Chile or most of the other Latin American countries. Therefore, it is necessary to explain and briefly place in context what happened in Chile on September 11, 1973. It must be said that, on that day, all of the revolutionary forces in Latin America and the rest of the world were dealt a hard blow.

However, as has been aptly pointed out, that fact, like what has happened in Uruguay, is not indicative of the prevailing spirit of this period in Latin America or of the other processes taking place in this region. Revolutionaries are encouraged by factors that to some extent compensate for the bitterness of the setback in Chile: the crisis of the OAS; the failure of the policy of blockade and isolation that the United States is trying to impose on our country; the provisional breaking off of the dialogue between the United States and the rest of the hemisphere; the independent stance of confronting imperialism as expressed in the foreign policies of various governments in the area; and the consolidation of our revolution.

These facts assure us that the struggle in Chile will continue to be very hard. But the conditions for a great and united mobilization, for the formation of a broad anti-fascist and anti-imperialist front, have been created, both in Latin America and in the world balance of power. The people of Chile have the solidarity of the socialist camp, headed by the Soviet Union, and of the other peoples of Latin America, Asia, Africa, Europe and the rest of the world.

There is no doubt that, even in the midst of situations such as that of Chile, Latin America is entering a new stage. It is developing in the midst of another phase of the crisis of the capitalist system, which contrasts with the upsurge in socialism, the struggles of the working class and the new triumphs of the national liberation movements. Events such as those taking place in Cambodia, Laos, South Vietnam, Portugal and Greece[2] and the independence of the former Portuguese colonies in Africa are part of those fundamental changes.

Comrades, as Comrade Armando Hart, member of the Political Bureau of our party, pointed out: when hopes have been dashed; when revolutionaries are murdered, imprisoned and forced to leave their homeland; when the bloody boot of bourgeois dictatorship is trampling

---

[2] This reference is to the fall of the long-lived military dictatorships that had ruled in Portugal and Greece for several decades and to the political strength shown at that time by the people's movements — including their respective Communist Parties — in both countries.

on the constitution, the laws and democratic freedoms — Chile has, dramatically, become another source of hope for revolutionaries of Latin America and elsewhere.

Now, the unity (and, consequently, the enormous strength) of the struggle being waged by the revolutionaries in Southeast Asia — especially in Vietnam and Cambodia — is an example to be followed. There, as in other latitudes, it has been shown that the sharpening of the national class antagonisms has intensified the political instability of capitalism and imperialist rule.

These new phenomena confirm the analysis that Lenin made of imperialism. They show that capitalism is not being "transformed" and that the process of its weakening, the sharpening of its contradictions and the increase in its decay and crisis are continuing and becoming ever more serious.

Asia, Africa and Latin America — our part of the world — are rising up now to control their own destinies. The national liberation movement, with its ups and downs, its greater or lesser depth and in different ways, is taking up the task of consolidating political independence, waging an offensive on economic backwardness and destroying all forms of dependence on imperialism.

But that road is not, nor will it be, an easy one. Even though imperialism is losing the battle with no quarter given, it still has weapons and is employing ever more refined methods. It is implementing long-term plans for retaining and consolidating its position in the underdeveloped countries, hiding its real intention of binding the Third World nations to the control of imperial interests.

The road of noncapitalist development isn't taken spontaneously. Only the active struggle of the working class and other workers and the unity, in certain tactical situations, of all the democratic forces in a broad national front can lead the peoples to the attainment of genuine national and social liberation.

This doesn't mean underestimating the role of imperialism — especially in Latin America, the scene of important future confrontations. U.S. imperialism and its executive branch, the CIA, facilitated and directed what happened on September 11, 1973, and they are now the main external supports of the military dictatorship. U.S. imperialism also invaded the sister Dominican Republic in April 1965, massacring its people who, led by the heroic Colonel Francisco Caamaño, opposed the invasion.

We revolutionaries have the duty to look history in the face. It is true that there are disagreements between the main powers, but history has shown that war is inseparable from imperialism. It has also shown that, with the new balance of power, imperialism is using all of its weapons, from the crudest to the most subtle and sophisticated in the ideological sphere, to try to neutralize the revolutionary forces.

This is why it we must achieve unity in leading the struggle. This is why we must create parties that can consolidate their unity of action and ideological unity and maintain permanent revolutionary vigilance. A working-class party that always looks ahead and is constantly revitalized from the masses, their energy and intelligence, completing and enlarging its own experience, can meet any test and emerge victorious from it.

In certain revolutionary processes, there is a stage in which the struggle may go through intermediate, democratic goals. Together with other strata of the people, the vanguard must then struggle resolutely for broad, true democracy. The goal, then, is to mobilize the masses to carry out actions against the policy of the financial oligarchy, which tries to suppress democratic freedoms and to go on to other forms of exploitation and oppression.

The alliance of the working class with all other workers is forged in that struggle. It draws together the farmers, who are its main allies, and broad strata of other sectors that are also exploited by capitalism and that become aware of the need for thoroughgoing changes in the economic, social and political spheres. Thus, they become allies of the working class. Far from separating us from the revolution and its final goal, this struggle for democratic goals brings us closer to them.

Moreover, when the exploiting classes resort to violence against the peoples, and peaceful roads and possibilities are exhausted, we must remember that Leninism teaches, and historical experience confirms, that the ruling classes will not cede power voluntarily. In those conditions, the forms of the struggles will depend not so much on the determination of the revolutionaries as on the degree of resistance that the reaction puts up against the will of the vast majority of the people.

Thus, the success of the revolutionary movement will depend on the extent to which the vanguard mastered all forms of struggle and are prepared for the rapid substitution of one form for another, depending on the changes that take place.

Chilean comrades, on behalf of our party, I reaffirm to you that, now more than ever, you can count on our active and militant solidarity in these efforts.

Many of us revolutionaries from various parts of the world, who are fighting for the same ideals as you, believe that the dictatorship now oppressing you — and imperialism, which supports it — will draw back only in the face of the unity of the Chilean revolutionary movement. That unity must create a polarization of social and political forces around it. If that anti-fascist front is centered on the cohesion of the parties of the Chilean left, the first great goal of the struggle will have been reached.

Within that necessary unity, the unity of socialists and communists is absolutely necessary. This will bring the working class, the Chilean people and all the forces and parties of the left closer together.

As Fidel has said, we have confidence in you and in the Chilean people, in your ability and experience in struggle; we have confidence in the ability and experience of the Socialist Party of Chile, which, in the 42 years since its founding, has always been one of the main detachments of the Chilean left and that, on more than one occasion, in its struggles to build a better life for the Chilean people, has joined with the Communist Party of Chile to oppose the forces of the right and the reaction.

Other parties of the left that were created in the Chilean process joined with the socialist and communist forces. Linked by deep aspirations and ideals, they waged victorious battles, such as that of the 1970 election, in which Popular Unity (UP) emerged triumphant, taking Salvador Allende to the presidency.

In Chile, many members of all political forces are heroically withstanding torture. Others were killed in combat or have been murdered. Many are in prison. They include Luis Corvalán[3] and Aníbal Palma,[4] whose lives are in serious danger. Others, such as Bautista Van Schowen,[5] have disappeared. And, in those adversities, no political or ideological distinctions can be noted. There is only one enemy, one kind of barbarity, one crime, one kind of abuse. Therefore, the hatred of the people, of the working class, should also be focused. The objective conditions for revolutionary unity exist. The military junta has helped us more than anyone else to create them.

Comrades, on the occasion of this anniversary, I would like to convey a militant greeting to Ezequiel Ponce,[6] who is leading the party in the underground. But, above all, I would like to pay well-deserved tribute to the socialists who died in the struggle to defend the people's

[3] Luis Corvalán was general secretary of the Communist Party of Chile. After the September 11 military coup, he was captured by the repressive forces and interned in the concentration camp on Dawson Island. International solidarity managed to get him released in 1976. He went to Moscow, where he continued the struggle against the dictatorship of Augusto Pinochet. In 1983, he returned clandestinely to Chile. Now 82 years old, he is a member of the Central Committee of the Communist Party of Chile.

[4] Coming from the ranks of the Radical Party of Chile (PRC), Aníbal Palma was Minister of Education in the Popular Unity government. After being arrested, he was confined in the concentration camp at Ritoque. He was released thanks to international solidarity. From exile, he continued struggling against Augusto Pinochet's dictatorship. He now lives in Chile.

[5] Bautista Van Schowen was a member of the Political Committee of the Movement of the Revolutionary Left (MIR) of Chile. He was captured while struggling in the underground against the dictatorship. His body has never been found.

[6] Ezequiel Ponce Vicencio was a member of the Political Committee of the Socialist Party of Chile. He was arrested on June 25, 1975. His body has never been found.

achievements and a socialist future for Chile — especially Arnoldo Camú, Luis Morambuena, Eduardo Paredes, Arsenio Poupín, José Rojas, Víctor Zerega and José Tohá,[7] all members of the Central Committee of the Socialist Party. Together with Salvador Allende, they are symbols for the struggle that lies ahead.

On marking this anniversary of your party's founding, we also pay tribute to the members of the Communist Party, Movement of the Revolutionary Left, Unitarian People's Action Movement and Worker-Farmer Unitarian People's Action Movement, Christian Left and Radical Party who lost their lives[8] — in short, to all of Chile's martyrs. All are worthy sons and daughters of their homeland. All are martyred sons and daughters of Latin America, men and women whose blood has flowed to enrich this earth in which thousands of fighters for our peoples' liberation — whose best example is Ernesto Che Guevara, the Heroic Guerrilla — are buried.

These Latin American lands, inspired by their martyred best sons and daughters, will struggle at your side to build a new Chile that has been freed for good from national, political and social oppression and to build the "broad avenues" of which Comrade President Salvador Allende always dreamed.

Long live the unity of the Chilean revolutionary movement!
Glory to the martyred members of the Chilean resistance!
Eternal glory to Salvador Allende and his immortal example!
Long live proletarian internationalism!

---

[7] Arnoldo Camú was detained and shot to death on a public street on September 24, 1973. Luis Morambuena, José Rojas, Víctor Zerega, Eduardo Paredes and Arsenio Poupín were arrested and murdered; their bodies have never been found. The last two were captured on September 11, 1973, in the (Presidential) La Moneda Palace. That same day, José Tohá, who had been Minister of the Interior and of Defense in the Popular Unity government, was also captured. After being interned in the concentration camp on Dawson Island, in southern Chile, he died on March 15, 1974, as a result of torture and the harsh living conditions to which he was subjected.

[8] Miguel Enríquez founded the Movement of the Revolutionary Left (MIR) of Chile and headed it until his death in combat. The Unitarian People's Action Movement (MAPU) and the Worker-Farmer Unitarian People's Action Movement (MAPU Obrero-Campesino) were founded in the early years of the 1970s as offshoots of the Christian Democratic Party, which also gave rise to the Christian Left, which was headed at that time by Bosco Parra.

Puerto Rico

Address given at Pedro Albizu Campos Junior High School on September 23, 1976, during a rally of solidarity with the people of Puerto Rico.

E ven though, traditionally, solidarity sessions wind up with a closing ceremony that sums up all of the activities carried out by the various political, social and mass organizations and governmental agencies in our country, I would like to say that this ceremony in no way means an end to our activities in solidarity with the struggle of the fraternal Puerto Rican people. We will hold that kind of closing ceremony only after Puerto Rico has attained its full independence.

It is the most natural, logical thing for us to meet today, September 23, to reaffirm our determined solidarity with Puerto Rico. Today, we are celebrating the 108th anniversary of the Cry of Lares, an event that clearly expressed Puerto Rican nationality and the moment when the first Republic was proclaimed in 1868. On that occasion, brave Puerto Ricans were waging an unequal battle against Spanish rule. A few days later, on October 10, Carlos Manuel de Céspedes rose up in Cuba against Spanish colonialism, as well.[1]

Throughout history, the peoples of Puerto Rico and Cuba have forged indestructible links in their respective struggles for national and social liberation. The feats of Lares and Yara — as part of our peoples' shared desire to expel Spanish colonialism from the Antilles and, by so doing, to protect Latin America's future — are well known, for we have learned about them in history. José Martí's exceptional foresight was expressed when the Cuban Revolutionary Party was founded in 1895 to bring about, "with the joint efforts of all men of goodwill, the absolute independence of the island of Cuba and to promote and help Puerto Rico to attain her independence."

After the triumph of the Cuban Revolution, it was possible to know,

---

[1] Carlos Manuel de Céspedes, the Father of his Country, proclaimed Cuba's independence on October 10, 1868, with the Cry of Yara. That statement began the Ten Years' War (1868-78), which ended with the Cubans' defeat.

with greater historical accuracy, how very many children of Puerto Rico took part in our efforts to attain independence. The name of Major General Juan Rius Rivera symbolizes the dozens of men who were officers and soldiers in our Liberation Army and who, in that era, already expressed a lasting internationalism. It wasn't by chance, therefore, that the dedication and passion of Betances — his example of revolutionary action — should turn his love for his homeland's independence into a dedication and passion for the independence of the Antilles and, specifically, for Cuba's independence.

How right was Major General José Lacret Morlot of Cuba's Liberation Army when, referring to the pledge to help Puerto Rico win its independence, he said:

> There is a pact, and it is natural that it trusts in us, because it is smaller; and it is correct that we help, because we are stronger. For years, it has been a proving ground for all the reforms Spain has come up with for covering up reality, but it has also been a place where our iron has been forged. It is childish to think of helping it when we have won our independence, because Spain will guarantee its dominion over and exploitation of it... while, now, it would prove to all the world that we have more than enough vitality — for Puerto Rico, it would prove the honesty of our offer; for Cuba, it would prove our humanity; and for Spain, it would be the most convincing proof that we are stronger than she is.

Those words formed part of a document presented to the Government of Cuba in Arms dated August 13, 1897, which was written to comply with Martí's internationalist precepts — contained in the bases of the Cuban Revolutionary Party — of helping and promoting the revolution in Puerto Rico.

In spite of his desires, and aware of the adverse objective and subjective conditions that existed in his homeland for the development of the armed movement that would put an end to Spanish rule, Betances devoted a large part of his life to the outbreak and development of the revolution in Cuba. Betances considered that working for the cause of Cuba was equivalent to working for the cause of Puerto Rico.

What does the history of those years teach us? That the uprising at Yara had its successful culmination with the triumph of the revolution on January 1, 1959, but also that the declaration of Lares on September 23, 1868, hasn't come to a successful conclusion yet, and the sons and daughters of Puerto Rico, as our Martí said, are still dying for the cause of real freedom.

The year 1898 marked the end of Spanish rule and the beginning of the U.S. occupation of Puerto Rico. Therefore, with the Puerto Ricans' and Cubans' desires for independence frustrated, the patriotic links between the two sister islands were renewed with the coming of the new century. The cause of Puerto Rican independence, guided by the legacy left by Pedro Albizu Campos,[2] is amassing new strength, and Cuba, following the principles of Martí, is once more expressing its solidarity in various ways with the legitimate cause of the Puerto Rican people.

You, the students of this beautiful school named after Pedro Albizu Campos, should be more familiar than anyone else with his heroic life and with the process of struggle that has been going on in Puerto Rico ever since U.S. soldiers first set foot on its soil.

The colonial status that the United States imposed on Puerto Rico still remains in effect. The various forms implemented during the process of domination cannot hide that reality. Therefore, it is important, on this occasion, to reiterate the real characteristics of the Puerto Rican situation, because the history of that sister nation is simply that of a dependent country that is colonized in all aspects, with economic, political, military, cultural, institutional and juridical elements that constitute that colonial status, turning it into the farce that they have called the Commonwealth of Puerto Rico.

All of us are aware of the degree of penetration and economic control that the U.S. monopolies exercise over Puerto Rico. We also know of their fruitless efforts to destroy Puerto Rican culture and, with it, its people's desire for independence — efforts that are fruitless because they have failed and will always fail to change the Puerto Rican people's determination to be independent.

The First International Conference of Solidarity with Puerto Rico, that was held in Havana last year, was proof of the universal recognition of Puerto Rico's plight and of the high degree of solidarity with that cause among revolutionaries and progressive bodies from various parts of the world. On that occasion, representatives of governments; political, social and religious institutions; outstanding individuals; and international agencies issued a general call to be alert to the colonial case of Puerto Rico.

Now, a year later, the congress's efforts have borne fruit. A short while ago, the Puerto Rican people consolidated a new victory in the Fifth Summit of Nonaligned Countries, which was held in Sri Lanka, and in the meeting of the Special Committee on Decolonization of the United Nations. Even though that Committee decided by consensus to

---

[2] Pedro Albizu Campos (1891-1965) was the main leader of the Nationalist Party and of the independence movement in Puerto Rico between the 1930s and 1950s. After being falsely accused and condemned by a colonial court, he was imprisoned in the United States in 1936. Poor prison conditions destroyed his health. A very sick man, he was returned to his homeland to continue virtual imprisonment. He died on April 21, 1965.

reaffirm Puerto Rico's right to self-determination and independence and to next year consider appropriate measures to implement its previous resolutions, some reactionary spokesmen tried to hide that reality.

After the UN meeting, the wire services reported on an editorial that appeared in one of the most important newspapers in the United States. Among other things, it said that common sense had finally prevailed in the deliberations that, without any grounds, had taken place in the Decolonization Committee about Puerto Rico's political condition.

What does "without any grounds" mean? Here are some data for those who tend to forget.

More than US\$13 million — more than a million dollars per square kilometer — of U.S. capital has been invested in Puerto Rico. U.S. companies control over 80 percent of the manufacturing industry and 85 percent of the retail sales outlets; they control both sea and air transportation and communications; they also own more than 60 percent of the housing construction industry and 90 percent of the industrial products for export.

What does "without any grounds" mean? I would remind those who seek to hide the facts that U.S. bases control most of the arable land in Puerto Rico and that the United States still keeps Lolita Lebrón, Irwing Flores, Andrés Figueroa Cordero, Rafael Cancel Miranda and Oscar Collazo[3] — the prisoners who have been imprisoned longer than any others in the western hemisphere — in prison. From Cuba, free territory in the Americas, we send those heroic fighters an emotional, militant greeting.

The conditions for Puerto Rico's colonial status have existed since September 23, 1868. The United States intervened in Puerto Rico in 1898, just as it did in Cuba.

University students were killed in Río Piedra on October 24, 1935; in response, Puerto Rican patriots executed Colonel Francis Riggs, the chief of the colonial police, in February 1936. Then there was the massacre at Ponce. Puerto Rican patriots lost their lives heroically attacking the home of the colonial governor and brought the world's attention to the case of Puerto Rico by the shooting at Blair House and the U.S. Congress in Washington, D.C. The nationalist revolution began in 1950, and Pedro Albizu Campos was imprisoned in the United States.

---

[3] Oscar Collazo took part in an attack on Blair House, the temporary residence of U.S. President Harry S. Truman, in 1950 to give publicity to the Puerto Rican desire for independence. Tried by a U.S. court, he was sentenced to life imprisonment. Irwing Flores, Rafael Cancel Miranda, Lolita Lebrón and Andrés Figueroa Cordero were tried and imprisoned in the United States after making an armed protest in the U.S. Congress on March 1, 1954. Thanks to an intensive international solidarity campaign and the rise in opposition all over the world to the continuation of Puerto Rico's colonial status, the five Puerto Rican nationalists were released in September 1979.

And, if those who tend to forget such things don't consider these things to be sufficient grounds, let them recall the tremendous legal superstructure — the Foraker Act, the Jones Act, Law 600 and the Constitution of the Commonwealth — passed by the U.S. Congress as living tools of colonialism. Every single minute of Puerto Rican life is controlled by some law of the U.S. Congress or regulated by the federal agencies of the U.S. Government.

The thousands of students who can't continue their studies, the thousands of unemployed workers and the 40 percent of the Puerto Rican people who are forced to leave their homeland and go to the crowded ghettos of large U.S. cities because they have no way to make a living at home all know this very well indeed.

Comrades, today, recalling the Cry of Lares, I have referred to the ties that link the Cuban and Puerto Rican people, because our two islands have had the same history of exploitation and struggle. The Cuban people had to fight hard to win their full independence. Our people suffered from capitalist exploitation and imperialist intervention. Our people knew what it meant to have thousands of workers with no jobs and thousands of students with no schools to go to. They knew what discrimination was, and the worst form of the exploitation of women.

The revolution did away with that shameful past, and now we are building socialism. Our students study in schools just as beautiful as this one. Our workers and students, men and women — all of us are striving to create the material and spiritual assets of a better, socialist society.

Never, in these years of hard struggle against the attacks of all kinds undertaken by the U.S. imperialists in their vain attempts to crush our revolution — never, in these years of heroic work to build a new society, have our people forgotten their sacred duty of solidarity with our Latin American, African and Asian brothers and sisters, who are also struggling to build a better world. Educated in Marxism-Leninism, in the principles of proletarian internationalism, our people have done their duty — simply, and with honor.

We have been inspired — and we say this with pride — by our party and our Commander in Chief. We have been inspired by the example set by Major Ernesto Che Guevara, the Heroic Guerrilla. We have been inspired by the feats of the Cuban internationalist combatants who, together with their Angolan brothers, made the South African racists and their puppets bite the dust of defeat.

Today, September 23, the 108th anniversary of the Cry of Lares, we reaffirm what our President, Comrade Osvaldo Dorticós, said just a year ago:

On behalf of the Cuban people and their Communist Party and

Revolutionary Government, I would like to take this singular occasion to state — with the authority given me by the history of our ongoing solidarity with the Puerto Rican cause and the historical identification of the revolutionary processes of the two countries — that Cuba unhesitatingly reaffirms those sentiments of solidarity and ratifies all of its pledges to provide unlimited support to the Puerto Rican people's cause.

Long live free Puerto Rico!
Homeland or death!
We will win!

History of the Americas

Remarks at the University of Havana in September 1977 during the ceremony inaugurating the graduate course on the history of Latin America and the Caribbean

Today, we are inaugurating this graduate course on the economic, political and social history of our America, sponsored and directed by the American History Department of the School of Philosophy and History of our beloved University of Havana.

We are pleased to observe that many comrades whose work is linked to our government's and party's foreign relations with the area of the Americas will participate in the course.

I know of the special effort that the professors who will give the course have made in order to offer this Marxist-Leninist panoramic view of Latin American and Caribbean history. This is the first time that a course on Latin American history is being given at this level of specialization in Cuba.

On a day such as this, four years before beginning Cuba's War of Independence — which he considered to be the first step in a national liberation process that would involve all of Latin America — José Martí wrote in his well-known essay "Our America," "The European university should give way to the American. The history of the Americas, of the Incas, should be taught thoroughly here, even if that of the Athenian magistrates is left out. Our Greece is preferable to the Greece that isn't ours. We need it more."

For us — revolutionaries and Marxist-Leninists — the study of history is, first of all, a weapon in the struggle. It means knowing the past so we can better interpret the present and struggle to transform the future. And, again, I will cite Martí: "Only the wealth that is created and the freedom that is won with your own hands is lasting and good. He who fears this does not know our America."

That teaching of Martí's is demonstrated practically in the courageous history of all the Latin American countries, one of whose best examples was the internationalist struggle waged by Major Che

Guevara, the Heroic Guerrilla, the anniversary of whose death in combat we will be noting with sorrow soon.

With the same spirit as Che, with the desire to contribute to the liberation of the rest of Latin America, wherever this may be necessary, let us ready ourselves selflessly and unassumingly, in this trench of ideas, to continue the struggle for the second, definitive independence of our America.

I wish you success and express my satisfaction over the enthusiasm and interest that all of you have expressed concerning this course. I am sure that this enthusiasm shows your individual and collective determination to get the most out of this opportunity that the University of Havana has provided to extend and improve the training of the revolutionary professionals who work in the various institutions linked to the international work of our people's government and the Communist Party of Cuba.

Thank you.

10th Anniversary of the Death of Che Guevara

Address given at the headquarters of the Central Committee of the Communist Party of Cuba on October 8, 1977, during the ceremony held on the 10th anniversary of Che's death in combat

Beloved relatives of the Internationalist Combatants, who lost their lives together with Che,

B
arely a year before leaving for Cuba to begin the struggle for our homeland's liberation, José Martí stated in a speech in honor of Simón Bolívar, "I bring the unworthy homage of my words, which are less profound and eloquent than that of my silence."

In Revolution Square on October 18, 1967, Fidel spoke on behalf of a saddened and brave nation when he said, "Tonight, we have gathered — all of us — to try to express in some way our feelings regarding a man who was one of the best known, most admired, best loved and undoubtedly most extraordinary of our comrades of the revolution."

Only Fidel could have brought out all of the deep yet subtle dimensions of Che's revolutionary qualities. After the conceptual descriptions and evaluations made by Fidel, I can add very little about Che's magnificent and stoic life.

Words seem paltry; silence is how best to pay tribute to Che, because only the people can express the homage for Che that our Commander in Chief requested, in their daily struggles in building our new way of life and in internationalist solidarity.

Our revolution was the clean, pure crucible in which those two singular men, the sons of Our America, forged their close revolutionary friendship — Fidel as the leader and guide and Che among the first men in his vanguard, the most extraordinary of his comrades of the revolution.

A soldier faithful to his beloved leader, Che summed this up in his farewell letter: "If my last hour should come under other skies, my last thought will be of this people and especially of you [Fidel]. I thank you for your teachings and your example, to which I will try to be faithful to the last consequences of my actions." The affection of a brother, his strong respect and unbounded confidence in Fidel was, then, another permanent teaching from the Heroic Guerrilla's legacy.

Ten years have passed since his death in Bolivia, and, in this time, our people have written countless pages of daily sacrifice and heroism in the difficult task of socialist construction, in the deepening of revolutionary awareness and in the inspiring practice of proletarian internationalism. This has had its highest expression in Africa, where Che also helped to show — with his example and Marxist-Leninist view of history — the road to the liberation of that continent in its interrelations with the anti-imperialist struggles of Latin America and with the victories of socialism all over the world.

Our Party's First Congress[1] was the most important historical event in the last decade. It produced the agreements and resolutions that our party, our Union of Young Communists (UJC), our government and our social and mass organizations — that is, our people — will strive to implement, confronting dissimilar, complex objective difficulties. Those difficulties, however, will neither lessen nor weaken their enthusiasm and creative firmness.

Therefore, now, on the 10th anniversary of Che's heroic and exemplary death, we who work in the Central Committee, like all the rest of our people, have the duty to reflect on our revolutionary actions. Che said that revolutionaries have the right to get tired but not to stop being the vanguard. It is in this effort to overcome difficulties and to implement the mandates of the [Party] Congress that Che — that model revolutionary — challenges us to do better, to improve ourselves and to make each workday a victorious battle.

In the last paragraph of his report to the First Congress of the Communist Party of Cuba, Fidel, with his excellent revolutionary pedagogy, exhorted, "May the most absolute honesty, unlimited faithfulness to principles, selflessness, ability to make sacrifices, revolutionary purity, spirit of self-improvement, heroism and merit always prevail in our party." Che summed up those qualities.

Addressing an impressive multitude of Cubans wracked by militant sorrow over the irreparable loss of their Heroic Guerrilla, Fidel said:

> As a revolutionary, Che summed up the virtues that may be defined as the fullest expression of the virtues of a revolutionary: an integral man in every respect; a man of supreme honesty, of absolute

---

[1] The First Congress of the Communist Party of Cuba was held December 13-18, 1975.

sincerity; a man with a stoic, Spartan way of life; a man whose conduct was impeccable. Because of his virtues, he constituted what may be called a true model of a revolutionary.

Therefore, what better homage could there be than to constantly increase our respect for the people, to pay systematic attention to the social and human problems with which our people are faced, to struggle to raise the level of economic efficiency, to raise the quality of the services and education, to increase internationalist awareness, to improve our knowledge of Marxist-Leninist theory and to do our specific jobs the best we know how?

Comrades, this 10th anniversary of the death in combat of Major Che Guevara coincides with the 60th anniversary of the glorious October Revolution. The triumph of the ideas of socialism in Lenin's homeland and the brilliant revolutionary teachings of the immortal guide of the world proletariat marked a new course in the history of humankind: the working class was able to seize political power and build a better, fairer society.

Those ideas went deep in Che's political awareness; starting very young, he suffered from the social injustices to which others were subjected and celebrated the victories of other peoples. Consistent with that way of thinking and feeling, Che often emphasized the historic meaning of the October Revolution and the role of Vladimir Ilyich Lenin, its brilliant leader. As he said, "After the October Revolution of 1917 — Lenin's revolution — humankind acquired a new consciousness." And then Che added, "And, since World War II, the bloc of countries that constitute the camp of peace and socialism has been very strong. There are a billion human beings who are directing and building history and know what they are doing."

With this ceremony, we are initiating the Camilo-Che Ideological Period[2] in our Central Committee. Their names, deeds and lives form part of our most inspiring revolutionary traditions. Their legacies are inscribed in the purest standards that generation after generation of Cubans will continue to follow as models of communist conduct.

Comrades, allow me to wind up this ceremony of remembrance by referring to Che as an Americanist, a citizen of that large homeland of which he felt permanently a part and to which he dedicated all of his efforts and intelligence, including his life. Time will pass, and the political conditions of the stage on which he lived may be reformed, but the justice of his concepts and his consistent attitude toward them will

---

[2] The reference is to the period of ideological training that is held in Cuba every year between October 8 (the anniversary of Che's death in combat) and October 28 (the anniversary of the legendary guerrilla commander Camilo Cienfuegos's disappearance in the sea after a plane accident).

retain their timeliness, because they were based on the scientific precision of Marxism-Leninism and on the continuity of the historical experiences of our patriots who fought for independence.

Speaking of Bolívar, Martí — a sensitive man who truly understood Our America — said something that seems to ignore time and clearly appropriate in describing Che. Martí said, "Thus, from generation to generation, as long as America lives, the echo of his name will resound in the most virile and honored of our men."

Eternal glory to the brave combatants killed in Bolivia!

Major Camilo Cienfuegos and Major Ernesto Che Guevara:
Ever onward to victory!
Homeland or death!
We will win!

Nicaragua

Excerpts from the address given in Managua, Nicaragua, on November 2, 1980, during the ceremony founding the local committee of the Communist Party of Cuba

F ulfilling one of the principles of democratic centralism, you have elected the comrade members of this party committee that we are officially constituting.

It isn't difficult for all of us who are here today and for the communists whom you represent to understand the political and organizational importance of the creation of this party organization.

This important decision meets a need that was first manifested when, in response to a request by the Sandinista National Liberation Front and complying with our internationalist duty to Sandino's heroic homeland, the first contingents of our magnificent health and education workers — a significant number of whom were members of or aspirants to membership in the Communist Party of Cuba — began to arrive in free Nicaragua. With them, the first party nuclei began to be organized in the ranks of the Cuban civilian workers.

The assistance to this sister nation has been growing, and so has the number of members of and aspirants to membership in the Communist Party of Cuba who are taking part in that assistance. There are already 665 Cuban communists participating in the noble and humane work of helping to rebuild Nicaragua in the spheres of education, health, construction, agriculture and communications.

It's only natural that this should be. I would even say that it couldn't have been otherwise. The party's position as the organized vanguard of our working class and as the most important agency guiding our society is expressed in its active participation in each and every task taken up by our workers, especially those which include fulfillment of our internationalist duty.

The number of party members and aspirants to party membership in the large group of workers who are now working in this country is important, but the dedication and selflessness with which, I am sure, you are carrying out your missions and the persevering work of conveying this attitude to the rest of your comrades and imbuing them with it are much more important.

As you know, this isn't the only group of Cuban workers who are providing solidarity and assistance to other peoples right now, nor is it the only Party Committee that is being created outside our country to direct and channel the activity of the nuclei and communists toward fulfillment of the proposed objectives. However, the special significance of the work you are doing in this country, Nicaragua — the second country in Latin America to have freed itself of imperialism and which is waging its struggle in very difficult specific circumstances — must be obvious to you.

Referring to Nicaragua in his address in the ceremony held on the 27th anniversary of the attack on the Moncada Garrison, Fidel said:

> It doesn't have a socialist regime; it has a mixed economy and a multiparty regime, with the Sandinista Front and other leftist groups and some parties of the right. Therefore, we can't imagine Nicaragua in a situation exactly like that of Cuba.
>
> There is a new revolutionary project in Nicaragua in the sense that, in this stage, they have set themselves the goal of national reconstruction with the cooperation of all sectors. As they announced on July 19, they also propose to have an agrarian reform, which will be applied to the land that is lying idle. But they are trying to provide incentives for the private industrialists who have remained in the country and for the medium-sized, capitalist farmers. They are appealing to them, asking them to contribute as much as possible to national reconstruction. This is a new experience in Latin America...

He went on to say:

> Last year, we issued a challenge to the western world, to see who would help the Nicaraguan people most: a kind of competition in assistance. We said we were willing to cooperate to the utmost, and we asked all the capitalist, oil-producing and socialist countries to give the revolution in Nicaragua their maximum support, which is really needed.

Later, in a meeting with the first group of the contingent of Augusto César Sandino internationalist teachers who went to Nicaragua, Comrade Fidel called on them to set an example for the workers, revolutionaries and teachers. He said:

We know that you are good, but you must be better there. I know that you are going to do an excellent job; I ask that you do an even more excellent one. I ask that you be even more exemplary.

I am confident that you will develop the most fraternal relations with the Nicaraguan people and that your contact with that noble, kind, courageous, long-suffering and struggling people will be an incentive for carrying out this mission of support for the Sandinista Revolution.

I sincerely believe that this mission that you are going to carry out is a history-making one of enormous value for Latin America and for the international revolutionary movement.

These words of Comrade Fidel show that of all the Cuban workers, Cuban communists, who are in other parts of the world, those in Nicaragua are especially duty-bound to demonstrate, in the way they approach their daily work, the values of our socialist society, our revolutionary people and our working people and the principles taught them by our party and Fidel, by the example he sets. Here, that duty is multiplied and takes on greater value from the political and ideological point of view.

It is extremely important that each group of workers carry out the specific task assigned to it successfully and with the required quality. This will acquire its full political and ideological value only to the extent that each one of you maintains an unassuming, disciplined, natural, humane attitude of respect for the Nicaraguan workers' and people's traditions and customs in your daily relations with them.

The actions of each of you and those of each of the other comrades who aren't here today — party members and non-party members, aspirants to membership in the party and in the UJC — will determine whether or not what Comrade Fidel said becomes a daily reality.

This is the history-making mission assigned to you. It is why we have created this local Party committee and why there are 60 party nuclei throughout the country. It is the goal for which the hundreds of communists in those nuclei should strive. To carry out this mission, it is absolutely necessary to pay close attention to the activities of the internal functioning of the party, keeping in mind that they are means, not ends, in our work; that they should help to prepare you to reach the goals set, working closely with the masses...

The efforts and results in construction, transportation, education and health have been equally important. In spite of difficulties, we have advanced and will continue advancing in the construction of our socialist society under Fidel's wise leadership, holding high the banners of proletarian internationalism; true to the legacy of Marx, Engels and Lenin and to the thought and actions of José Martí; and true to those who, like you in Nicaragua and other countries, are making this an inspiring reality.

Comrades, I salute you for the meritorious revolutionary work that you are doing alongside the fraternal people of Nicaragua. As Comrade Fidel said, "Being an internationalist means helping to pay our debt to humankind." I ask you to convey this idea to the rest of the communists whom you represent and to the group of workers to which you belong.

I wish those of you who have been elected to serve on this committee and its leadership body success in your work. I am sure that the selflessness and dedication with which you will carry out the tasks assigned to you will lead to success.

In closing, comrades, I would like to emphasize the significance that meeting with you here in Nicaragua, in the heroic, combative land of Augusto César Sandino and Carlos Fonseca Amador, has for all of us Cuban communists. This was made possible thanks to the rebelliousness and bravery of its sons, the revolutionary courage of its men and women, who took the road of armed struggle with tenacity and determination and achieved the tremendous victory of July 19, 1979, under the wise leadership of the Sandinista National Liberation Front (FSLN).

It was a very high honor for you to have been chosen to carry out the internationalist missions that our revolution assigned to you and for which we are meeting here today. Therefore, comrades, because of the great significance of this history-making time, I call on you to hold high our banner of struggle and combat, firmly and in solidarity, setting examples of performing daily duty. Be worthy of our revolutions, of the heroism of this people and of our history. By so doing, we also honor our own martyrs; our own heroes; Ernesto Che Guevara, the Heroic Guerrilla; and Major Carlos Fonseca Amador, who continued Sandino's work and founded the FSLN.

Long live our Communist Party and its Second Congress!
Long live the heroic FSLN!
Long live proletarian internationalism!
Long live the peoples' heroic struggle for their definitive liberation!
Long live Fidel!
Homeland or death!
We will win!

The Current Crisis of Imperialism and the Revolutionary Process in Latin America and the Caribbean

Revolutions of National and Social Liberation

Each period leaves its imprint on the social revolutions that occur within it. The same is true for national liberation struggles. Lenin stressed this idea when he said: "The period 1789-1871 was of special significance for Europe. This is irrefutable. We cannot understand a single national liberation war, and such wars were especially typical of that period, unless we understand the general conditions of the period."[2]

In the pre-monopoly stage of capitalism, national liberation revolutions were part of the great anti-feudal transformations that were bourgeois-democratic in content. Their social character was predominantly capitalist. Consequently the tasks they carried out were part of the worldwide development of the capitalist system. We should not overlook the fact that these anticapitalist national liberation struggles occurred within the context of the expansion and development of the capitalist socioeconomic formation. At the same time, however, we should note that each process had its own particular features. These particularities were conditioned by the character of foreign domination, the historical circumstances and the specific economic and sociological make up of the countries involved. The national factor thus represented the particular, distinctive ingredient of these revolutions, while the

---

[1] This essay was published in the form of an article in *Cuba Socialista* No. 4, Havana, September-November 1982, 15-53. It was presented to the International Theoretical Conference on "General and Specific Characteristics of the Revolutionary Processes in Latin America and the Caribbean" held in Havana on April 26-28, 1982.

[2] V.I. Lenin, *On the Caricature of Marxism and "Economic Imperialism"*

insertion of these countries within the capitalist system represented the more general framework.

In examining the many experiences of the liberation struggles of the 19th century in our own countries, we should keep both these factors in mind. Thus we can avoid the error of viewing these struggles as equal with the European revolutions of the same historical period.

It would not be valid — neither then or now — to mechanically apply to each specific situation, without distinction, a generalized conception of revolution. This emphasizes, perhaps more clearly than in any other field, the well-known Leninist assertion: Concrete analysis of the concrete situation is the soul of Marxism.

In our era, national liberation revolutions have also presented particular characteristics. These are determined by the general crisis of capitalism, the existence of a powerful and developing socialist system, and the historic confrontation between those two systems. These factors are the origin of the great differences between the present national liberation struggles and those of the pre-monopoly stage of capitalism. Imperialism creates and sustains the oppression of nations through new relations of domination — centered on state monopoly capital. But it is also true that the revolutions taking place in underdeveloped countries are fundamentally aimed at destroying these premises. Accordingly, their distinctive feature is their anti-imperialist character.

At the same time, and because of their anti-imperialist nature, current national liberation revolutions are also links in the process of transition from capitalism to socialism. And precisely here the most important characteristics of these revolutions originate, both in terms of their objectives, social composition, and tasks, as well as their strategic historical direction. They are more advanced than their predecessors; yet they also maintain a continuity with these earlier revolutions that culminates in a dialectical leap. Sooner or later, and in many different forms, the dominant material realities impel these countries to liquidate the foundations of their entire oppression. This is the inevitable outcome for dependent countries facing the crossroads that imperialist exploitation has brought them to.

This explains why the national liberation revolutions of our time have a profound social content that converts them into events of worldwide importance. They are an indivisible part of a single international revolutionary process in which the fundamental contradiction — socialism *versus* capitalism — is in turn sharpened by the very advance of these revolutions.

Their anti-imperialist course and their anticapitalist tendency place them among the principal forces to transform the bourgeois system, alongside the world socialist system and the international workers' movement.

The revolutions for national and social liberation in Latin America and the Caribbean are a clear expression, as well as key elements, of these general circumstances.

They also embody characteristics that are significant in relation to the present liberation process in Africa and Asia. Our revolutions, like those of Africa and Asia, are also advancing along the world historical path that began in October 1917. They form a part of the three underdeveloped continents that are confronting imperialism. But the material premises created by capitalist domination in our countries (a level of development that on average is superior to that of Asia and Africa) have created better conditions for a more intense and radical advance of our revolutions. In their dialectical course, these revolutions take on tasks of a democratic, popular, and anti-imperialist content in their first stage. As they develop, they tend to carry out clearly socialist tasks — as an indissoluble part of their own process and in accordance with their general historical character.

On this point, the [1975] Programmatic Platform of the Communist Party of Cuba says: "There is no insurmountable barrier between the democratic-popular and anti-imperialist stage and the socialist stage. In the era of imperialism, both are part of a single process, in which national-liberation and democratic measures — which at times have already a socialist tinge — pave the way for genuinely socialist ones. The decisive and defining element of this process is who leads it, which class wields political power."

This is why the national and social liberation movements on this continent have to confront imperialism directly and immediately. This means U.S. imperialism, in particular, in its role as the system of domination conditioning the physiognomy of capitalism in Latin America and the Caribbean. Despite their distortions, bourgeois-national states (formed more than 150 years ago) have matured in the majority of our countries. There exists in these countries a formidable variety of experiences in national and class struggles. This was brought out most clearly with the triumph of the first socialist revolution in the hemisphere, which unmistakably reveals the degree of maturity reached by these societies.

In Our America the proletariat — the main historical agent of the new society — is the most important social force. This is true not only because of its qualitative merit but also because of its size in various countries of the region, a point that in no way diminishes the extraordinary significance of the poor peasantry and other popular forces. Finally, to note another relevant factor: foreign domination on this continent is exercised by the strongest imperialist power, which, because of its overall interests, attributes a geopolitical strategic character to the struggle. This makes the liberation of our peoples more difficult — but also more radical and urgent.

These realities have not ceased to be expressed in a contradictory fashion over the last 25 years, with advances and retreats. But at the end of the last decade and increasingly in the early years of this one, our region demonstrated the revolutionary movement's highest level of acceleration in the underdeveloped areas, including on a world scale.

From the factors we have pointed out, there flows a unique combination of democratic and popular tasks on the one hand, and economic, political, and social demands on the other — all of which contribute to the historic socialist course of the revolution. It is a combination of anti-imperialist, national liberation tasks alongside the consolidation of power by workers, peasants and other toiling sectors against latifundist and capitalist exploitation. In a nutshell, what we have in some countries is a complex and dynamic overlapping or interweaving of the class struggle and the anti-neocolonial or anti-colonial struggle. In his main report to the [1975] First Congress of the Communist Party, Commander-in-Chief Fidel Castro referred to the experience of Cuba: "Our national and social liberation were indissolubly linked, to advance was a historical necessity, to stop was cowardice and treachery that would have again turned us into a Yankee colony and slaves of the exploiters."

It is worthwhile to investigate the material and historical realities that explain the intensity, scope, depth and perspectives of the present class struggle in our societies. This will help identify the objective and subjective factors that lie behind the present structural crisis of capitalism on the continent, the rise of various revolutionary processes, and the growth in the militant movement of the popular masses.

The Crisis of Capitalism and the Revolutionary Processes in Latin America and the Caribbean

Reflecting what is happening in reality, in Latin America and the Caribbean there is a crisis in the capitalist models of economic development. Schemes for independent development (efforts by the national bourgeoisies of various countries from the 1930s to the 1950s, along with a few later development-oriented variants) have been frustrated one after the other because of the asphyxiating limits imposed by foreign monopoly capital. With the cancellation of these options, variants for development were reduced to a single alternative: either the imperialist transnational enterprises and the international economic relations they represent; or the revolutionary program of the popular classes, in the first place the proletariat: the socialist path. The first choice operates within the network of capitalist structures imposed by region-wide imperialist domination; it involves the reproduction of well-known deforming and deformed socioeconomic conditions. It also accentuates and complicates the contradictions of underdevelopment in Latin America and the Caribbean. Fundamentally this leads to a polarization of the class struggle as an inevitable expression of the concentration and centralization of capital. The other choice allows independent development — that is, genuine development — and flows from the very contradictions generated by the system of oppression and exploitation. Socialism thus emerges as the sole historical solution making it possible to overcome the tremendous obstacles of underdevelopment, obstacles that are insoluble under capitalism.

As part of the worldwide capitalist system, since the 1970s the economies of Latin America and the Caribbean have been subject to the process of the establishment of a new capitalist international division of labor, promoted by the leading countries of this system. This has brought about, first and foremost, the consolidation of the domination of big monopoly and finance capital, which has definitively become the decisive axis of the majority of the region's economies. In this way, and as never before, the fate of the economic evolution of the area depends on the overall dynamic of capitalism on a world scale. Moreover, the prolonged crisis that has affected capitalism in recent years has repercussions in Latin America and the Caribbean that are even more direct and brutal.

Scarcely a single country has been spared from the process of transnationalization of the Latin American and Caribbean economies. For example, this is reflected in the final integration — or rather in the structural dependency — of the continent's bourgeoisies in relation to big monopoly and finance capital.

In this way the pattern of capital accumulation inherent in the establishment of a new capitalist international division of labor has given rise to a greater integration of the national economies for the developed countries. This new capitalist international division of labor presupposes specialization in the production of more technologically complex goods and the perfection of science and technology, with the aim of maintaining control over the most advanced technology. At the same time, the service sector grows, and there is a general increase in the parasitic activities of the monopoly economy, thus confirming the tendency of imperialism that Lenin pointed to.

The underdeveloped countries are "elevated" to a more modern rung of the ladder through the incorporation of new methods of production. Such techniques are channeled there by the industrialized countries because of the greater relative density of the work force these techniques require. This is why it is more profitable to exploit labor in dependent countries, where the working class has much lower wage levels. Accordingly, one of the formulas that in recent years has received the most support from transnational capital is the return to liberal economic relations. As the Chilean case clearly shows, this represents an extreme variant of dependency on foreign capital; of concentrating and centralizing national wealth in its hands, in association with "national" big capital; and of enforcing the highest rates of superexploitation of workers ever registered in the history of our region. Some variants of state capitalism, including state monopoly capitalism (which are also dependent because of the nature of the society from which they emerged) rest on the same principle of modernization through attracting foreign capital. Occasionally, however, contradictions arise with foreign capital as a consequence of potential different interests that can become quite significant.

Although the complexity of this process cannot be discussed extensively here, it is important to recognize the contradictions and new consequences that arise. These include, in particular, the tendency toward reducing bourgeois democracy and the establishment of repressive military regimes. Such consequences, in our opinion, increase conditions that are favorable for the tasks of the revolutionary vanguards. At the same time, they demand of these vanguards the highest capacity of struggle on all fronts and a scientific understanding of capitalism's new adjustments in its various manifestations, both global and national.

In this context we would like to point out some of the contradictions that can be observed in this process. In one form or another, they are present in the majority of countries of the region.

There is an initial contradiction that arises between the necessity of the area's economies to increase investment so as to attain development, and the limits imposed on these economies by the narrowness of the internal market — precisely because of the domination of that market by the foreign monopolies.

Paradoxically, the effects of the modern technology used in new investments by the transnational enterprises are minimal in terms of the internal market of the country on the receiving end. This technology does not tend to increase sources of employment. And at times, in displacing old technologies and artisanal activities, its impact on the internal market is totally negative.

On the other hand, as a consequence of their monopoly control of prices, their absolute domination of finances, and the possibility of expansion because of the bankruptcy of competitors, the transnational enterprises have no special interest in breaking up traditional agrarian relations based on latifundism.

So these archaic agrarian structures continue to survive, although with relative modernization as a result of other factors that we will analyze later. There is a sustained increase in unemployment and underemployment, whose most obvious manifestation are the inhuman marginal barrios. Both factors impose very strict limits on the expansion of investment. And this in turn results in greater stagnation of the economy.

Another significant contradiction arises out of the transnational enterprises' primary interest in attaining high profits. They seek to recover rapidly the capital they have invested and to increase dividends. The profits they make are not reinvested in the country from which they originate. Therefore, the limits of that country's internal market determine that the transnational enterprises must channel their profits toward new markets in other countries. This is the origin of an antagonism between the underdeveloped countries' need to increase investments, and the interests of the transnational enterprises to increase their overall profits, including by deepening the decapitalization and financial dependency of the underdeveloped countries.

One result of the new capitalist international division of labor is endemic deficit in the Latin American countries' commercial balances and their balance of payments. These in turn are manipulated even more intensively by the International Monetary Fund and private international banks. This is done with the systematic aim of imposing a policy in accordance with the interests of big imperialist capital.

This type of modernizing neodevelopment of dependent capitalism has elevated to higher and decisive levels the trans-nationalization of our economies, affecting nearly all the countries of the continent. On the one hand, the dominance of monopoly and finance capital within the economies in the region has been consolidated. On the other, there has been a strengthening of the alliance between foreign capital and sectors of big local capital, in a process where denationalization is reflected in greater degrees of submission to the pattern of imperialist accumulation. Such a dynamic, unfolding in the present stage of capitalist crisis and recession, has definitively exhausted the previous stages of relative national industrial development, which were based on import substitution and broadening of the internal market. In the political sphere, it has tended to provoke a crisis in multiclass groupings of a populist nature, as well as in the bourgeois-democratic state order.

There has been an accelerated tendency toward class polarization in the social structure, resulting in clearer demarcations between the conflicting forces. Defined more clearly in the majority of our countries are two large class blocs: first, the classes and sectors linked organically to foreign capital; the second, broadly based, is made up of the working class first of all, the peasantry, the unemployed, the underemployed, and growing segments of what are called the middle sectors.

The crisis of capitalist development models in the region has thrown into sharper relief the question of socialist development as the only alternative to the underdevelopment capitalism generates.

In the last two decades, economic and political reformism has put into practice different policy variants aimed at diminishing the effects of the new pattern of capitalist accumulation. All these variants, however, have met failure one after the other, since they were too weak to confront the economic, political and social structures that sustain the system of capitalist domination in the region. One aim of the reformist schemes has been to attenuate the class struggle. But this has been achieved only in a few cases and for brief periods of time, as the masses tend to radicalize even more when they are unable to resolve underlying problems, and this in turn increases their consciousness concerning the way to resolve them.

One fact has been demonstrated in different countries and at different times: reformism's aspirations are limited to destroying the traditional export economy and sharing economic power with the foreign monopolies, counterposing the forces of state capitalism. There is no question of attaining independence, which they know to be unobtainable. They accept the premise of dependency on foreign capital and try to achieve maximum profit for the national economic interest they claim to represent.

The social layers that sustain this position are normally the civil and military bureaucracies, backed in a partial and temporary way by strata of the middle sectors. Under the new conditions, they seek to inherit the functions of the national bourgeoisie, whose schemes failed in the decades from the 1930s to 1950s. Today, the dominant material situation renders more fatal the negative results of those schemes. Accordingly, their weakness is not just economic. In the political sphere they are also accustomed to accepting as inevitable the imposition of restrictions on bourgeois democracy and the use of state repressive mechanisms, which are seen as necessary to assure the high levels of exploitation and poverty to which the popular masses are subjected.

Coinciding in recent years with the deepening of the world capitalist economic crisis, the negative consequences of the new capitalist international division of labor have become visible in the area. These include the exhaustion of reformist efforts, the decline of bourgeois-democratic regimes, and the tendency of dictatorial military governments to replace such regimes. All of this marks the end of a historic stage on the continent and foreshadows a new scenario for the class struggle in which the peoples and their revolutionary organizations encounter greater possibilities for developing their struggles. These struggles are more radical because of the nature of the material bases that condition them. And, as a consequence, they become more complex and diverse in their national expressions. They have a common objective: the definitive solution of the contradictions of the system of imperialist oppression and exploitation through the path of revolutionary transformations of their economic and political structures. This road is already being taken by Nicaragua and Grenada — at their own pace and with their own forms — while El Salvador and Guatemala can be seen advancing in a very promising way. Cuba, in the vanguard historically, has shown the viability of the alternative and continues successfully on this alternative course.

Thus, in the mid-1970s, Latin America and the Caribbean began a stage of deep polarization of their social structures, heightened political confrontations, and an increasingly well-defined antagonism between revolution and counterrevolution.

To sum up, the material bases of the present revolutionary processes in Latin America and the Caribbean have been created by the changes that occurred in economic and social relations in our countries, especially since the 1950s. These transformations have brought levels — and means — of capitalist development of a deformed and distorting-variety that must be very carefully considered so as to define the character of the revolutions for national and social liberation in this part of the world.

The economic growth of capitalism in the region has provoked the spread of underdevelopment because of imperialist domination and the lack of a challenge to archaic agrarian relations based on latifundism. These circumstances accentuate without interruption the contradiction between the character and development of the productive forces and the relations of production, both of which are molded by foreign capital in association with the local bourgeoisie and landowners. What has occurred is a process of capitalist socioeconomic formation subordinated to the world imperialist system through neocolonial relations.

Here precisely lies the historic nature of the present crisis of Latin American and Caribbean societies — historic because, in addition to being economic and social, there will be no substantial change in the continent's future without anti-imperialist and anticapitalist transformations.

That is why the present crisis in the region is at one and the same time a crisis of imperialist domination, of obsolete agrarian relations, and of the system of dependent capitalism's relations of production. It is simultaneously a crisis of all these structures linked to a political, juridical and ethical crisis. It is an overall crisis of the society, deepened by the growing negative effects of the general crisis of capitalism.

The convergence of these factors and processes determines the historical character of the contemporary revolutions of our continent. This character, rather than excluding, presupposes the possibility of varied forms and rhythms of moving toward socialism, and of different national paths facilitating an initial anti-imperialist, democratic, and popular stage of the revolution.

It is important to stress, however, that in the majority of the countries on the continent the material bases created by capitalist development have established the conditions necessary to permit triumphant revolutions to advance in an uninterrupted manner — although by stages — in a single historical process, toward socialism.

The many experiences accumulated by our peoples in their intense and varied struggles, especially since 1959, are a factor favoring this possible outcome. Since then, we have witnessed the collapse of bourgeois-democratic reformist movements and various nationalist experiments, followed by the search for options for obtaining development, independence, and self-determination. Working class activity has been incessant, along with the advance of the rest of the people's movement. Formidable examples have been accumulated in the revolutionary use of arms by vanguards and the peoples. We have lived through an interesting and useful experience toward achieving socialism — in Chile. Military dictatorships of the old and new type have proliferated. There have been uprisings by patriotic military men and the establishment of nationalist governments led by them. There has been a notable incorporation into the struggle of Christian, progressive, and revolutionary sectors. Nicaragua and Grenada, with their victorious revolutions, have reaffirmed the validity of the road to power opened by Cuba and have enriched the heritage of the continent's revolutionary culture.

These nearly 25 years of battle and sacrifice, impregnated with the blood of thousands of combatants, represent today's best school for the revolutionary movement of Our America. Today, in addition to the theoretical and scientific certainties and the rich experiences accumulated by our peoples since the wars of independence, they also have at their disposal a number of revolutionary situations that various revolutionary generations in struggle have lived through — experiences that have been sufficiently broad and clear in their fundamental lessons. This diversity of experiences and situations includes both undeniable advances and temporary setbacks. But one truth has been reaffirmed again and again, and is now irrefutable: The historical course toward socialism does not depend solely on the objective laws of the capitalist system; in crystallizing this course, the revolutionary vanguards have the first and decisive responsibility for impelling the process forward, and this must be demonstrated above all in their capacity to lead the peoples to the conquest of power. This is the cardinal problem of every revolution. It synthesizes the different aspects that must be considered and correctly resolved, in order to increase the possibilities of that crucial moment — the end of a complex process and the guarantee of its development.

Among the many factors linked to the struggle for power, we consider it essential to examine first the structure of the classes and social forces that objectively tend to participate in the revolution.

Structure of the Classes and Forces that Are Motors of the Revolution

We are not going to spend a great deal of time on this theme because we have already discussed it at some length in the theoretical conference held in 1980.[3] Our interest here, in connection with the main objective of the conference, is to identify the principal actors in the present class struggle on our continent.

When analyzing the structure of classes one cannot isolate the struggles of these classes. For these struggles, in the course of their development, modify all of the society's structures. Accordingly, the first element to be considered is imperialist domination, which we view as the main conditioning factor in the class structure and class struggle on our continent. Let us look first at the bloc of ruling classes.

The modernizing economic processes we described earlier have led in recent years to the formation of a new oligarchy representing the different factions of the big bourgeoisie — industrial, commercial, financial and agrarian. This new oligarchy is subordinated to and shares the same strategy of development and domination as imperialist capital. Occasionally, however, there may appear certain differences of interests that should not be overlooked in terms of the tactical struggle of the revolutionary movement.

Another element of the bloc of exploiting classes is the declining middle, or national, bourgeoisie, substantially weakened by the rigors of its alliance with the big bourgeoisie and the transnational enterprises. In general, this middle bourgeoisie has been reduced to the most traditional industrial sector — non-durable consumer goods — and is gradually losing its potential for economic reproduction. These circumstances mean that many sectors of the middle bourgeoisie may become important allies of the revolutionary process. This, however, does not always depend so much on correct tactics toward them as on the interweaving of their interests with different branches of the economy, ideological factors and specific situations of struggle.

The third element is the landowners. In some countries they have retained their power, based fundamentally on control of landed

---

[3] This refers to a paper presented in the name of the Americas Department of the Cuban Communist Party to the International Theoretical Conference on "The Structure of Classes in Latin America" that took place in Havana in March 26-28, 1980. This paper appeared under the title "Modernization of Capitalism and Social Classes in Latin America."

property. In other countries, however, various capitalist reforms carried out in the countryside have affected this class, disintegrating or modifying it in one way or another. In almost all cases a capitalist agro-export business sector has arisen, that is, a sector of modern ranchers and agro-industrialists. However, a layer of landowners of the traditional type still exists — latifundists — many of whom turn to renting out their land.

This process of dissolution of the landowning class is incomplete in the majority of countries and will continue at many different paces and rhythms, depending on the circumstances in each country. But in its general direction, the modernizing faction (the big rural bourgeoisie we mentioned) tends to tighten its links with sectors of the local commercial and financial bourgeoisie. And they too, in the last analysis, subordinate themselves to the interests and accumulation patterns of the imperialist bourgeoisie, which becomes the beneficiary and principal center of the new relations of capitalist exploitation in Latin American agriculture.

It should be noted that this process of transformation in the countryside generates contradictions between the sectors of "modernizing" capital and the landowners who defend traditional latifundism. The latter react strongly against certain aspects of agrarian reform, and above all against those modifications that alter their position. This accentuates their reactionary role in class struggles, and in many countries they make up a significant part of the counterrevolution.

To sum up, there is an noticeable tendency toward homogenization of the ruling classes, as never before seen in the history of the continent. This is determined by the international processes of capitalism mentioned above. At the same time, however, it should be kept in mind that varying levels of economic development in subregions and countries preclude an absolute generalization — for example, in comparing the situation in some countries of Central America and the Caribbean with others on the continent. It is also useful to point out, because of its evident practical value, that the transformations operating in the capitalist system in our region are generating various contradictions inside the bloc of ruling classes. Among them, we can point to the following:

- The struggle between sectors of the local big bourgeoisie and foreign monopoly capital, as both seek the best economic opportunities in the international market.
- Differences of interests between the latifundists and the big agrarian bourgeoisie.
- The conflict of the middle bourgeoisie with the big bourgeoisie or new oligarchy, as well as with transnational capital.
- Middle sectors that are part of the system and defenders of it, but

who also aspire to reform and renegotiate their dependency on transnational capital.

It is useful at this point to take a general look at what are called the middle sectors. In Latin American societies, perhaps even more than in other capitalist countries, defining these forces is an extremely complex task. This stems from their diversity of composition, the limited economic stability of many of them, and other factors in the dynamic of the class struggle. Because of these characteristics, it is very difficult to place all these sectors in either the bloc of ruling classes or in the bloc of exploited classes. It is valid, however, to identify them on the basis of their class standpoint. We share the assessment that they, in and of themselves, do not represent an organic social class. The fundamental component of this social force is the urban petty bourgeoisie, comprising small businessmen and entrepreneurs, professionals with private practices, and so forth. Added to this are such diverse layers of the population as government functionaries, students, public employees, skilled workers, professionals, etc.

The distinctive feature of the middle sectors is their socioeconomic heterogeneity, which determines their extremely contradictory content. Flowing from this, the middle sectors are incapable of formulating an independent historical program, and it is common knowledge that they have to make an alliance with one class or another.

On the one hand, they have an average standard of living that is higher than that of manual workers. They are usually susceptible to influence by bourgeois ideology and assume values and expectations that stem from this ideology. Some of these layers serve as administrators of the capitalist state and have fully committed themselves to this.

On the other hand, many members of these sectors are wage earners or small entrepreneurs who are not linked with either monopoly capital or the local oligarchy. In both cases they suffer the consequences of the system's crisis and of the imposition of the new pattern of accumulation. This either reduces them to poverty or diminishes considerably their standard of living. Furthermore, the absence of individual guarantees and institutionalized democracy is keenly felt by these sectors when they come up against the system. These factors, among others, give rise to the possibility that many members of the middle sectors will adopt a progressive stance, including identifying with the interests of the working class.

It is the task of the political forces of the bourgeoisie on the one hand, and of the exploited classes on the other, to win over this middle sector, which — for the reasons noted above — leans toward one direction or the other, or one or another class point of view. In these sectors (which are numerous in the majority of our countries and have a qualitative role that is still quite important) there is to be found a force that can be decisive for the victorious outcome of the Latin American revolutions. This explains the priority given them by the parties and organizations that represent the exploited classes. The aim is to isolate the reactionary layers, neutralize and draw in as much as possible the ambivalent elements, and win over to the revolution those who are objectively in a position to be incorporated into this historical undertaking. Often, large components of the middle sectors can become part of the leading force. They can serve as catalysts in the revolutionary struggles of their peoples, with a significant presence in the vanguards.

Along with the transformations that have taken place in recent years in the capitalist structures in Latin America and the Caribbean, there have also been some changes in the relationship of forces inside the bloc of exploited classes. There has been a notable increase in the level of relative and absolute pauperization among all the oppressed classes and sectors.

Because of the new process of industrialization we have already discussed, the working class tends to be more heterogeneous. This contributes to making the class more representative of the overall interests of the people. At the same time, it is necessary to understand that the industrialization process under way tends to concentrate the sector of workers associated with it, and to stratify them in relation to the rest of the class. This is heightened wherever the importance of other economic sectors (such as medium and small national industry, or the mines) either disappears or is reduced. It is useful to take such differences into consideration in order to avoid having them become obstacles to the unity of the industrial working class.

The rural sector of the proletariat is also changing. The expansion of capitalist relations in the countryside gives rise to a relative increase in this vital segment of the working class. Even more importantly, it generates a greater concentration of such workers within the framework of the big haciendas. This increases their capacity for class organization, which on occasion is also enhanced by attainment of greater skills and by links with the urban industrial proletariat.

The broad peasant masses — poor peasants — constitute the other fundamental class within the popular bloc. The peasantry in our countries continues to be made up of diverse segments: tenant farmers, sharecroppers of various sorts, small proprietors, those who simply make use of property whose ownership is not defined, and so forth. But the common factor is their extreme and growing poverty. The most inhuman forms of this poverty continue to be concentrated among the Indian masses, who are subjected to the highest levels of exploitation and social marginalization.

In various countries of the region the peasantry remains numerically the most important class within the rural population. In other countries this is already no longer the case because of the capitalist transformation of agriculture. One impact of this transformation is that peasant proprietors suffer the pressure of competition from the big productive haciendas, often resulting in their ruin or displacement from their parcel of land. In general this process implies a tendency toward elimination of the peasantry, since capitalist modernization of agriculture tends to reduce the size of this class. This occurs through proletarianization and semi-proletarianization of part of it, and expulsion toward the cities (mainly to their marginal outskirts) of another part. At the same time, in a number of regions the amount of land the peasants have access to has either been notably reduced — or remained the same. This combined with the population increase means that the smaller properties can no longer serve as the basis for family subsistence farming. This whole complex situation develops the consciousness of the peasantry about the need for profound agrarian reforms. It increases the potential of their struggles for economic demands and those of a revolutionary character. And it objectively increases the potential for development of their alliance with the working class.

Alongside these exploited classes — often part of one or another of these classes, or with subtle distinctions — is the urban and rural subproletariat. This sector is numerous in Latin America and the Caribbean, unstable by nature, and in transition toward either the marginal population and lumpen proletariat or toward joining the productive system. These social forces are pressing to resolve their problems — for urbanization of their settlements, among other things — pressure that is occasionally dramatized by violent explosions. Because of its composition and conditions, this subproletariat is usually inconsistent and subject to manipulation by the parties of the system. But it has also been shown that it is possible to orient them toward revolutionary objectives when effective work is carried out, for example, in the marginal settlements.

To complete the broad range of forces that make up the social base of the present revolutionary processes on our continent, it is necessary to include the large and growing mass of unemployed — extreme victims of the capitalist system who do not have access to even minimal possibilities of subsistence.

This group shares a similar standard of living and exploitation, with no possible solution under the reigning system. In addition, it is often subjected to the terrible severity of reactionary dictatorial governments. These layers can only enter into radical contradiction with the existing socioeconomic system.

These forces thus constitute the historical protagonist of the present revolutions on our continent. The working class is the fundamental center of this multifaceted collection of forces, but all are important in the struggle for power and in the later development of socialist construction. It is impossible to define uniformly the role of each one of these forces in all countries. It is up to the vanguards in these countries to make this analysis and to develop the correct relationship in its tactics in order to gain their effective participation in the different stages and settings of the struggle.

In the particularities and nuances of this relationship, conditioned by the general and decisive historical confrontation of our time — that between the bourgeoisie and proletariat — there is to be found indispensable support for the triumph of revolutions on the continent. In this regard, it is worthwhile to stress the outstanding role peasants have played in revolutions that have been victorious, and in those today developing in El Salvador and Guatemala. In the latter country, incorporating the Indians is decisive to the struggle for power.

Strategy and Tactics of the Revolution: General Considerations

Let us begin with a fundamental truth: The class struggle can neither be planned nor programmed; the triumph of revolutions even less so. We should also base ourselves on another well-known truth: When revolutions are authentic, they always respond to universal laws; but their very authenticity also makes them unique in terms of their national outlines.

It is not our intention to examine exceptional factors or the contributions that have been made by Latin American revolutions that are victorious, postponed or under way. This task is of great importance for the revolutionary movement of this continent's collective heritage of political culture, and we will surely have analysis here by other delegates on this theme.

We would simply like to consider a few more general factors and problems that are present in the processes occurring today in the region. These common ingredients, while also exhibiting their national characteristics, have been confirmed with the triumph of Cuba, Nicaragua and Grenada. They are also being clearly repeated in El Salvador and Guatemala; and they are evident in other developing processes.

For Marxist-Leninists, the central problem of the revolution is the seizure of power. This means encouraging the material and subjective conditions that will make it possible to advance the process, in an uninterrupted manner, toward the socialist stage. The first and most important of these conditions is the destruction of the bourgeois state apparatus and its replacement by a revolutionary state based on the hegemony of the proletariat in close alliance with the other popular classes and sectors. In any genuine revolution there is no substitute for this historic break.

Not all components of the bourgeois state can be destroyed at the same time, or with the same methods. However, the nucleus of the state apparatus — its repressive force — is the key to attaining domination over the rest of the state body. Hence its destruction is the indispensable and definitive priority for the triumph of any revolution. The repressive apparatus is, in the last analysis, what guarantees the bourgeoisie its continuation in power, what it turns to in situations of crisis. It is possible, to be sure, to encounter substantial differences when comparing the forms of political and ideological domination of various bourgeois regimes. But differences are minimal when it comes to the forms of organization and use of the repressive apparatus by this type of state. So, the problem of power rests above all on the validity of the strategy for reaching this goal. Accordingly, revolutionary strategy must at least fulfill the following requisites: defining the character of the revolution; assessing the world, regional and national relationship of forces; identifying the main enemy, its allies, and the contradictions among them; defining the leading class of the revolution, its allies, and the points of convergence and divergence among these forces; elaborating the main outlines of the fundamental path of the struggle that has been chosen, as well as of other complementary forms that are indispensable for advancing the revolution.

The strategy of the revolutionary movement is based on scientific considerations that are, for this very reason, effective only to the extent that they are adapted to the specific realities of each country. Development of the revolution presupposes the maturation, over a more or less lengthy period, of the forces that will lead the dual task of destroying the old order and building the new one. The multiple tasks faced by these forces range from economic struggles to political and military objectives. These in turn generate, at a determined moment, the opening of a pre-revolutionary period, characterized by a high degree of class confrontation and by a crisis of bourgeois power. In this process the incessant activity of left parties and organizations is decisive.

It is then that wider possibilities for the revolutionary triumph emerge. The attempt to seize power becomes the definitive test of the effectiveness of the strategy that has been worked out, and of the tactical capacity of the vanguard to lead the masses to the decisive goal.

In the first instance, the basis of all strategy lies in the objective conditions that define it and provide its historical viability. Consequently, if the subjective conditions do not correspond to the strategy that has been outlined, this does not mean that the strategy has to be replaced by one of lesser scope. In such cases — and this in fact is what happens most often — what is required is the use of tactics that are adequate to bringing about a *practical* understanding of the *viability* and *necessity* of the chosen strategy. This understanding emerges out of a complex and dynamic direct participation by the masses who, consciously or unconsciously, assimilate and adopt as their own the strategy worked out and led by the vanguard.

The masses do not act solely out of conviction injected into them from outside — without belittling the importance of revolutionary propaganda. They do not enter into combat because of simple faith in the promise of a better world or a future ideal. It is the experience they accumulate in the confrontation between their own vital interests and the economic and political realities they experience that serves as their main school. That is how they learn the strategic road to their liberation and the practical means for advancing along it. In short, the problem of how to bring the strategy to fruition can only be resolved through the various tactics of struggle.

Consequently, the elaboration and victorious application of revolutionary tactics is the most complex and definitive test of a vanguard. In real life there is no task more difficult than deriving tactics that are adequate to the strategic line that has been adopted. For while the latter rests on a scientific analysis of reality, the former must also take into account a multiplicity of factors that are both difficult to control and scientifically unpredictable. Day-to-day activity, then, requires a vanguard that is both well grounded in theory and has a special capacity and sensibility for capturing concrete reality. Only in this way is it possible to master the dialectic of struggle with sufficient flexibility to be able to implement rapid and effective decisions as events develop. This is especially true in revolutionary periods, which frequently present situations of a brand new type.

In reality, vanguards and individual leaderships emerge precisely where, in addition to a correct strategy, correct tactics of struggle are defined and developed at each moment. This, therefore, is the fundamental attribute of a legitimate vanguard.

That is, the decisive challenge for every vanguard is the elaboration of tactics adjusted to both concrete circumstances and to the strategic objectives of the revolution. We do not seek to standardize the factors that must be taken into account in formulating tactics. But experience indicates that there are certain points of reference that are useful to consider because of their general value. These include, among others: the relationship of forces at every moment of the struggle; contradictions inside the ruling classes; tactical objectives of the enemy's political gambits; the organization, consciousness, tradition of struggle, and social psychology of the masses; and the overall cohesion and strength of the vanguard.

As is well known, none of these factors are static. For example, it would be a metaphysical approach to always attribute to the ruling class a strength superior to that of the oppressed classes. In actuality the relationship of forces is characterized by its dynamism. Timely and audacious action by revolutionary detachments can, with the support of the masses, bring about abrupt changes in their favor. The same thing occurs, but inversely, when revolutionary actions are inadequate or do not match the level and creativity demanded by a given conjuncture. History shows the high price paid by the peoples in such cases, because each error, deficiency and failure of the revolutionary movement is exploited to the hilt by the adversary.

Finally, it is important to note that it is often not possible to define the limits between strategy and tactics. They are interrelated and complement each other.

In elaborating their strategy and tactics of struggle, the revolutionary movements in Latin America and the Caribbean confront two conditioning factors that are fundamental and permanent: the character of imperialist domination on the continent and the policy of the U.S. Government.

For the United States, our region is part of the internal nucleus, the core, of its world strategy. U.S. imperialism has an integral policy toward our continent, containing all elements necessary for the conservation of its control of the hemisphere. Being part of an overall strategy, the policy of the United States with respect to neighbors to the south is based on principles that are both international and continental. In addition, in a few cases, there are particular approaches to relations with given countries and subregions.

Alongside the economic, military and political importance the United States attributes to our countries, its arrogance in refusing to accept the triumph of liberating revolutions inside what it considers to be the borders of its national security is also a factor.

These circumstances determine the increasingly sharp confrontations between the democratic, popular and revolutionary processes on the one hand, and U.S. imperialism on the other.

That is why, on the level of strategy, the popular vanguards pay special attention to anti-imperialist objectives. Such objectives become the principal line of revolutionary combat, both strategic and tactical.

Revolutionaries also know that the crisis of U.S. imperialism will engender internal political currents and forces with varying points of view as to the most adequate forms for resolving the crisis and maintaining world domination. Thus, it may be possible to note genuine subtle differences between one and another U.S. administration — as well as within each of them — differences that will logically be expressed in their policy toward our region. Experience teaches that in their handling of tactics, revolutionaries must pay the most painstaking attention to the policy developed by U.S. administrations so as to identify its weakest aspects and draw from them the greatest fruit. Both Cuba and Nicaragua have given us valuable experiences in how to correctly understand and use appropriate tactics in taking advantage of openings provided by different U.S. governments.

From all the above it follows that in the strategic conception and tactics, the revolutionary processes of Latin America and the Caribbean must adopt, as their principal line, unity in the effort to defeat the overall enemy. This point of view is shared by all revolutionary parties and organizations in the region.

The socioeconomic and political changes these societies require have as a prerequisite the liquidation of U.S. imperialist domination over each one of these countries. This in turn requires removing imperialism's representatives from power.

To accomplish this, solidarity between all anti-imperialist forces is a historical necessity, an unavoidable condition for achieving the national and social liberation of our peoples.

Unity, the Masses and Arms in the Struggle for Power

The experiences of the victorious revolutions and of the many processes that are developing on this continent confirm the general criteria formulated by Comrade Fidel Castro regarding the three ingredients decisive to attaining revolutionary triumph: unity, the masses and arms.

It is useful to examine the specific importance of each one of these factors separately.

Life shows that it is not enough to proclaim the need for unity in order to advance toward achieving it. It is precisely in this manner that the real maturity of a vanguard and its full commitment to the cause of its people is tested. Individual passions, sectarian deviations, and other limitations must bow before the collective interests of the masses.

The process of building unity encompasses all the motor forces of the revolution and the allied democratic sectors. But its vital nerve center is the solid unity of the vanguard. The truth is that when the different detachments of the left succeed in cementing unity in action, have a consistent strategy, and put forward common tactics of struggle, the popular masses — who are instinctively for solidarity among themselves — increase this unity, to the point of making it virtually irreversible. And the broader the scope of the forces — national and international — taking part in the struggle against the immediate enemy, the greater is the imperative for the unity of the vanguard.

At this point in Latin American and Caribbean revolutionary history, this means objectively recognizing that in the majority of our countries other left parties and organizations have grown up alongside the experienced communist parties. These organizations have won in struggle the respect of their peoples, and many times also represent exemplary detachments in leading the people along the road of their final liberation. Therefore, the unity of these parties and organizations amongst themselves, and their unity with the communist parties, is the primary guarantee for advancing the democratic, popular and anti-imperialist revolutions in our continent.

It is necessary to realistically understand the processes of unity, and to avoid taking superficial steps that later turn out to be counter productive. It is indispensable, at the same time, to make sure that the nonsectarian spirit of effective collaboration spreads through all levels of the parties and organizations, bearing in mind that many times in real life, the various groups carry out their activities in geographical spaces and social sectors that turn out in the long run to be complementary in the development of the revolution.

In those countries where military dictatorships rule, the field of unity broadens. It embraces even sectors interested solely in the destruction of the repressive, fascist-like structures, and in the return to bourgeois-democratic constitutional norms. In those cases the ground is even more fertile for the creation of anti-dictatorial democratic fronts, but on the condition that the revolutionary parties and organizations succeed in previously consolidating the leadership nucleus in such fronts.

We must emphasize that the proletarian revolution in Latin America and the Caribbean is at the same time eminently a people's revolution. To take power and keep it, the working class needs to weave close political, ideological and military ties with the rest of the masses. The unity of the working class and its allies must be pushed strongly through a mass policy, because that unity will not arise spontaneously from common economic interests, nor from the propagandistic invocation of those interests.

Certainly, the potential for unity in action by the popular masses exists in the economic basis of the system. But the process that leads to this unity in the political and ideological fields depends on the action of the vanguards; it is these vanguards, and not some economic determination, that are responsible in practice for the achievement of democratic and revolutionary unity.

Today in various countries of the region the problem of unity is the principal obstacle to the advance of the revolution. But there is evidence that it also represents a spur for overcoming the harmful tendency toward the division of the left in some of our countries. Every step toward unity is a step forward on the road of the revolution.

Inertia, delay or deviation from the united road is a gift from the revolutionary movement to the enemy.

It is common knowledge that the best form of advancing unity is through collaboration in concrete struggles. This direct relationship between the development of the revolutionary processes and the levels of unity of the vanguards is right now being demonstrated in El Salvador, Guatemala, and elsewhere in Central America, such as Honduras. The Sandinista triumph reaffirmed, among other important questions, the crucial value of the unity of the vanguard as the nucleus providing cohesion and orientation to the anti-dictatorial, democratic, anti-imperialist, and revolutionary forces as a whole. We also see in Chile advances toward unity that are promising for the future of the struggles of this people.

The unity of the revolutionary movement within the borders of a country is a contribution to the broader unity on a continental and world scale. In regard to our region, the historic and economic factors, the confrontation with a similar enemy, and the political interrelation of our societies fosters an identity in proposals and reciprocal solidarity of the left. But here too, these elements are potential, and by themselves they cannot move forward the effective collaboration of the revolutionary forces in action.

There has to be an individual and collective will that demonstrates in action the proclaimed Latin Americanism and internationalism. There are numerous examples of solidarity and they are well known. We Latin American and Caribbean revolutionaries have offered convincing demonstrations of our understanding of internationalism. However, internationalism is of such importance for achieving the triumph of national revolutions in one or another historical moment, and the role of concrete solidarity toward one or another process is so complex and dynamic, that we must still ask ourselves how far we have to go to advance and perfect the collaboration between all the revolutionary parties and organizations of the area.

Sometimes, there are confusions or deviations regarding the necessary and healthy independence that parties of the left have the right and the duty to preserve, although in Latin America it does not occur to the same degree as in other regions. Real sovereignty of these parties and movements, however, far from excluding it, presupposes the need to join collectively to confront common international problems and to collaborate in support of the revolutionary processes that most need solidarity at a given moment.

Finally, together with united work, it is indispensable to give special emphasis to activity to take advantage of the contradictions within the ruling classes in each country and those that arise on an interimperialist scale or between the countries in the region.

The Latin American experience confirms the ideas of Lenin:

The more powerful enemy can be vanquished only by exerting the utmost effort, and by the most thorough, careful, attentive, skillful and *obligatory* use of any, even the smallest, *rift* between the enemies, any conflict of interests among the bourgeoisie of the various countries and among the various groups or types of bourgeoisie within the various countries, and also by taking advantage of any, even the smallest, opportunity of winning a mass ally, even though this ally is temporary, vacillating, unstable, unreliable and conditional. Those who do not understand this reveal a failure to understand even the smallest grain of Marxism, of modern scientific socialism *in general.* Those who have not proved *in practice,* over a fairly considerable period of time and in fairly varied political situations, their ability to apply this truth in practice have not yet learned to help the revolutionary class in its struggle to emancipate all toiling humanity from the exploiters.[4]

Although there are many differences in the various countries and subregions, it is possible to offer a general characterization of four fundamental forces with which revolutionary forces in Latin America and the Caribbean have to develop tactical or strategic alliances. We are referring to Social Democracy, Christian Democracy, the Christian movement and progressive military sectors.

Our position in regard to the activity and ideological and political content of the Social Democracy was clearly expressed by Comrade Fidel Castro in the main report to the Second Congress of the Communist Party of Cuba.

We take into account that Social Democracy is not a homogeneous political current but rather one that inevitably reflects the different social forces that make it up on a world and regional scale, as well as inter-imperialist contradictions. This explains why, despite common political and ideological views, these parties adopt stances that are not always identical, and on many occasions notoriously divergent, with regard to the various revolutionary struggles. For that reason, an alliance with Social Democratic forces has to be based on clear and honest principles of collaboration, without impairing the final objectives the revolutionaries are fighting for. Accordingly, we must stress this collaboration in the political aspects that unite us rather than stress the ideological differences that separate us. For while the latter cannot be avoided, they should not be allowed to become insurmountable obstacles to united action in favor of coinciding objectives.

In contrast, the most general tendency of Christian Democracy is to

---

[4] V.I. Lenin: *Leftwing Communism: An Infantile Disorder*

lean toward active collaboration with the policy and interests of U.S. imperialism. But it is not correct to deduce, from such an extreme, a position that excludes all Christian Democratic forces. Inside the Christian Democracy there also exist important sectors that are genuinely democratic and Christian, and on occasion these sectors are forced to break openly with the official, compromised leaderships of their parties. In such cases, keeping in mind specific national situations, it is our responsibility to approach them frankly and free of prejudice, with the aim of working in common agreement on all tasks wherever possible. This includes the strategic line for the conquest of power and the construction of a new society.

It is well known that we take a broad approach to the Christian movements, that include priests and members of the Catholic hierarchy who identify with the human, political and economic aspirations of their peoples. On various occasions Comrade Fidel Castro has stressed the decisive character of unity between Marxist-Leninist forces and Christians who are acting together with their peoples for essentially the same objectives. These Christians we consider brothers in struggle for great historical changes on the continent. There will be no victorious revolutions without the participation of the immense Christian masses that populate our countries. Consequently, it is natural for the vanguards to open their doors to rank-and-file Christians, to priests and members of the church hierarchy who are committed — often at the cost of their lives — to the struggle for the emancipation of Latin America and the Caribbean. We believe that in a number of countries the revolutionary movement has not yet made the advance that is both necessary and possible in terms of collaboration with and integration of these forces. In some cases, it is these Christian forces who show a greater readiness for unity, and a more correct understanding in practice of their revolutionary role.

Another question that is important to take up is that of relations with progressive military sectors. In our opinion, the conduct of the armed forces cannot be analyzed apart from the historical context of each country or from its class confrontations.

Regardless of the general function that the military apparatus is supposed to carry out within the bourgeois state, it would be erroneous to view every man in uniform as an unconditional servant of the state. In this aspect as well, accumulated experiences indicate the usefulness of making a distinction with regard to the progressive elements of the armed forces, an important sector in some countries. The aim should be to get to know the practical possibilities of collaboration with them in the development of anti-imperialist, democratic and revolutionary struggles.

A correct policy toward the military sectors cannot be based on rigid, exclusionary schemas. It must emerge from each specific reality and take into account all the factors that make up such an institution. Nor would it be valid, on the other hand, to overlook the fundamental principles of Marxism-Leninism, which teach that it is imperative to destroy the repressive machinery of the state in order to achieve complete control over the state and replace it with one of a new type.

We should now focus on the role the masses must play. The incorporation of the masses into the revolution is the sole motor force capable of guaranteeing the achievement of power and its subsequent preservation. But as we know, it is not enough simply to call on the working class and the rest of the people to overthrow the bourgeoisie for the masses to respond to that call. Lenin taught us, and life confirms, that propaganda and agitation are not sufficient by themselves to make the people understand and become involved in revolutionary activity. For this, the political experience of the masses themselves is needed, Lenin asserted. And he concluded that this is the fundamental law of the great revolutions.

The problem, then, is to contribute to these experiences of the masses, to help them develop their revolutionary energies through the most fitting channels at each stage of the development of the class struggle. This cannot be derived from the desires and final aspirations of the revolutionary movement.

Subjectivism can lead to substituting the vanguard for the role of the masses or to precipitating decisive actions of the masses, which should occur at the most opportune moments. Just as bad, subjectivism can also lead to a metaphysical view of repeatedly postponing certain actions arguing that the masses are not adequately prepared to move toward the conquest of power.

There are no recipes or general formulas to resolve the crucial question of incorporating the masses into the tasks of their revolution. Nevertheless, there are experiences that are useful to consider. For example the revolutions in Cuba, Nicaragua and Grenada show that a program of struggle against the dictatorship and for democracy has the greatest possibilities to mobilize the broad masses of the people and other allied political forces.

We think that under present conditions in the majority of our countries, the decisive thing is not to stress the final or long-term objectives of the struggle, but rather unifying slogans linked directly to the circumstances that most strangle the life of the people, in the economic, social and political realm.

Focusing the central activity of the masses on achieving their anti-dictatorial, democratic aspirations, and on solving their most pressing human problems — jobs, health, education, among others — increases the possibility of their acting. With this comes an increase in the revolutionary movement's potential in the struggle to achieve power and initiate the democratic and anti-imperialist phase of the revolution.

The third and final factor — along with unity and the masses — that guarantees the triumph of genuine revolutions is the correct and timely use of arms. This does not represent a dogma, but rather results from the system of domination that exists in the majority of Latin American and Caribbean countries. It would be a grave voluntarist attitude to try to sketch out a single continental strategy for such a geographically extensive span of national societies, enriched by their own historic struggles and sociological peculiarities. But at the same time, there are certain principles of every revolution that cannot be forgotten.

Arms are indispensable to securing the victory of any liberating revolution in the continent, and, even more important, to preserve its continuity and achieve its full realization. This statement does not disregard the objective reality of different countries. In some countries where there are regimes of the far right — nearly always military dictatorships of a fascist nature — the use of forms of armed struggle or the correct preparation of the vanguard for their use is a virtually inescapable imperative.

In other countries, where democratic norms of life predominate and the vanguards have constitutional channels adequate for carrying out their activity, the role of arms will be shaped not by their inopportune use but rather by psychological preparation and the creation of the consciousness in all militants that — at some point, in some form — military confrontation will be indispensable, even though it may not be valid under existing circumstances. What is involved, therefore, is to create an attitude in all revolutionaries, and to move forward as much as possible in the revolutionary military preparation of the cadres and militants.

Furthermore, at the moment when political conditions demand the selection of the armed road, that decision must not be subordinated to the survival of some democratic forms, which would compromise the strategic actions of the revolutionary and people's movement.

And, finally, in the daily events of the class struggle, one must tenaciously forge the conditions that will help to advance along the road to the conquest of power. This conquest of power, in one or another variant, and with its national modalities, has always been due to the creation and development of its own military force.

Occasionally, of course, false dichotomies have been put forward that counterpose armed and non-armed forms of struggle. A struggle is not reformist simply because it is legal or because it seeks to open a democratic space; nor can a struggle be called revolutionary simply because it has an armed character. In our opinion, the revolutionary content of any form of struggle is measured by its results, that is, by the advance or retreat it implies for the final objectives of the popular masses.

The leadership capacity of the vanguards rests in their overall preparation to utilize all forms of struggle, permitting them to articulate energetic and appropriate responses to the diverse twists and turns that the class confrontation imposes. In that respect, the experiences of various revolutionary processes in the area show that a division between the political and military functions — particularly when determined and popular use of arms is required — gives rise to a distortion of both functions. Therefore only a political-military strategy, and the corresponding formation and preparation for it, provides the vanguards with the flexibility to undertake a new form of principal struggle in accordance with the stage and conjuncture of each national process.

At times the necessary use of arms is incorrectly identified with the mechanical application of one or another experience of armed struggle. The revolutions in Cuba, Nicaragua and Grenada present well-known differences, but, among other similarities, have the common mark of the use of arms. At the same time, along with specific common bases (especially in the cases of Cuba and Nicaragua), they show differences in military tactics employed, in insurrectional forms, etc. For example, in El Salvador creative revolutionary formulas are being applied in the use of arms, based on the closest links with the masses and in adverse geographic conditions — including among other factors the country's small territorial dimensions.

All the revolutions of our continent will have their own characteristics and will undoubtedly bring with them new contributions to the world revolutionary heritage. There won't be schemas capable of guiding the processes of national liberation and the construction of socialist societies in the Americas. Each people will make their revolution and will reach socialism by taking nourishment from the roots of its own national, Latin American and Caribbean history. And this will not be a contradiction, because every real social revolution is, at the same time, also a daughter of the universal laws discovered by Marx, Engels and Lenin.

In that sense, our Commander in Chief Fidel Castro asserted:

Modern revolutionaries are indebted to the theoreticians of scientific socialism — Marx, Engels and Lenin — for the immense treasure of their ideas. We are absolutely sure that, without them, our people would not have been able to achieve such a tremendous leap in the history of their social and political development. But, even with them, we would not have been capable of achieving it without the fertile seed and the unlimited heroism sown among our people and in our spirits by such giants of our country's history as Martí, Maceo,

Gómez, Agramonte and Céspedes. That is how the real revolution was made in Cuba, based on its unique characteristics, its own traditions of struggle, and the consistent application of universal principles.

Struggle in Central America

Article co-authored with Jesús Montané Oropesa, then Alternate Member of the Political Bureau of the Communist Party of Cuba, and published in International Review, *No. 4, Prague, April 1982*

A n examination of the present situation of Latin America and the Caribbean shows a terrible crisis throughout the region and is aggravated by the Reagan Administration's insane, aggressive policy.

Events in Latin America following the Second Congress of the Communist Party of Cuba confirmed the view expressed in that important meeting on the serious and immediate consequences of the presence of Ronald Reagan's team in the U.S. Government. The consequences of the Reagan Administration on the political life of our peoples reaffirms yet again the irreconcilable nature of the contradiction between U.S. imperialism and the interests of the Latin American and Caribbean countries.

The actions of the present U.S. administration in the region are characterized by its overt support for and promotion of the most reactionary governments and forces; outright hostility toward those processes and causes that express the people's feelings and interests; and virulent anti-Cuban propaganda, with which it tries to blame Cuba for the revolutionary political eruption in Central America.

However, as Comrade Fidel Castro said,

World public opinion and the progressive, democratic forces all over the world know that it isn't Cuba, with supposed subversive actions, that is destabilizing Central America. It is U.S. imperialism which, in the past, imposed atrocious governments and systems of merciless exploitation in the region. It is U.S. imperialism which, now, is rejecting all possibilities of a political agreement in El Salvador, supplying the repressive forces of that country with new armaments, hypocritically trying to hide the genocidal barbarity of its partners in crime. It is U.S. imperialism that threatens to intervene militarily either directly or through the equally reactionary and homicidal regimes that are its lackeys in the area — and, therefore, is responsible for the lack of peace in Central America.[1]

It is clear that the United States doesn't have any solutions to offer for the serious problems with which the region is faced, and it is impossible for it to maintain its hegemony and impose its dictates as it used to do. The only "solution" that it offers as an alternative, together with the language of threats and force, is "free enterprise," the massive flow of private investments and the expansion of the rule of the transnationals. These are formulas, which, as has been shown in practice, lead only to a deepening of the accentuated structural deformities of our countries' economies, to the pillaging of our peoples' natural resources and wealth and to an ever more alarming foreign indebtedness.

The exacerbation of the general crisis of imperialism, its absolute inability to solve it and the impossibility of its offering alternatives to our peoples' legitimate demands have led the most aggressive circles of monopoly capital to resort to fascist methods and actions, thus stirring up tensions and prolonging the sufferings of the peoples of this part of the world — who, with ever greater firmness, are refusing to put up with imperialist rule and are rebelling against those plundering policies. It is an unquestionable historical truth that no formulas can contain the peoples' insurgency.

The victorious revolutions in Nicaragua and Grenada — true expressions of the rupture of the structure of imperialist rule and unequivocal proof of the qualitative development and advances of the people's democratic, revolutionary movement in the region — reflect this reality. Both revolutions constitute the most important events in the Latin American and Caribbean peoples' struggles since the triumph of the Cuban Revolution; they contribute new teachings and profoundly demonstrate the possibility of defeating imperialist control and drawing up an independent future in line with the interests of their people.

The triumphs of Nicaragua and Grenada stimulated our peoples' anti-imperialist feelings and desires for independence. In addition, they encouraged the efforts of the revolutionary, progressive Latin American movement in its struggles against oligarchic-imperialist oppression and for democracy and peace.

In the face of attempts by the U.S. Government and most reactionary regimes in the area to destabilize them, the Nicaraguan and Grenadian processes are growing stronger, making tremendous efforts to carry out their programs of transformation for the people's benefit. In the midst of

---

[1] Fidel Castro, address to the 68th Conference of the Interparliamentary Union, Havana, September 15, 1981.

the growing hostility of their neighbor to the north and of their minority domestic reactionary forces — hostility that has even taken the form of threats of military aggression — both revolutions are holding firm to their pluralistic, democratic guidelines, supported by the masses of the people.

Although an important, increasing growth in the class struggle can be observed in Latin America, it is clearly in Central America where the people's revolutionary struggle is expressed with the greatest strength and intensity at present. There, together with the redoubled efforts that the Nicaraguans are making to carry forward their victorious revolution, the Salvadoran people — led by their vanguard, the Farabundo Martí National Liberation Front (FMLN) — are writing heroic pages in the history of their struggle against the genocidal Christian Democratic military junta that is supported and kept in power by the United States.

In that tiny Central American country, U.S. imperialism is bent on demonstrating its clout, implementing militaristic "solutions" based on force while rejecting international efforts at mediation to find a negotiated political solution for the Salvadoran conflict — efforts in which the revolutionary forces of that country have expressed their willingness to participate in a dialogue and negotiation.

In contrast, the initiative of the governments of Mexico and France to recognize the participation of the patriots who are fighting in El Salvador; the resolution adopted in the latest session of the UN General Assembly calling for a political solution; the peace talks that the Farabundo Martí National Liberation Front and the Revolutionary Democratic Front (FDR) presented to the international community through Daniel Ortega, member of the Junta of Reconstruction of Nicaragua; and the efforts made by the Socialist International have come up against systematic resistance from the U.S. Government and the Salvadoran military junta, which are bent on continuing their policy of extermination.

The explosive Central American situation is also reflected in Guatemala, where repression and death are being extended to ever larger sectors of the population. In an inevitable reaction to the escalation of repression, the Guatemalan people's democratic and revolutionary movement is becoming more united and is dealing important blows against the military regime, strengthening its legitimate struggle for national and social liberation.

In the face of U.S. arrogance, the fraternal people of Panama also raised high their banners of struggle for compliance with the Panama Canal agreements and the definitive recovery of their sovereignty over that part of their territory.

It is unquestionable that the upsurge of the revolutionary forces in Central America is speeding the breaking of the oligarchic-imperialist control of this subregion and has multiplying effects on the rest of Latin America.

This is shown even more clearly in the Caribbean, where, together with the advances of the Grenadian Revolution, a revival of the peoples' movement, of the progressive forces and of the entire left can be seen, in spite of attempts by the United States and its loyal followers to reverse that process.

The legitimate struggle that the Puerto Rican patriots are waging for their independence and sovereignty, the Haitian people's signs of resistance against the dictatorship that oppresses them, and the goals of changes in the Surinamese process are unequivocal expressions of the advances of the people's democratic forces in the struggle to win their legitimate rights.

Meanwhile, in the South American countries — especially those in the Southern Cone — a growing revival of the mass movement can be noted in the face of the failure of the economic model established by the oligarchic groups and the transnationals and in response to the repressive actions with which they are trying to keep social tensions under control. The revolutionary forces and the peoples' movements are making progress in Colombia, Chile, Uruguay and Bolivia, and, after an ebb, the masses of the workers in Argentina are once more rising to their historical levels of combativity, struggling for recognition of their democratic rights.

These advances of the Latin American peoples' revolutionary movements — which have different levels of development, rhythms and specific characteristics — confirm the approach of the Final Declaration of the Conference of Communist Parties of the area that, "The forms of the sociopolitical processes in the Latin American countries are different, as is the degree of the people's participation in the direct leadership of the sociopolitical transformations."[2]

However, in the effort to bring about revolutionary transformations, the battle against fascism and in defense of democratic achievements is combined dialectically with the confrontation of imperialism and the oligarchies, objectively forming a single process of struggle. The battle to recover democratic rights and the demands for thoroughgoing structural changes and for socialist goals is integrally linked to the struggle against the rule of the monopolies and imperialism, which maintain the forces of the oligarchy and the reaction. In this way, the tactics and strategy of the Latin American revolutionary movements are essentially guided by the struggle against their common main enemy: U.S. imperialism.

The close links between the movement of the masses and the revolutionary vanguards have been a key component in the

---

[2] *Granma*, June 16, 1975.

development of this process, showing the level of development achieved by the movement of workers, farmers, young people and others, on the one hand, and the level of the crisis of the system of imperialist and regional bourgeois rule, on the other.

The rise in the labor unions' struggles and the ever greater influence of the organized workers' movement, the many instances of the radicalization and activation of the farmers' movement, the actions carried out by young people — especially young workers and students — and the progress women have made in their struggles to achieve recognition of their rights are realities that confirm the advances of the Latin American people's movement and their revolutionary vanguards.

Another especially important factor in the advance of the Latin American revolutionary organizations, which is expressed in the Second Congress of the Communist Party of Cuba's resolution on international policy, is the unity they have achieved and the level of coordination and alliance with other democratic and progressive forces — especially their links with the revolutionary Christian sectors which support the people's struggle. The unity of all those anti-imperialist forces, with solidarity and coordination of the different efforts made in their common struggle, is the reply required in the face of the enemy's ongoing attempts to isolate and divide them.

Now, more than ever before, the progressive, peace-loving forces all over the world should remain alert and vigilant so that, with their actions of solidarity and denunciation, they can frustrate the present U.S. Republican administration's plans for intervening in El Salvador and attacking Nicaragua, Grenada and Cuba.

History shows — and the present circumstances ratify — that Latin America and the Caribbean have ceased to be U.S. imperialism's backyard. The strength of the people's revolutionary movement, the demands of vast democratic and progressive forces and the firm anti-interventionist positions of several governments in the region reflect the qualitative changes that have come about in this part of the world.

In the face of U.S. imperialism's aggressive policy, military threats, and irresponsible and anachronistic hegemonistic aims that seriously threaten peace and stability in our region and the world, the peoples of our America — heirs to the most noble and heroic Latin American and Caribbean traditions — are raising their banners of combat with greater strength and determination, inspired by the example of heroes such as Major Ernesto Che Guevara, who, with their actions, blazed the way to a new future of independence and justice.

Cuadernos de Nuestra América

Address given in Havana on August 30, 1984, in the ceremony launching
Cuadernos de Nuestra América *magazine*[1]

W e Latin Americans are living at one of the most important times in our history. As Cubans, we feel very concerned about the present situation and about the future of our brothers and sisters — especially, now, about that of the Nicaraguans and Salvadorans.

The imperialists' attempts to undermine the Cuban Revolution by means of an armed counterrevolution, diplomatic isolation, economic blockade and political blackmail have failed. The rulers of the United States have run out of means for suffocating Cuba and, exhibiting complete lack of political realism and of any wish for dialogue, have even gone so far as to believe — as some of them proclaim — that the only effective means to oppose our revolution is to engage in direct action. Obviously, our country is stronger, better organized and better able to defend itself now than ever before. In addition, Cuba isn't the only place where imperialist rule in the hemisphere has been broken. The Central American people's movement isn't just an incipient, inexpert, weak phenomenon. Somoza can tyrannize Nicaragua no longer, and the Sandinista National Liberation Front is directing its people's struggle against imperialist attack. The Salvadoran oligarchy can't drown in blood the people's uprising led by the Farabundo Martí National Liberation Front (FMLN) and the Revolutionary Democratic Front (FDR); the Guatemalan masses have an experienced political-military vanguard in the Guatemalan National Revolutionary Union (URNG); the Honduran people are opposed to seeing their country turned into a U.S. stronghold; and the Costa Rican people want no part of the warmongering plans of the United States.

In the Caribbean, in spite of the setback in Grenada,[2] whose people

---

[1] This address was published in *Cuadernos de Nuestra América*, No. 1, Havana, January-July 1984, 347-50.

[2] The reference is to the U.S. military invasion of the tiny island of Grenada in

are already beginning to recover, there are unequivocal signs of attrition in several Antillean regimes, which may well be suffering more than any others in the region from the consequences of the world economic crisis and from their dependence on imperialism. They are now demonstrating their inability to constitute viable models that may solve the serious social problems in the area.

It isn't by chance that the United States is trying to present a "mini-Alliance for Progress" with the so-called Caribbean Basin Initiative, a propaganda device that has already demonstrated its inability to tackle the serious problems of the foreign debt, the drop in production and the plummeting of the region's exports as a whole. Therefore, the democratic-representative regimes in Latin America no longer constitute the flock of sheep obedient to the wishes of the United States that they were 20 years ago. This is shown not only in the relations that many of them now have with Cuba but also in their stands against military intervention and in favor of a negotiated political solution for the conflict in Central America.

Opposition to the dictatorships and authoritarianism in Latin America also reflect the growing contradiction between the Latin American peoples and the imperialist system of rule. We should also consider who is in power in the United States. Emboldened by its own rhetoric and by the manipulation of public opinion, the conservative group, symbolized by Ronald Reagan, now constitutes the opposite pole of the critical international and regional situations.

Now, when the U.S. position toward Latin America — which is becoming increasingly aware of its own interests — should be more flexible, intelligent and open to negotiation, the rulers of the United States are instead demonstrating their arrogance, ideological dogmatism and ignorance of the real situation in Latin America. With the atmosphere filled with predictions of crisis and war, the multiplicity of trouble spots and the diversity of international participants implicated, this time in which we men and women of our America are now living is more critical than any other preceding it.

The First and Second Congresses of the Communist Party of Cuba identified the most burning problems in the region of the United States, Latin America and the Caribbean. Comrade Fidel has spent considerable time reflecting on these subjects in the last 25 years. Our people are aware of the high priority which Latin American affairs have in our foreign relations, so they don't constitute sophisticated topics of concern only to specialists. Therefore, I think that their analytical and objective discussion, their attentive and systematic examination, their

October 1983. As will be recalled, that invasion and the internal political events which preceded it (including the assassination of Maurice Bishop, leader of the New Jewel Movement) destroyed the Grenadian revolution of March 1979.

documented and profound interpretation and their correct dissemination carry out a function which we should evaluate in all of its dimensions. The party considers that the social sciences make a very important contribution to social, cultural and political development.

Comrade Fidel reaffirmed a few days ago, in his address on the most recent anniversary of the attack on the Moncada Garrison, that considerable attention should be given to the research institutions and to their development, since, as he said, they are of decisive importance for our country's development.

Naturally, the vast and complex economic, political and social problems of the Americas are such that they call for a multidisciplinary approach and cannot be the exclusive sphere of a single scientific institution, no matter how large. We must continue working to improve the links between the centers, so that the results of work are used jointly; avoid a duplication of efforts; and, at the same time, stimulate a healthy spirit of emulation between institutions, so that, as in other sectors of social life, the quantity and especially the scientific quality of the results obtained are increased. The achievements and capacity of our scientific institutions which carry out studies on the Americas will be measured by this quality, expressed in the specific work that they do.

As Comrade Fidel has pointed out, we want our researchers to be the best, in an all-around way. They should be exemplary in terms of effort, dedication and self-sacrifice, increasing their scientific and political-ideological level in line with the complexity, responsibility and social prestige of the work they do.

Therefore, the specialists on the Americas shouldn't limit themselves to knowing Marxist-Leninist theory in general but should strive to make creative use of its enormous conceptual and methodological possibilities, applying them to the analysis of the specific problems posed by reality. Mastering these theoretical tools and, at the same time, the most advanced techniques of the specific social sciences should be a permanent spur to those studying in this field.

As Fidel said on July 26, it is also necessary to give maximum attention to the use of computer techniques, because, in the future, it will be impossible to direct any endeavor without the use of computers. We must struggle to keep up with contemporary science and technology, to make the activities carried out in our research centers on the Americas more efficient and rewarding.

Before concluding, I would like to salute the appearance of *Cuadernos de Nuestra América*, not only as the organ of the American Study Center (CEA) but also as a publication of key importance to the studies focused on the Americas in our country. This achievement, in my opinion, marks a qualitatively new stage in the development of these studies, for, as we all know, this specialized publication has been in great demand among our specialists, cadres and students in general and an institutional need that has been expressed for quite some time. In the specific case of the CEA, I think that its publication is the result of a sustained effort by all its workers and others who contributed to it — a result which the party holds in high esteem.

However, I would like to say to the CEA workers and all the specialists and representatives of institutions who are here today that we can't be satisfied with this. The future of this publication depends on the effort and rigor with which everyone works every day to make it an ever more worthy continuation of an intellectual tradition which reached its peak in Martí, Mella, Che and Fidel. May those studying the Americas be inspired by those great figures in our history who, with their thinking and action, showed us in practice that it isn't enough to interpret the world — we must also transform it.

Thank you.

El Salvador

Address given on October 11, 1989, in the ceremony marking the Ninth Anniversary of the founding of the Farabundo Martí National Liberation Front [Frente Farabundo Martí para la Liberación Nacional, FMLN] of El Salvador

This is the ninth anniversary of the founding of the Farabundo Martí National Liberation Front (FMLN) of El Salvador, which has great revolutionary importance and, coincidentally, took place on October 10, the same day as the beginning of our revolutionary struggles for independence, the 121st anniversary of which we celebrated yesterday.

The anniversaries of those two events are close to yet another — one of grief and glory, for October 8 is the anniversary of the death in combat of Major Ernesto Che Guevara, the Heroic Guerrilla. Moreover, on October 11, we gather to remember the day on which General Omar Torrijos took an important nationalist and patriotic military stand in Panama.[1]

In contrast to the stupidity and arrogance of the U.S. Government's policy, the seed of dignity and courage that Torrijos sowed in the Panamanian people — and especially in the Defense Forces — has taken root. They have written pages of Latin Americanist, anti-imperialist glory, challenging and defeating — not without difficulty — all of the U.S. Administration's intrigues and acts of aggression. The aggressiveness of U.S. policy can be clearly seen not only in its opposition to the Panamanian people's determination to recover and

---

[1] On that day the Panamanian people's struggle to recover their sovereignty over the Panama Canal entered a new stage. On September 7, 1977, after more than a decade of intensive negotiations between the U.S. and Panamanian governments, the Torrijos-Carter Treaty (named for Presidents Omar Torrijos, of Panama, and James Carter, of the United States) on the Panama Canal was signed. The U.S. Senate ratified it with some amendments in 1978. In spite of those amendments, the Treaty — which has extensive support in the international community — established Panama's absolute sovereignty over the Canal and called for the gradual withdrawal of all of the U.S. military bases in the Canal Zone and the return of all installations to the administration of the Panamanian Government starting on December 31, 1999.

consolidate their national sovereignty and to implement the Torrijos-Carter Treaties but also in its opposition to the consistent policy of peace that the FMLN of El Salvador has proposed and defends.

The Salvadoran revolutionaries, sure of their people's strength and trusting in the political and military power amassed by the revolution in the past nine years of war, have frequently expressed specific forms for moving toward a negotiated political solution to the armed conflict.

Barely four months ago, an ARENA Party administration, representing the most reactionary political interests and the fascist sectors in the country, was inaugurated. Since then, that administration has increased the repression against the people's movement; gradually established a neoliberal, IMF-approved economic policy, further exacerbating the terrible living conditions of most of the Salvadoran people; and worsened the historic anti-democratic, genocidal political climate in El Salvador.

El Salvador's unjust sociopolitical and economic structure, the key cause of the revolutionary people's war, hasn't changed at all during these years. The ARENA Administration's policy is greatly exacerbating the causes of the conflict and expresses a resounding refusal to seek true peace.

The United States tested a counterinsurgent model in El Salvador under the concept of reforms and repression, in an attempt to undermine the people's support for the revolution. That policy failed. The substantial difference between the earlier counterinsurgent project that the United States had promoted and ARENA's political program makes some think that the Bush Administration is separating itself from Alfredo Cristiani's Administration or at least attaching strings to its support for it.

However, the facts fully confirm that the interventionist U.S. policy is capable of using anybody to achieve its ends and purposes, yet is determined to always consider the fascist, most reactionary groups in El Salvador as its most loyal allies. The Bush Administration has already hallowed its alliance with the reactionary ARENA Administration and with the high command of the Salvadoran Armed Forces, a fundamental tool of its antidemocratic, counterrevolutionary policy.

To cover up its reactionary political program and try to gain legitimacy and sympathy both inside the country and internationally, Alfredo Cristiani's Administration sent its representatives to Mexico to talk with a delegation of the General Command of the FMLN. The meeting showed the FMLN's flexibility and firm desire to agree on a peace policy and the intransigence and obstinacy of the ARENA Administration, which has little or no interest in seeking peaceful formulas. Even so, the agreements that were signed in Mexico — which were basically the fruits of the FMLN's peace policy — have given rise to hope in the search for a negotiated political solution.

However, the U.S. Administration and the reactionary civilian and military sectors in El Salvador — which are vainly bent on defeating the FMLN militarily — still lack political realism. These sectors are trying to ignore the powerful political-military force of the revolution and are trying to get the Salvadoran revolutionaries to surrender at the negotiating table — something which they haven't managed and won't achieve on the field of battle.

No one can ignore the lesson that the tenacity, daring, shrewdness and courage of the FMLN, the Salvadoran revolutionary vanguard, has taught in the past nine years. For decades, the democratic path for attaining the most legitimate and deeply-felt aspirations of the Salvadoran people was closed in El Salvador. Every attempt to achieve freedom and social justice and to recover the country's independence and sovereignty and the most basic rights to life was cruelly drowned in blood by the repression, which has taken more than 50,000 lives.

In the face of the violence and oppression imposed on the people by the ruling classes — supported and egged on by the United States — the Salvadoran revolutionaries, consistent with their glorious historic feats, took up arms to defend the purest desires of the masses of the exploited. We should never forget that if the revolutionary forces hadn't defended themselves arms in hand, they would have been wiped out by the fascist forces — with the approval of the U.S. administrations.

Nobody should be confused: if hope is dawning for a negotiated political solution in El Salvador that will put an end to the conflict and create the conditions for eliminating the causes that originated it, this is because the Salvadoran people have a tested, solid political vanguard, whose military strength and capacity cannot be questioned by any sensible person.

The Salvadoran people know better than anyone else that the only guarantee for achieving their noble historic goals lies in their own strength. This has been shown many times during these hard years of the revolutionary people's war. The Salvadoran people also know better than anyone else that the political-military force that has been amassed by and for their revolution by the Farabundo Martí National Liberation Front is an indivisible part of their interests and purposes and the basis of their guarantees for building a more equitable future.

True peace in El Salvador rests on the unpostponable need to implement a political program that sums up the interests and desires of the Salvadoran people without foreign interference of any kind. How can anyone speak of peace if the prevailing unfair socioeconomic order is maintained? How can anyone speak of peace with death squads? How can anyone speak of peace without recovering the country's sovereignty and independence, which are brutally insulted by the U.S. policy and its humiliating meddling in all of El Salvador's internal affairs? How can anyone think about peace with the chilling figures on infant mortality, illiteracy, unemployment, underemployment, lack of health care, poverty and hunger from which the Salvadoran people suffer? How can any honest person really believe that those who have been exploiting and torturing these heroic people are willing, of their own free will, to offer them the peace with social justice for which they have been fighting with exemplary generosity?

The Cuban people, who endorse the Salvadoran revolutionary cause, reaffirm their fraternity and militant solidarity with that exemplary people and reiterate their confidence in and respect for the FMLN of El Salvador, its prestigious revolutionary vanguard.

Comrades, the aggressive policy of the U.S. Administration is expressed not only against Panama and El Salvador but also includes the overt aims of continuing to hinder the process of peace that was begun in Nicaragua. The Sandinista National Liberation Front has shown its proven capacity for flexibility and its wish to achieve peace in the difficult, adverse conditions through which that revolutionary process has had to pass, under permanent attack by the United States. This is a propitious occasion, filled with revolutionary symbolism, to reiterate our solidarity and support for the Sandinista people's revolution and the Sandinista National Liberation Front, its legitimate vanguard.

The U.S. Administration's policy of aggression also continues against Cuba. The permanence of the criminal economic blockade, the systematic campaign of defamation and smears against our revolution and people and the planned attack on our sovereignty — in flagrant violation of international law, through television broadcasting are clear expressions of that wrong and unsuccessful policy.

Dodging difficulties and dangers, the Cuban people, under the wise leadership of Comrade Fidel, our Commander in Chief, are developing and deepening their process of rectifying mistakes and doing away with negative tendencies. The fabulous revolutionary reserves and morale, tenacity and fighting ability of our people, now organized to stand firm and defeat attack by applying the concept of a war of all the people, are the greatest wealth our party has with which to confront these complex times.

Along with developing and improving our own ways and means for promoting the consolidation and advance of socialism in our homeland, the Cuban Revolution staunchly maintains its Latin Americanism — resolutely supporting the struggle against the foreign debt and for a new international economic order and fighting to achieve the economic integration of the Latin American and Caribbean countries. The defense of and support for the democratic processes that are taking place and the firm rejection of all kinds of imperialist intervention in our countries is added to the struggle to rescue the sovereignty and independence of our great American homeland.

All Latin Americans have the duty to denounce and isolate that imperialist aggression.

That battle and the denunciation of the Bush Administration's policy now take the form of the defense of the Sandinista people's revolution, the struggle to demand respect for Panama's sovereignty, support for the search for a negotiated political solution in El Salvador and resolute condemnation of the escalation of repression of the Guatemalan people and the Guatemalan National Revolutionary Union (URNG).

Comrades, before concluding my remarks, I would like to extend a fraternal, revolutionary greeting to the heroic sons and daughters of the Salvadoran people who are living here, in the July 26 Camp, healing their war wounds in our country. To all of you and to the selfless guerrillas, fighters in the underground, cadres and leaders of the mass organizations and militant Salvadoran women, I convey our people's affection and respect.

Allow me to recall and share the mourning and grief of the mothers and other relatives of the thousands of men and women who have disappeared, been wounded or been killed in the criminal war that the United States has imposed on El Salvador. I salute the respected, beloved comrades of the Revolutionary Democratic Front (FDR), who are opposing the repressive machinery, and each and every one of the members of the Farabundo Martí National Liberation Front — especially the comrades of its general headquarters with whom we have strong ties of revolutionary fraternity and militant solidarity.

Long live the heroic Salvadoran people!
Long live the Farabundo Martí National Liberation Front!
El Salvador will win!
Homeland or death!
We will win!

Solidarity with
the Salvadoran People

Address given on January 29, 1990, in the closing session of the rally of solidarity with the Salvadoran people

This is the final day of the Rally of Solidarity with the Salvadoran People in our country. In fact, the Rally is symbolic. The Salvadoran people's uprising headed by Agustín Farabundo Martí and his determined followers took place in January 1932, and the Communist Party of El Salvador was founded in that month, as well. Both actions were brutally and bloodily repressed by the Salvadoran oligarchy and Armed Forces, faithful allies of U.S. imperialism. In addition, on January 10, 1981, the heirs of those patriots, organized in the Farabundo Martí National Liberation Front of El Salvador, unleashed their first general offensive, shaking the foundations of the unfair order prevailing in the country.

In the 1980s, the Salvadoran people waged a daily, unequal battle for freedom, independence and peace with social justice, against the considerable financial, military and other resources emanating from the U.S. Government's aggressive policy against that tiny Central American country. In those years, the Salvadoran people's heroism multiplied, and thousands followed the example of the fighters of 1932. Each and every one of those killed in continuing that struggle nourished with their blood the seed of patriotic rebellion.

It wouldn't have been possible for the Salvadoran revolutionaries to stand firm against the military potential unleashed by the enormous assistance the U.S. Government gave the Armed Forces of El Salvador if the five revolutionary organizations hadn't built and consolidated their unity in leadership and action. Revolutionary unity enabled them to achieve a single political-military strategic leadership that was able to provide quick, effective responses to the complex problems that have characterized the Salvadoran people's war and the difficult international situation in which it has developed.

The Salvadoran revolutionary leadership has boldly, consistently and tenaciously defended the people's interests and principles, combining them flexibly and with political astuteness and adapting to the reality of each specific situation and circumstance in both the political and military fields. The ability to adapt and readapt military tactics to each theater of operations and whenever the circumstances made this necessary shows the FMLN's proven political-military leadership.

Several times, without losing sight of the Salvadoran people's legitimate interests, the Salvadoran leadership has proposed new formulas that constitute the basis for a political solution for the conflict. The Salvadoran revolutionaries' creativity and initiative have also been shown in their ability to propose and establish formulas for alliances and of cooperation with all other political and social forces that want peace in El Salvador and in their proven political and diplomatic ability to defend the achievements and interests of the Salvadoran revolutionary process and to obtain and receive international support for and solidarity with their legitimate struggle.

The latest U.S. administrations — those of Reagan and Bush — have maintained the unsuccessful policy of trying to defeat the guerrilla forces in El Salvador militarily. For this purpose, they have used military resources of all kinds, saturating the armed forces with weapons, fighting techniques, sophisticated means of extermination, modern planes and advice, trying out counterinsurgent plans and ideas. Far from solving the armed conflict, all of those formulas have only made it worse. They have also exacerbated the socioeconomic and political causes for that conflict. The results of that insane imperialist policy have been state terrorism, violent repression, an absence of democratic freedoms and of individual and human rights for the Salvadoran people and the aggravation of the prevailing socioeconomic ills.

In spite of the tight control over the mass media — which have been placed at the service of a psychological war based on lies and propaganda against the authenticity and justice of the Salvadoran revolution — the people's forces are gathering with ever greater strength in the defense of their legitimate interests. They are challenging the prevailing order, joining in the different forms of struggle and swelling the ranks of the guerrilla detachments in ever greater numbers.

Only a few weeks ago, when the forces of the reaction and of imperialism got puffed up and started boasting that the Salvadoran revolutionaries had been reduced to insignificant groups of rebels, the Farabundo Martí National Liberation Front launched an offensive against the main military and political objectives in the country.

The various meetings that have been held between representatives of the ultrarightist ARENA Party and the guerrillas have shown the government's complete lack of interest in a serious dialogue that would make it possible to reach a real negotiated solution for the armed conflict. The government, the Armed Forces and the U.S. administration not only turned a deaf ear to and refused to accept the Farabundo Martí National Liberation Front's proposals but also violently increased the repression of the people's movement — providing a sample of the genocide that would occur if the guerrilla forces were to be defeated in El Salvador.

Last November 11 [1989], the FMLN began a large-scale military offensive throughout Salvadoran national territory. The actions carried out by the guerrilla forces, especially in the capital of the country, constituted an impressive page of heroism and glory in Latin American history. They showed not only the strength and dimensions of the revolution in El Salvador to those who still harbored doubts about the FMLN's political and military ability but also the impossibility of governing the country without the participation of the people's forces. The revolutionary forces won an important political victory based on their military ability and unmasked the brutality and the reactionary nature of the administration headed by Alfredo Cristiani.

The international community witnessed the massacre, the indiscriminate bombings of the civilian population and the generalized crime, symbolized by the savage murder of Father Ignacio Eyacuria and five other members of the Jesuit Order.

If any doubts existed prior to November 11 about the fascist nature of imperialist rule in El Salvador, no thinking people have any doubts now about the legitimacy and justice of the revolutionary people's war and about the need to find a negotiated political solution that will put an end to the conflict and lay the bases for a lasting peace with social justice, as proclaimed by the FMLN.

Early on the morning of December 20, the U.S. Government launched its fury and criminal imperialist arrogance against another tiny Central American territory. Counting on their numerical superiority and better weapons, U.S. combat forces with air and naval support invaded Panama in a brutal, traitorous attack from Panamanian soil, where they have maintained their military enclave against the will of that people.

The U.S. forces didn't hesitate to crush the Panamanian people's heroic, unequal resistance. The United States brutally humiliated the Panamanian people, trampled upon Latin American dignity, didn't even respect international norms or the diplomatic protocols in effect, and paid no heed to the revulsion caused by their vile invasion.

The events in Panama leave no room for mistake. Imperialism is untrustworthy, and, however hard it may be to accept this, the only option the peoples have for confronting and defeating it is that which comes from the ability and determination to stand firm and use all possible means against the forces of aggression.

The imperialists and their lackeys are emboldened. They think they are omnipotent, the lords and masters of humankind. In the last few days, the U.S. Government has increased its propaganda threats to use its military might and to attack other Latin American countries, this time under the pretext of fighting the traffic in drugs — as in Colombia.

In El Salvador, the fascist right feels safe and is continuing to murder leaders of the people's, democratic sectors with impunity. A few days ago, Héctor Oquelí Colindres — a Social Democratic leader, prestigious political figure and outstanding leader of the Socialist International for Latin America — was murdered in Guatemala. We pay tribute to Oquelí and to all social and political fighters, whatever their ideological positions and beliefs, who have contributed and continue to contribute to the Salvadoran people's most profound longing for freedom and justice.

For our people — who have confronted, stood firm against and defeated attacks of all kinds that imperialism has thrown against the Cuban Revolution and against our homeland — the development of recent events fully confirms the justice of Fidel's postulates and the need to consolidate and increase the country's defense with the participation of the masses in a war of all the people.

By its crowing, imperialism is stepping up its despicable plans for directing television attacks against our sovereignty and national dignity. As we have said many times, we won't let any imperialist attack against our people go unanswered. We don't want war; we want to live in peace and to consolidate and develop our socialist society's magnificent future. However, we will always be willing to defend our revolution and its principles and to make imperialism pay a high price for any adventure it may assay against our people.

Comrades, on concluding this rally of solidarity with the heroic Salvadoran people, we reiterate our firm support for and solidarity with their legitimate struggle, confident that, in spite of the complex circumstances prevailing in the international arena, the Salvadoran revolution will win. We base this feeling on our confidence in the Farabundo Martí National Liberation Front, their veteran vanguard, and on the tenacity and stoicism of the admirable Salvadoran people.

Honor and glory to those killed in this struggle!

The Salvadoran people will win!

Homeland or death!

Socialism or death!

We will win!

Epilogue

A Final Reflection
on Che and Bolivia

*Tribute paid to Commander Manuel Piñeiro Losada
by a new generation of students*

The First National University Seminar on Che and the Challenges of the Third Millennium was held February 25-28, 1998, sponsored by the *Che Lives* Group (Grupo CHE VIVE) of the University of Havana. The organizers and Dr. Juan Vela Valdés, Rector of the University, invited Commander Manuel Piñeiro Losada to address the participants and other Cubans and foreigners who were invited to attend this important student seminar, and he did so on the morning of Saturday, February 28, 1998, speaking for almost two hours in the Manuel Sanguily Auditorium of the School of Philosophy and History.

After some brief introductory remarks, Piñeiro, with his customary directness and informality, answered questions from the floor. Unfortunately, not all of his comments were recorded. Andrea Salvagno, of Uruguay, one of those invited to attend, was the only one who taped his replies, on her own tape recorder. The transcription of the tape she kept and the notes taken by the editor of this book made it possible to reconstruct a part of the dialogue, which was the last time Commander Manuel Piñeiro Losada spoke about Che's Bolivian feats.

That same evening, the renowned Cuban internationalist and Latin Americanist attended the closing session of the student seminar, which was held in the Aula Magna of the University of Havana. The organizers of and participants in the seminar greeted him with a simple but emotion-packed ceremony — a well-deserved tribute paid to the legendary Commander Red Beard by the new generations of students.

Because of the importance of both those events, we are presenting an edited summary of some of Commander Manuel Piñeiro Losada's reflections on that memorable occasion.

– *Luis Suárez Salazar*

****

Commander, did the leaders of the Cuban Revolution intend to send new members to reinforce Che's guerrilla column in a second stage?

Piñeiro: There was talk of this. Criteria had been drawn up for selecting some of the comrades with whom Che had spoken and who wanted to join the struggle in a second stage. Logically, it would take time to send them, by ones and twos, depending on Che's decisions and how events developed in Bolivia.

The problem was quality, not quantity. The combatants who were selected had to be experienced, both militarily and politically. They had to be trustworthy in political terms. In their selection, we also had to consider how determined they were to struggle and their physical condition. Those are very important factors in a guerrilla struggle, and especially in the first stage of the survival of the guerrilla unit. Of course, we had all the possibilities and backing for continuing to support Che's guerrilla effort when he should ask for it and when the conditions made this possible – beginning with Fidel and with the support of all the party and, above all, of the Cuban people.

Why did Che decide on Bolivia?

Piñeiro: I've already explained this several times. The 1964 coup triggered a rise in demonstrations, protests, strikes by the miners and repression against many leaders of the leftist and other people's movements. Some of those leaders were taken to concentration camps outside La Paz. When we analyzed that situation, we saw that it wasn't entirely favorable to the enemy. A guerrilla project that would move the scene of struggle from the cities and mines to the mountains, with a guerrilla column of Bolivians, some Peruvians and a group of Cuban comrades with guerrilla and other military experience, led by Che – with all his experience – would open the way for a revolutionary offensive.

Another factor was the existence of a group of cadres of the Bolivian Communist Party and other leftist organizations that were willing to join that internationalist project – as some of them did. Therefore, as I have said before, I think that, if Che had managed to survive the first stage of the guerrilla struggle, which is the most difficult one, the prospects for struggle in Bolivia and eventually in the Southern Cone could have been different.

What do you believe caused that defeat?

Piñeiro: I've already gone into that quite thoroughly, too. I think that one factor was Mario Monje's negative attitude and the split which that caused in the Bolivian Communist Party. It meant that the Bolivian young communists and some cadres of the Bolivian Communist Party who were committed to Che's project couldn't join the guerrilla struggle in the end. It also meant that the urban support, information and logistics network for purchasing certain things that the guerrillas needed (such as medicines) was hit prematurely. In the first stage, lack of support from the urban networks, from the cities nearest the guerrilla area, plays an important — though not decisive — role...

Commander, excuse me, but in the interview you gave Tricontinental *magazine, you said that Che made some mistakes in military tactics.*

Piñeiro: No, that isn't what I said. You're interpreting my words. What I said was that, on analyzing the situation, you come to the conclusion that Che's decision to divide the guerrilla column in two, one part headed by himself and the other by Comrade Vilo Acuña, was based more on humanitarian reasons than on military ones...

But, if I'm not mistaken, in that part you said that he wasn't very familiar with the area in which he was operating. However, other versions that aren't as authoritative and reliable as yours state that, before Che left for Bolivia, Régis Debray visited several areas and that it was Che himself who chose the area in which they would begin the struggle. Would you go into this in more detail, please?

Piñeiro: In the interview you mention, I spoke of the analysis and decisions Che made before leaving for Bolivia. I also said that, after operating in an unfavorable area for five or six months, looking for Comrade Vilo Acuña, Che decided to head north from Ñacahuazú. I think that, when Che spoke of the possibility of going to another, more favorable area, he was thinking of the area that Debray had studied from the political and sociological points of view.

Independently of the rather unethical attitudes which that French intellectual adopted later on and his positions opposed to the Cuban Revolution, it must be said that he did make a good study of that area from the viewpoint of land ownership, the agrarian contradictions, the composition of the military forces, the number of officers and weapons, the tradition of revolutionary struggle, and the topographic and climatic conditions. In short, it was an exhaustive, integral analysis of the characteristics of that area in terms of its potential for guerrilla operations.

Che read Debray's report while he was here in Cuba. I emphasize this because, if I'm not mistaken, Debray said somewhere that he doubted that we had passed his report on to Che and that Che had read it before leaving for Bolivia. What happened was that, when Che read it, it was already urgent that he enter Bolivian territory. I myself think that he ruled it out at first without completely rejecting that possibility. Remember that those of us who have been guerrillas and revolutionary leaders don't give full credence to the information we're given until we have verified it and seen things on the spot. Logically, the analysis that somebody else makes can be objective to some extent, but it may also be somewhat subjective. And, in revolutionary projects, any degree of subjectivism, no matter how small, may cost human lives or even wipe out the project itself.

I can say, however, that Che liked the analysis, and I'm quite sure he thought it was an area where the guerrilla struggle could be developed in Bolivia later on. But there was a contradiction between that assessment and the urgency he felt for going to Bolivia as soon as possible. Perfectly logically, he felt that, the more time that passed, the greater the risk of the enemy's hearing of the project. Moreover, some. cadres of the Communist Party, the Cuban comrades who were in Bolivia and the sectors that were pledged to the plan had already taken many steps. The logistical support was already at Ñacahuazú, the farm had been bought, weapons had been moved there, etc.

Che was worried about possible betrayal and about the possibility that one of the comrades who had taken part in those movements might be captured, causing a situation that would end or delay his plan. That would have implied that he would have to wait longer to go to Bolivia, and that wasn't in his plans. I think that those psychological factors meant that he was tense and worried, which multiplied the contradiction I've already mentioned. The comrades who were there had already looked for resources and considered that the Ñacahuazú farm was a good place to use as an arms depot and as a reception and transit point for the Bolivian, Peruvian and other comrades. It was hard for Che to give more weight to a report of Debray's — that, in any case, should be verified on the spot — than to those realities.

Now, regarding Che's decision to keep looking for Comrade Vilo Acuña and the other members of his small column for five or six months, the question arises: Was that decision correct militarily, with a view to reconstituting the column and, after it was strengthened, setting out for an area that had better conditions, or was it based only on solidarity with the comrades?

Considering Che's personality, I think that his sense of solidarity, not wanting to abandon any comrade, weighed heavily in that decision, as did his determination to keep the promise he had made to Vila Acuña and the other comrades that they should meet in 15 or 20 days. With the facility always provided by retrospective analyses of events and their results, I think that that decision was governed by humanitarian factors of solidarity rather than by military ones.

Obviously, you would have to be on the spot to make a better analysis of the various alternatives, but I still think the facts show that too much time was lost and that the guerrilla column suffered seriously from attrition during those five or six months, when other Bolivian combatants couldn't join it because of the obstacles created by Mario Monje, general secretary of the Bolivian Communist Party.

As I have said on other occasions, that attitude of Monje's prevented many young Bolivians, both members of the communist youth and members of the Communist Party — including around 15 or 20 Bolivian scholarship students who were here, had been trained and were ready to go — from joining Che's guerrilla column. The students couldn't be sent, because the channels established for their entering Bolivia — and especially the guerrilla area — weren't functioning. Some of those who left ahead of the main group told us that they weren't given replies or facilities for joining the guerrilla struggle.

Therefore, that was another key factor which meant that, at the same time that Che's guerrilla column was suffering from serious attrition because of battles with the army, it couldn't receive the reinforcement of a group of Bolivian comrades who were well prepared from the military point of view, in good shape physically and politically motivated to join the internationalist column headed by Che.

Would you clarify the role played by the Bolivian Communist Party?

Piñeiro: By sectors of the leadership, to be more precise, since we are in a university atmosphere...

Some of the things I've read contain information showing that, before Che's arrival, there were plenty of signs pointing to the negative attitude that Mario Monje would adopt. For example, Monje came to get training here and dropped out before completing the course. Another group of comrades from the Bolivian Communist Party did the same. And, at one point, I've been told, Monje also expressed a measure of opposition to guerrilla struggle, stating that he preferred an insurrectional approach. Were all those signs taken into account — and, if so, to what extent — or did the desire for struggle that usually sweeps all revolutionaries prevail at that time?

Piñeiro: Without that desire, we would all stay home reading the newspaper...

Exactly, but I'd like to know your opinion of the other Bolivian comrades who took part in the struggle and of the Bolivian Army. I think it contained a revolutionary seed, especially after its reorganization following the 1952 revolution headed by the Revolutionary Nationalist Movement (MNR). At that time, the Bolivian Army drew on the people. How did you view that situation at the time?

Piñeiro: My god, comrade, you take the cake with your questions! That's about seven in one...

Let me give you some background. Our relations with the Bolivian Communist Party — like those with the other Communist Parties in Latin America — were very close. As you surely know, Cuba had an embassy in La Paz up until 1964. The diplomatic relations between Cuba and Bolivia were broken that year, but we continued to have very good relations with all the Bolivian political forces: with all of the leftist and other progressive political parties; the people's, student, miners' and farmers' movements; and even officers — some of them high-ranking — of the Bolivian Armed Forces. Some of them expressed their solidarity with the Cuban Revolution and cooperated with us, either by giving us information or by carrying out some actions against the U.S. policy in Latin America.

That is, ever since the 1960s, there has been great liking for and support of the Cuban Revolution among the people in Bolivia, and even within the Army and the military high command.

Moreover, when Che was thinking of his internationalist, continental project, he analyzed and discussed with Comrade Masetti the idea of having a guerrilla column in Argentina. On the basis of that commitment, other Argentine and Cuban comrades were chosen, some of whom were killed in the struggle.

To succeed in that effort, they needed the support of comrades who were familiar with the area, logistics and training for the combatants, so they went to the Bolivian Communist Party and Mario Monje, who decided to give them the support they requested. At that point, even though he was in Moscow, he kept the promises he made. That — plus the support of certain solidarity structures of the National Liberation Front of Algeria — enabled Masetti and some other comrades to go from Algiers to Argentina, via Bolivia. A group of Bolivian cadres — including the Peredo brothers — who would later play a courageous, heroic role in the guerrilla column which Che commanded, did outstanding work in support of those efforts.

On that occasion (that is, while they were preparing for the guerrilla struggle in Argentina), some of the weapons were obtained from friends in the Army and from agrarian leaders who had kept weapons of various calibers since the 1952 revolution.

After Barrientos's coup, some of them formed armed columns of farmers and small landowners to keep the military government from taking away the land that the 1952 revolution had given to them. They were very good fighters. They also provided some of the weapons that Che's guerrillas used. Some of them lived in the Santa Cruz de la Sierra area, which was relatively near the area in which Che was operating. Unfortunately, no actions could ever be coordinated with those forces. I'm sure that, if that had been achieved, it would have dispersed the enemy and would also have served as a stimulus to the revolutionaries and to the Bolivian patriots. Some of those agrarian leaders — such as Sandoval, in the Santa Cruz de la Sierra area — had a lot of political prestige.

There were some other factors that I don't think I should reveal as yet. What I mean by all this is that the traitorous attitude that Mario Monje adopted after his meeting with Che wasn't as clear then as it is now, especially because of the promises he had made to the top leaders of the Cuban Revolution. We had a lot of information about the contradictions that were developing within the Bolivian Army and about the revolutionary potential of some of its officers. Obviously, the fact that Che's guerrillas didn't manage to survive the first stage aborted both those possibilities and the help that the more combative sectors of the Bolivian farmers and the miners' and student movements could have given them.

Commander, what is your opinion of the most recent biographies of Che?

Piñeiro: Many of them contain insidious elements, based on the subjective thesis that Che was isolated, left alone and abandoned by the leaders of the Cuban Revolution — especially because of the supposed differences that existed between Che and Fidel and because of the pressure that the Communist Party of the Soviet Union had supposedly brought to bear on our country. According to those authors, those contradictions and pressures forced Fidel to get rid of Che and offer him a way out through revolutionary, internationalist projects. Those insidious suppositions can be considered calumny in many cases. They are the main theme of many of the books that were brought out on the 30th anniversary of Che's death in combat — some more obviously and others more subtly, but those ideas are definitely there.

There are other books, which, though not based on that theme, contrast the political personalities of Che and Fidel and the course of the construction of socialism in Cuba with Che's thinking. In general, they try to show the existence of contradictions between Fidel and the rest of the Cuban revolutionary leadership, on the one hand, and Che, on the other. They take isolated ideas out of context to shore up this thesis and try to prove that there were ideological differences between the two revolutionary leaders and between Che's thinking and the subsequent course of the Cuban Revolution. I think that such fallacies should be challenged and shown up for what they are.

How did the first reports of Che's death reach Cuba?

Piñeiro: By a wire photo that came in through the Cuban Institute of Radio and Television (ICRT), which Comrade Papito Serguera headed at the time. Later, another wire photo came in through the Prensa Latina news agency. They were immediately sent to me, and I called Comrade Fidel and showed them to him. Logically, our first reaction was to doubt them. Even though we recognized that the body in the photos was very similar to Che, they were images that you don't want to accept.

Then another, more detailed wire photo came in. It convinced us that it was Che's body. Fidel called Celia Sánchez and asked her to find Comrade Aleida March, who was in the Escambray mountains at the time. Aleida came by plane, and Fidel went to see her and explained the situation. You can imagine what a sad task that was. Then, after that, we began to work on how to convey that terrible news to the Cuban people and to other peoples in the world. We knew it would have a terrible psychological effect on our people, all revolutionaries and people all over the world — which was why it was important to give them the news carefully, for Fidel to choose just the right words with which to tell the Cuban people and others.

Commander, one final question: What can you tell us about the present situation of the guerrilla struggle in Latin America, especially in Colombia and Chiapas?

Piñeiro: Right now, the Colombian situation is an exception to the rule in Latin America. In Colombia, there are thousands of armed men with experience in the struggle and with veteran cadres who are waging a political and military offensive. The system is filled with internal contradictions. The Army is being hit hard. There are signs of demoralization. How long will this last? What rhythm will it have? How will it advance, and at what speed? This depends on the specific conditions and the outcome of the plans held by the Colombian guerrilla movement.

Objectively, it is the only revolutionary armed movement right now that has possibilities for developing and becoming a political-military force with which, in my judgment and according to what the Colombian press says, the government will have to seek rapprochement, discussion and dialogue if it really wants to guarantee peace and stability in Colombia. As you know, the Colombian guerrilla leaders don't want just any kind of peace. In view of the goals they have sought in their long struggles and of the present balance of power, they want and are calling for a peace that will mean better living conditions for all Colombians.

Peoples' struggles are on the rise throughout Latin America. Most of them are legal, unarmed demands aimed against neoliberal policies. Those struggles create the possibility that, basing itself on its specific conditions, the political vanguard in each country may use the conditions that are being created by those policies which exclude and marginalize the people — generating more unemployment, alienation, repression and hunger — to stimulate, channel and organize their resistance. That is, those struggles may make it possible for the political vanguards to gather political strength and gain new ground for struggle in those nations.

In many Latin American countries, the revolutionary left has gained political ground by having its representatives elected to positions of responsibility such as mayors, municipal councilors, grassroots leaders and governors in a longer-range plan. In that process, they gain experience as leaders, administering resources, building and gaining strength from the political point of view, based on the destabilization that neoliberal policies are generating in almost all the governments in the region. Because of steadily declining budgets, they decide to sell national resources to private interests and decentralize public administration. As a result, discontent is increasing, not only in the capital cities, against the central governments, but also in other regions — the provinces outside the capital.

This has made it possible — for example, in Brazil — for the left to control an important number of governors' offices, state governments and mayor's offices in areas with several million inhabitants. Logically, there are differences among them. Some fall into political opportunism and pragmatism, but others have more encouraging, longer-range plans aimed at gathering the strength required to challenge the power of the ruling classes. What are their immediate prospects? It isn't easy to say. I think you have to view them in terms of the circumstances in each country and the growing discontent and resistance that neoliberal policies are generating. The situations in Venezuela, Mexico, Argentina, Brazil and Uruguay are all different.

However, I think that — with an intelligent, correct policy — the strength required for the left to become an important factor in the Latin American and Caribbean political arena will gradually be amassed. Of course, this will be achieved only by persevering in the struggles against the status quo and against imperialist oppression. As Che said, the peoples' revolutionary struggles and broad anti-imperialist unity are absolutely necessary to create the subjective conditions that will make new victories of the peoples' causes possible some day.

Thank you.

Also from Ocean Press

CHE: A Memoir by Fidel Castro
Edited by David Deutschmann
Preface by Jesús Montané

For the first time, Fidel Castro writes with candor and affection of his relationship with Ernesto Che Guevara, documenting the Argentine-born doctor's extraordinary bond with Cuba from the revolution's early days to Che's final guerilla expeditions to Africa and Bolivia.

Castro vividly portrays Che, the man, the revolutionary and the thinker, and describes in detail his last days with Che in Cuba, giving a remarkably frank assessment of the Bolivian mission.

A preface by veteran Cuban leader Jesús Montané recalls the first encounter between Guevara and Castro in Mexico in 1955.

Illuminated by many newly published photos – including the first and last of Guevara and Castro together – this is a revealing portrait not just of its subject but of its author as well.

168 pages, photos ISBN 1-875284-15-X

Available in Spanish as "Che en la memoria de Fidel" (ISBN 1-874284-82-6)

CHE GUEVARA AND THE FBI
U.S. political police dossier on the Latin American revolutionary
Edited by Michael Ratner and Michael Steven Smith

Published for the first time are the U.S. secret police files on the legendary revolutionary Ernesto Che Guevara, showing how the FBI and CIA monitored his movements and activity in the United States, Mexico, Cuba, Africa and Latin America.

A Freedom of Information Act request succeeded in obtaining the FBI files, CIA and other secret documents on Guevara. With an introduction by the editors, U.S. attorneys Michael Ratner and Michael Steven Smith, this book poses the obvious question: why did the FBI have such a dossier?

"Che is fairly intellectual for a Latino," reads a 1958 CIA document on Guevara during the period of the guerilla war in Cuba. Watched closely after the 1959 revolution, Guevara's every public word was recorded and transmitted to the FBI and CIA, with particular note taken of his anti-U.S. statements.

These secret files add to suspicions that U.S. spy agencies were plotting to assassinate Guevara when he was a Cuban government leader and suggest that they were involved in the pursuit and murder of Guevara in Bolivia in 1967.

For all those interested in Che Guevara, Washington's relationship with Latin America and the workings of U.S. spy agencies, this book is a significant new contribution.

213 pages, photos ISBN 1-875284-76-1

Also from Ocean Press

CHE GUEVARA READER
Writings on Guerilla Strategy, Politics and Revolution
Edited by David Deutschmann

Three decades after the death of the legendary Latin American figure, this book presents a new selection of Ernesto Che Guevara's most important writings and speeches. It is the most comprehensive selection of Guevara's writings ever to be published in English.

This wide-ranging selection of Guevara's speeches and writings includes four sections: the Cuban revolutionary war (1956-58); the years in government in Cuba (1959-65); Guevara's views on the major international issues of the time, including documents written from Africa and Latin America after his departure from Cuba in 1965; and a selection of letters written by Guevara, including his farewell letters to Fidel Castro and his children and family.

This anthology provides an opportunity to assess Guevara's contribution to the Cuban revolution in its early years. As the most authoritative collection of the work of Guevara, the book is an unprecedented source of primary material on Cuba and Latin America in the 1950s and 1960s.

Included is an extensive chronology, glossary and a complete bibliography of Guevara's writings.
400 pages, photos   ISBN 1-875284-93-1

CHE IN AFRICA
Che Guevara's Congo Diary
By William Gálvez
With an introduction by Jorge Risquet

A year before his fateful Bolivia mission, Che Guevara led a group of guerillas to support the Congolese liberation movement in 1965. Considerable speculation has always surrounded Guevara's disappearance from Cuba and why he went to fight in Africa.

The story behind the Congo mission is now revealed in this book, which includes Guevara's previously unpublished "Congo Diary". Guevara's diary assesses the role of figures within the African liberation movements, among them Patrice Lumumba and Laurent Kabila, leader of the 1997 overthrow of the Mobutu regime in Zaire (Congo).

Author William Gálvez quotes recently declassified CIA documents showing how the CIA assembled a mercenary band of white South Africans and others to pursue the Guevara column.

Che in Africa presents a generally unknown chapter in the anticolonial struggle and sheds light on events in Central Africa today.
307 pages, photos   ISBN 1-876175-08-7

Also from Ocean Press

CUBAN REVOLUTION READER
A Documentary History
Edited by Julio García Luis
An outstanding anthology presenting a comprehensive overview of Cuban history and documenting the past four decades or revolution.
300 pages   ISBN 1-876175-10-9
Also available in Spanish La Revolución Cubana *(ISBN 1-876175-28-1)*

FIDEL CASTRO READER
The voice of one of the 20th century's most controversial political figures — as well as one of the world's greatest orators — is captured in this new selection of Castro's key speeches over 40 years.
600 pages   ISBN 1-876175-11-7

JOSE MARTI READER
Writings on the Americas
An outstanding new anthology of the writings, letters and poetry of one of the most brilliant Latin American leaders of the 19th century.
300 pages   ISBN 1-875284-12-5

SALVADOR ALLENDE READER
Chile's Voice of Democracy
Edited by James D. Cockcroft and Jane Carolina Canning
This new book makes available for the first time in English Allende's voice and vision of a more democratic, peaceful and just world.
287 pages   ISBN 1-876175-24-9

CAPITALISM IN CRISIS
Globalization and World Politics Today
By Fidel Castro
Cuba's leader adds his voice to the growing international chorus against neoliberalism and globalization.
300 pages   ISBN 1-876175-18-4

LATIN AMERICA: FROM COLONIZATION TO GLOBALIZATION
Noam Chomsky in conversation with Heinz Dieterich
An indispensable book for those interested in Latin America and the politics and history of the region.
120 pages   ISBN 1-876175-13-3

Ocean Press, GPO Box 3279, Melbourne 3001, Australia
● Fax: 61-3-9329 5040 ● E-mail: info@oceanbooks.com.au

www.oceanbooks.com.au